Blasphemy in Modern Britain

For Joanne, Isabella and Colin.
All of whom contributed more to this than they will
ever know

Blasphemy in Modern Britain

1789 to the Present

DAVID NASH

Ashgate

Aldershot • Brookfield USA • Singapore • Sydney

© David Nash, 1999

Published by
Ashgate Publishing Limited
Gower House
Croft Road
Aldershot
Hants
GU11 3HR
England

Ashgate Publishing Company
Old Post Road
Brookfield
Vermont 05036–9704
USA

The author has asserted their moral right under the Copyright, Designs and Patents Act, 1988, to be identified as the author of this work.

British Library Cataloguing in Publication Data

Nash, David S.
  Blasphemy in Modern Britain: 1789 to the Present
  1. Blasphemy — Great Britain.
  I. Title.
  291.5'695'0941

Library of Congress Cataloging-in-Publication Data

Nash, David S.
  Blasphemy in modern Britain: 1789 to the present/David S. Nash.
    p.   cm.
  Includes index.
  ISBN 1–85928–023–4 (hb: alk. paper)
    1. Blasphemy—Great Britain—History. I. Title.
  KD8073.N37   1998
  345.41'0288—dc21   98–24459
                                                         CIP

ISBN 1 85928 023 4

This book is printed on acid free paper

Typeset in Sabon by Bournemouth Colour Press, Parkstone and printed in Great Britain by Galliards, Great Yarmouth

Contents

List of Figures

Acknowledgements

The writing of a book of this nature incurrs many debts from many quarters and it is only the act of collating them and placing them in print which makes the writer realise how lucky he has been to receive help, opinions, administrative assistance, comfort and love on the route to completing this work. During the course of this book I have also been the grateful recipient of support from the British Academy in the form of a personal research grant. I am grateful to the University of Leicester Social Sciences Research Fund which also provided funding which effectively launched this project. My own institution, the School of Humanities at Oxford Brookes University has also made available research funding and research leave to enable the project to reach its conclusion for which I offer grateful thanks.

I would like to record the help and assistance I have received from library staff at Oxford Brookes University Library, the Bodleian, the Bodleian Law Library, Rhodes House Library, the Oxford History Faculty Library, Social Science Faculty Library, Nuffield College Library, Wolfson College Library, York University Library, Manchester Central Library. Archivists at the following libraries and record offices have also provided much assistance: The British Library, Public Record Office, Bishopsgate Institute, Leeds Record Office, Bradford Record Office, The Co-operative Society Library (Manchester), The National Library of Scotland (Edinburgh) and Edinburgh Record Office (West Register House). My colleagues at two University departments have provided support of various kinds which has made this work possible. Thus I owe thanks to Rob Colls, Phil Cottrell, Nick Davidson, Rupert and Babette Evans, Norman Housley, David Williams, Shearer West and David Wykes at Leicester and my current colleagues in Oxford: Jonathan Andrews, Mark Clement, Mary Chamberlain, Anne Digby, Detlef Mühlberger, John Perkins, Steven King, Rob Pope, Lori Williamson and Richard Wrigley. Mike Daly saved me from making any serious misrepresentations of the law and the *Gay News* case whilst Roger Griffin gave me the benefit of his knowledge of the far right and made perceptive comments about Chapter 7. Steven Matthews offered important criticism of Chapters 2 and 8 for which I am most grateful. Edward Royle commented upon several chapters and made important suggestions which have significantly enriched this work and the author continues to be grateful for his astounding knowledge and scholarly integrity. I owe also a massive debt to John Stewart and Donal Lowry who have been ever reliable sources of unstinting help, encouragement and support. John Stewart never tired of reading draft chapters and contributing intelligent and wise criticism without which this work would be infinitely poorer. Donal Lowry has been a constant source of engaging ideas, comments and insights. This book has benefited significantly from the contributions of both these two very professional and highly dedicated scholars. Simon and Stacy Cordery were sources of inspiration and insight as well as warm and genial hosts. Simon's record as an informed yet kind critic of this author's work is one which I value and shall always value.

My other academic debts are numerous but I record my grateful thanks to the following: Lyn Abrams, Sarah Barber, Malcolm Chase, Laura Deal, Barry Doyle, Gail Gaskell, Michele Hawley, Martin Hewitt, Jo Hoffman, David Jasper, Bob Jones, Katherine McDorman, Rohan McWilliam, Joss Marsh (whose book *Word Crimes* unfortunately arrived just as this book was going to press), Shirley Mullen, Colin Pedley, David Starkey, Brad Verter and Stephen White. I also owe thanks to those in the contemporary secular movement who took time off from writing and campaigning to talk about the past and present of the issue of blasphemy. These include Norman Bacrac, Jennifer Jeynes, Terry Mullins and Barbara Smoker. I owe particular thanks to Keith Porteus-Wood, Jim Herrick and Nicolas Walter for sharing their opinions with me and being prepared to publish my own earlier formative thoughts on the subject. Alec McAulay was an enthusiastic and very supportive commissioning editor, who aided and encouraged the progress of the book from its very inception, whilst the excellent work of Caroline Cornish ensured the smooth passage of the manuscript into print.

I would also like to thank seminar audiences in Boulder, Chicago, Glasgow, Houston, Lancaster, Leeds, Leicester, Monmouth Illinois, Oxford, Seattle, Buffalo and Macomb Illinois for listening to my ideas and commenting upon them in the best possible spirit.

Last and most important I owe immeasurable debts to my parents-in-law Michael and Joy Meadows and to the support and encouragement of my wife Joanne who also (somehow) found time to give us both a dear and beautiful daughter. Thank you, thank you all.

Abbreviations

APU   Anti-Persecution Union

BBFC   British Board of Film Classification

DPP   Director of Public Prosecutions

NSS   National Secular Society

RPA   Rationalist Press Association

Introduction

In modern British society each successive generation complacently congratulates itself that blasphemy is a curious and even fascinating anachronism. It is manifestly a relic of a previous age but also is often seen as an enduring religious presence in an era in which such ideas and proposals seem precociously unfashionable. But the more religiously committed in society are repeatedly apt to see blasphemy as an important touchstone and legacy of a religious and moral golden age. This latter view can be used to nurture long-forgotten fears about moral collapse and invoke images of the blasphemy law as a didactic lingering *memento mori* of man's final destiny. Moreover this law's apparent anachronism, in its way, even engenders a familiarity that allows some to mourn its relative absence and others to fear its passing.

This view of the law as generally harmless is in part a consequence of the supposed infrequency of its use and application, a matter often alluded to by some commentators. Moreover those who fall foul of it and are prosecuted by it are seen to be a marginal minority, further reinforcing this view. This alone can persuade society that such laws are largely benign and used only *in extremis* for the benefit of the vast majority of citizens, if not ultimately for all of them. The argument runs thus: if blasphemy has been on the statute book since the middle ages without doing serious damage can there be any justification for those who complain about its effects or clamour for its removal?

Blasphemy has proved difficult to define for scholars and commentators from a whole range of disciplines. Even the legal interpretations of the crime in England, supposedly supported by case-law, cannot produce a coherent definition of the offence. Legal commentators themselves have noted that the offence's operation relies upon legal authorities which are not at all clear or reliable and are often ambiguous. An important example of how this works in practice is furnished by a brief investigation of which branches of Christianity are protected by the law of blasphemy. The Gathercole case of 1838, which involved libels of Catholicism, has been used to suggest that all forms of non-Anglican Christianity are not protected by the law. This was also recently cited as the precedent for denying such protection to Muslims. A close look at the precise words used at the start of the case's summing up seems to support this, yet there is a contradiction in the passage which follows declaring ' ... any general attack on Christianity is the subject of criminal prosecution, because Christianity is the established religion of the country.'[1] Thus this precedent could be used to argue that all of Christianity is protected or that only the Anglican Established Church is protected! Another commentator, however, suggests that the matter is even more complex since this authority, whatever it purports to say is based upon a dubious precedent gleaned from a judge's summing up which should not have the status of case-law.[2]

Whatever the confusing status of such precedents, most commentators agree that the offence consists of a systematic attack upon the sacred Christian beliefs of another, sufficient to cause a form of insult and injury. However, even here the evolving nature of the law allows legal authorities to give only a list of previous cases which suggest what precise ideas have been prosecuted in the past but offer no guide to what may be indictable in the future. Thus G. D. Nokes in his legal Treatise of 1928 noted that attacks upon the Trinity, the existence of God, the attribution of human passions to God, denial of Christ's birth, good works, teachings and resurrection had all been the subject of prosecutions.[3] Since this treatise was written the *Gay News* case will have added accusations of homosexual behaviour to this list.

Modern interpretations of the law insist that the motives and intentions of the blasphemer do not have to be investigated and proved in any prosecution. In England it is only Christianity which is protected; historically this has been closely identified with the Anglican Established Church and it seems clear that this institution was believed to embody this rather than to constitute it.[4] Whilst the Statute Law of Blasphemy was never used its provisions seem to have made the identification of the Anglican Church with the Christianity protected by the law much closer. Indeed this would not be surprising when the political context of the law's inception, the early years of William III's reign, is considered. It is thus no surprise to see many protagonists in blasphemy cases identifying the Anglican Church with the law because the two so frequently in practice appeared to be interchangeable.

Most recent cases have, however, suggested that a consensus of Christian feelings has been protected by the Common Law offence of Blasphemous Libel. The public participation in the construction of the offence which this invites means that the law is capable of being enacted at any time by an individual having sought permission from a judge. Thus prosecutions are deemed to be directly reflective of public opinion since they can only be brought by private individuals. Decisions in the cases rely upon judge-made law capable of being interpreted and re-interpreted to suit the outlook of an individual judge who is assumed to reflect wider societal norms. Taking these variables into account it seems that there is no intelligible standard of what is permissible and what is illegal that writers, journalists and speakers can refer to as a meaningful set of practical guidelines. It is thus tempting to conclude that the most realistic working definition of the offence is simply to consider that which was (and will be) prosecuted for the crime at any given historical juncture.

However, these laws are by no means a widely recognised standard of how to regulate the expression of religious opinion and would be considered draconian in most other European countries. Indeed the original function of the blasphemy law which survives in a modern, if truncated, form is that a central part of the apparatus of the state (in this case established religion) is protected from maliciously intended ridicule or, some would say, even reasonable criticism. Seen in this context it is clearly evident why such a law came into being at a historically remote juncture but equally this also produces a collection of perplexing questions concerning its contemporary retention.

This state of affairs, whereby British law appears to be the slave of older, sometimes medieval conceptions of law and morality, is further reinforced by a consideration of the legal situation in America. The chance afforded by the American Revolution to start anew was in this instance embraced enthusiastically when the American Constitution enshrined religious toleration, or more correctly the absence of state-protected religion, in its much-quoted First Amendment. Whilst blasphemy is not entirely absent from the religious history of the United States, the disestablishment of religion removed the pretext for much legal action against the irreligious and sceptical.

It has frequently been a mode of attack upon blasphemers to suggest that they are a threat to morality within society. Indeed an enduring theme that surrounds many blasphemy cases over the last two hundred years is the extent to which blasphemy has been a useful offence to cite in accusations against a range of politically dangerous and errant tendencies within society. This, however, does not indicate that those accused of the offence were entirely innocent victims of exceptionally crude forms of political and social coercion. The blasphemers who constitute the subject of this work tended in general to construct an elaborate counter-argument which suggested that Christianity itself had the potential to destabilise society through the irrationality and immorality of its own doctrines. Whilst English law, in the eyes of many blasphemers, effectively protected only the Church of England, the courts and the public sphere, as time went on, were accused of eliding this into a wider Christianity which was portrayed as the pillar of morality in a civilised country. This homogeneity was attacked by some blasphemers because it presumed far too much in its assumptions that Christianity spoke with one voice. The rise in the nineteenth century of new religious forms such as Salvationism constituted an attack upon lifestyles and opinions that significantly diverged from established Christianity. Even today the assumption that an extended blasphemy law will be of particular use to Muslims and other non-Christian groups relies upon the assumption that Christianity is itself dormant and homogenous. This discounts the recent appearance of sectarian, salvationist and millenarian Christianity as an important cultural and social force in Britain.

When addressing the subject of blasphemy the historian is invariably involved in an agenda conveyed by the phenomenon itself. Earlier historical accounts portray the laws of blasphemy and their operation as either a necessary weapon in the armoury of civilisation or as evidence of civilisation itself being significantly incomplete or precarious. Invariably the motivation behind these accounts is to contribute new arguments to a contemporary and important debate. As history they are informative and as indicators of progress and the significance of certain historical moments they are invaluable. Earliest on the scene were those closely associated with the leading protagonists of late nineteenth-century blasphemy. Perhaps this school of writing upon the subject can be traced back to John Foxe's martyr narratives of the Reformation.[5] Later associates of blasphemers, and the blasphemers themselves, have significantly been notable historians of the problem and constitute almost a roll call of religious radicalism. Henry Hetherington's account of his own trial for blasphemy, for example, attempts equanimity and impartiality, as indeed do some of the later writers. However the desire to prove the utilitarian nature of their sacrifice alongside their barely concealed contempt for the process of law leads many of these sources to be considered best as primary material.[6]

In many important respects the historiographical debate around blasphemy is a part of the debate itself – the issue, after all, has not been solved to the satisfaction of society leaving almost all historians of the subject duty bound to comment upon its future. The first systematic historian of the subject was Hypatia Bradlaugh-Bonner, daughter of the secularist leader Charles Bradlaugh. Bradlaugh-Bonner's work demonstrates a sort of inverted whiggism whereby the failure of successive governmental and legal authorities to banish the remnants of medieval thought represents a massive oversight that has produced the worst of all possible worlds. Bradlaugh-Bonner's work is a particularly outspoken dialogue between the past and the present as she continually rails against what she sees as an anachronistic, yet manifestly contemporary, crime. This has a poignant contemporary relevance since the first edition of *Penalties Upon Opinion* was written and published in 1912 in the aftermath of the Boulter case and the continuing blasphemy of J. W. Gott, Ernest Pack and T. W. Stewart. The book was intended to be a highly popular introduction to the history of the suppression of opinion and was eventually published in the RPA series 'The Thinker's Library'.

Arthur Calder-Marshall's 1972 work *Blasphemous, Lewd and Obscene* is an altogether more episodic history of blasphemy. Written in a sometimes overly masculine style it portrays its protagonists as simultaneously heroes and martyrs for what Calder-Marshall fetishises as the national obsessions of freedom of opinion, free speech and the notion of a free press. As such it is a history of obscenity as much as blasphemy and occasionally mingles the two less than comfortably. Each protagonist is given an obviously catchy sobriquet which enables the readership to identify with the characters and their virtues as well as their tragic flaws. All of this is completed with type and presentation which echoes the eighteenth-century chapbook. It is invariably upbeat and optimistic – as indeed it could afford to be since it followed the Chatterley and Oz cases but predated both the Whitehouse versus Lemon case and the later Salman Rushdie controversy. It too contains a modernisation motif which, from the comfort of the 1960s and '70s, looks back upon the trials as a series of rather masculine japes carrying a distinct whiff of the Junior Common Room.

More recently the work of Richard Webster demonstrates how inextricably linked blasphemy's past is with its present. The title of his *A Short History of Blasphemy* is in part a misnomer; the book in fact devotes most of its pages to supporting the post-Rushdie Islamic call for an extension of the blasphemy laws in England. It represents perhaps the apogee of blasphemy polemic as history. This work is equally a part of the post-Rushdie debate and in its interest in the cultural consequences of this episode there is a clear acknowledgement of the work of Edward Said. Webster views the history of blasphemy not in the traditional whiggish terms of the development or otherwise of tolerance but rather of western clashes with the East. This sees both crusades and medieval and later pogroms as implicit attacks by western culture upon an alien force within. The suggestion here is that liberal/intellectual western culture is not value free and has not brought an end to prejudice.

Representing almost a polar opposite to Webster, the work of Nicolas Walter has done much to present blasphemy to a contemporary audience from a rationalist perspective. Walter's pamphlets, articles and comments are an important reflection of modern secularist outlooks upon the issue of blasphemy and carry particular insight owing to the author's involvement in many of the latter-day incidents he describes. Walter notes how Christianity in particular contains its own blasphemous texts. Moreover he also emphasises that historically monotheistic religions are particularly prone to using blasphemy as a means to attack their polytheistic predecessors. Perhaps the most recent and wide-ranging work of historical scholarship in the area has been the work of Leonard Levy in his two volumes. The latter in particular is a monumental piece of scholarship which attempts to analyse the phenomenon of blasphemy in most of western society for a period stretching from antiquity to the Rushdie episode. This almost encyclopaedic work has been of considerable use to this author, although its sheer scope is both daunting to the general reader and weighs heavily upon his attempts to sustain an interpretation.

Blasphemy has also been approached from a literary studies perspective, notably in the form of David Lawton's *Blasphemy*. Using forms of literary theory this work attempts to view blasphemy as a series of texts and episodes of confrontation and transgression. As such it too engages with contemporary debates but these emerge as related fundamentally to issues in cultural studies. Themes and perspectives like Orientalism, transgression and the various approaches characterised as postmodernist echo through Lawton's work which is considered in some detail below in the chapter entitled 'Blasphemy and Theory'.[7]

This book is an attempt to update the history of this subject. As matters have turned out, this has necessitated considering incidents and interpretations that evolved during the course of the last months before publication. It is on one level a chance to offer some new perspectives and to consider the enduring 'problem' of blasphemy in British society in some new ways. This has been aided by fresh archive research and by an approach which tries to view incidents of blasphemy more clearly in their context. It is a contention of this book that blasphemy and blasphemers themselves are more readily understood when the mantle of victim is removed from them. An aid to this process is a reconsideration of the notion of secularisation within society which is an undercurrent throughout this work. This theory, which still informs and invigorates recent writing on the subject of religion, has too readily identified blasphemers as trail-blazers whose confrontation with a slower-moving moral climate makes them 'ahead of their time'. This is not to say that blasphemers appear from a void for each generation as blasphemy cases sometimes appear to. It suggests that a collection of defences and lines of argument were established almost organically, thus allowing their subsequent use by those accused in successive generations. The historian who neglects both of these facets will miss much. Likewise the establishment of a tradition, a trope or a discourse (all somewhat inadequate words in this context) should also not be allowed to undermine the individuality which blasphemers brought to the page, the platform and the courtroom. The collision between the value of courtroom evidence and that produced outside it, and the dichotomy between a tradition/discourse and the individuality of those in the dock are not irreconcilable opposites, as this book hopes to demonstrate. However, this is also a work of synthesis which acknowledges debts to the authors previously cited. Likewise, engagement with the work of other historians such as Ian McCalman, Marcus Wood and James Epstein who have worked long and hard to shed light upon the murky world of early nineteenth-century radicalism has also proved of benefit to this study.

One further insight as to why a book of this nature is needed is perhaps provided by a comparison of the state of the historiography related to blasphemy with the advances made in the study of an analogous area of socio/cultural and legal history – early modern witchcraft. In many respects the comparisons are suggestive. Both involve an individualised perception of offence on the part of the victim. Both appear at historical junctures where the nature of print culture and the audiences for it are in the process of profound evolution. Both are susceptible to moral and detection panics, and both phenomena are on occasions fuelled by a widespread perception of the dangers of creeping apostasy and the creation of a dangerous anti-social 'other'. Moreover the attitudes of authorities charged with policing these two offences prove to be remarkably similar. The conflict between localised and centralised forms of justice is inherent in both, as is the clear need for careful consideration of the wisdom of judicial or other (in)action. The pursuit of witchcraft has engaged anthropological scholars for many years, not simply because the subject matter appears so remote from our own time but because wider conclusions drawn from this study persistently show up new things to say about the society which produced the phenomenon. Drawing on this it is interesting to reflect on what an anthropology of blasphemy might be able to offer us.

Witchcraft was considered a *crimen exceptum*, with special jurisdictions throughout some parts of Europe, as well as a secular crime in which religious authority was expressly involved. Here there are clear parallels with heresy and later blasphemy, offences which were similarly identified as exposing explicit enemies of the prevailing social and moral order. Indeed Christina Larner's identification of how witches became 'Enemies of God' directly mirrors ways in which blasphemer's actions were seen as having the potential to destabilise civilisation and to point the way to the moral and spiritual abyss. As a crime, witchcraft had an explicitly political dimension, a clear parallel with the crime of blasphemy. Witchcraft became legally impossible after 1737 yet still retained important residues in popular culture and remained an important component of socialisation for those constructing a moral world for themselves. The disappearance of its legal existence did not destroy its cultural and intellectual existence since it was an enduringly powerful social reality.

Historians of witchcraft have themselves been alive to the last of these factors and have thus focused upon the dynamics of witch beliefs and witchcraft prosecutions within regions, societies and individual communities. This has included attempts to see how witchcraft 'works' in individual cases. In most respects this is indicative of a general trend to accept the social reality of witchcraft accusations as functions of societal strain, conflict and tension as well as conceivably indicating the function of particular social and psychological structures. Likewise the history of both witchcraft and blasphemy have contained discourses from contemporaries concerning their supposed anachronism, and historians of both are constantly faced with the temptation to discuss the two subjects in relation to the intellectual modernity of the societies in which they occur.

Thus the historian of blasphemy could do much worse than to follow the lead of the social historians of witchcraft. If the former were taken out of the courtroom, divested of its legal trappings and perspective, it would be allowed to live for historians actually in the society which created it. This would satisfy a desire to see how blasphemy 'works', not necessarily in a crude functionalist sense but to examine the dynamics which lead to the process of perception, the production of moral panics and the eventual naming and detection of such a crime. Moreover an attempt to at least acknowledge a 'dark figure' of blasphemy and possibly even to investigate the concept of informal semi-official justice is long overdue.

This book attempts to set this process in motion, if only by examining many of the standard cases anew. Whilst I would plead for a view of blasphemy that searches for a cultural context for its appearance it should be remembered that legal cases are the area in which the dialogue takes place. I would argue that prosecutions should be considered the cultural and legal flash points for issues rather than such courtroom dialogue, discourse and action being treated as the issues themselves. Thus, it seems reasonable to suggest not that the issues relating to the court and prosecution be denied importance or legitimacy but rather that they be considered to be only a part of the context.

The effectiveness of this approach has been emphasised for me in my interaction with other interested scholars. During the course of writing this book I have had the pleasure of delivering seminar papers and lectures on blasphemy. Invariably a commentator or member of the audience will invite me to speak upon the contemporary climate for blasphemy prosecutions. This usually consists of being asked to consider a collection of comic asides drawing upon paraphrases of biblical authority such as, 'Ten Reasons why Beer is Better than Jesus' or 'The Top 16 Biblical Ways to Acquire a Wife'. The following example will suffice and comes from the latter of these. Amongst the sixteen are the following:

Find an attractive prisoner of war, bring her home, shave her head, trim her nails, and give her new clothes. Then she's yours.

(Deuteronomy 21: 11–13)

Purchase a piece of property, and get a woman as part of the deal.

Boaz (Ruth 4: 5–10)

Wait for your brother to die. Take his widow.
(It's not just a good idea, it's the law).

Onan and Boaz (Deuteronomy or Leviticus, example in Ruth)

Don't be so picky. Make up for quality with quantity.

Solomon (1 Kings 11: 1–3)

A wife? ... NOT!!!

Paul (1 Corinthians 7: 32–5)

Become sinless, and die in atonement for others, and you can marry a whole bunch of people.

Jesus (Revelation 15)

The enquirer is usually American and, perceptibly shielded by first amendment protection, is anxious to know whether such utterances are punishable under the law of blasphemy as understood in England. It is at this point in the proceedings that I am reminded why the book you are about to read has the shape that it does. In answer to the inquirer I find myself drawn to diminish the role of what the law may 'think' in such matters. The first stage of offence has been accomplished by the observer drawing these items to my attention. This suggests that such an observer finds the matter potentially offensive. Already we are into areas of cultural response, which pushes me to answer that the application of the law has to wait until the cultural context persuades an individual to be offended. The context in which the offensive material is encountered can also be crucial. Whilst, in English law, the matter of the offence is arguably now once again more important than the manner, it is still true that the way a casual observer encounters such material can be crucial to the extent and depth of the offence felt. The depth of this feeling perhaps also depends upon the society's attitude to the phenomena (or, as literary scholars have it, tropes) of, in these cases, beer and marriage. Moreover I may even suggest that whether these texts are blasphemous is a considerably less interesting question than who produced them, for whom, and with what particular purpose in mind? By this stage the inquirer is perplexed and probably disappointed with an answer which amounts to 'that rather depends', yet their inquiry has reached into the heart of the problems associated with blasphemy. The history of blasphemy, whilst containing elements of legal history, would probably benefit from being understood as the history of a cultural phenomenon or a contest between cultures. In exploring the episodes in which these cultures conflict, the attention paid to context and prevailing social attitudes and 'atmosphere' (a clumsy but still useful word) is crucial to the enterprise of understanding them and the society which produced them. I thus hope that the reader will take away a realisation of the complexity of this topic which ultimately does, and rightly should, defy easy and unequivocal answers. Blasphemy is a many-sided phenomenon and searching for a simple definition risks destroying the multiplicity of ways in which it should be seen.

Questions of blasphemy invariably develop into questions about the precise relationship between religiosity and the State. How far are states prepared to protect religious culture from its opponents? Why do they defend this religious culture and how does this defence precisely reflect public opinion on the nature of society? These are large questions which have baffled philosophers and sociologists for many years. Whilst this book cannot hope to offer conclusions to the secularisation debate it may be able to assist other scholars in framing the questions in new ways. As such the relationship between blasphemy, State religiosity and public opinion as a reflection of popular religious mores represents a further underlying theme of this book. If we look at the contemporary world there are a number of fruitful examples to draw upon. Some modern religious organisations, in the United States in particular, manifest themselves as vehement opposition to state involvement in religion through the establishment of foundations to promote religious liberty (i.e. the liberty to be publicly religious in the face of a perceived atheistic or religiously neutral state). This response is manifested in almost every modern encounter between Church and state. The siege at Waco, the rise of televisual evangelism, the rampant state phobia of survivalist or vigilante anti-abortionist groups are all evidence of religion 'from below' seeking to divorce the realm of religion from the state. In Britain the Rushdie affair, whilst paradoxically seeking to produce a state sanction for religious laws, was proof self-evident that perceptions of religious values and the ownership of religion had passed to communities at large, leaving the state's previous role as protector/guarantor or promoter of religious culture as apparently ambiguous.

Related to this democratisation of religious power are the various analyses linked to postmodernism. These tend to suggest that blasphemy is itself a privileged discourse which the multiplication of narratives will ultimately destroy. The retreat from such privileged, or meta, narratives is accomplished by the multiplication of audiences and the destabilisation of these narratives. The different and increasingly enclosed cultural spaces in which forms of religion, atheism, pantheism etc. inhabit becomes, within this model, an increasing guarantee that they will not conflict with one another. This likelihood is enhanced, within the model, by the removal of privilege from religious narratives, so that religious and sacred texts become mere books, and religions themselves no more than sets of competing discourses. Although they did not know it, some blasphemers, it could be argued, would find themselves on the side of the current postmodern cultural theorists. One constant theme throughout this volume, is the variety of ways in which protagonists confront what might be called 'the culture problem'. This manifests itself in many ways. Prosecutors and defendants are each obviously themselves seeking, through their actions, to defend cultural precepts which they both hold dear. However, many blasphemers and their opponents are also arguing about the type of society and culture that their age should be host to. The defence offered by blasphemers such as Holyoake, Foote and Stewart contained references to other contemporary works which escaped prosecution for blasphemy because of their scholarly approach and content. In their argument for equal treatment they were trying to close the widening gap between polite and street culture. Early blasphemers wanted a level playing field where the source and medium of expression of ideas would count for less than their apparent utility. G. W. Foote, for example, hoped that the values of Freethought would cause Christianity to wither away – although we should note that he envisaged that there would be a victor and a vanquished.

The late twentieth century could be said to have produced a further defence of postmodern views, aired by some in the *Gay News* case, which postulates a set of imagined communities where diversity of opinion flourishes and is nurtured by wider and cheaper access to the raw materials, machinery and products of the mass media. Thus the gay community, like culturally marginal groups before it, could legitimately suggest that the Kirkup poem was intended for them and published for them in a magazine over which they had cultural ownership. Interlopers or those confronted by the consequences of a 'casual encounter' thus deserved to experience the offence they felt. More recently this argument and defence of such dissident cultures has gained credence with the appearance of many so-called blasphemous websites on the internet. These sites are known to atheists, are approved of by them and contain numerous disclaimers and warning screens which seek to prevent providing offence to the unwary. Moreover, the increasing sensitivity and sophistication of electronic screening devices strengthens this case for tolerance. What we as historians must ask is how such blasphemers have been so singularly unsuccessful in their cultural quest and ultimately whether their unsuccessful history questions postmodern theories about the past and future of world cultures.

At this point the reader may wonder why the main chronological focus of this book ends in 1980. Since this time there has been an important incident, the Salman Rushdie affair, which might be said to have altered the landscape of British society's perception of the offence, adding to it further questions regarding the justification for the law as it currently stands. Discussion of this case would add much to our understanding of the multi-cultural dimension of the offence. So why is substantial coverage of Rushdie, a manifestly important case, omitted from this book? Firstly, space is at a premium. Any consideration of the Rushdie case would have to establish, at some length, the context of religious multi-culturalism in Britain. Not only was this not the purpose of the book as originally conceived but pressure of space would have left it deficient in other coverage. Further, this would do a double disservice to the subject since I am acutely aware that others have produced, or are in a much better position to produce, analyses of the affair that are considerably more informed than any that might reasonably be attempted here. Lastly, the book and the expertise of the author concentrates upon the attacks upon Christianity which the laws of blasphemy were intended to protect. Whilst there is the briefest of discussions of the Rushdie case in the concluding chapter, this is solely to place it in the context of the previous two hundred years. Requests from British Muslims for an extension of the laws of blasphemy have provoked only a deafening silence from the authorities. I believe my review of the alternatives to the blasphemy law, as discussed by the Home Office in the first half of this century, will indicate why. I am conscious that this concentration upon anglocentric manifestations of religion in relation to the laws of blasphemy leaves me open to accusations of operating a contemporary form of academic Orientalism which might marginalise the subject of Islamic and other eastern religious responses. My answer to such accusations would be that this state of affairs is preferable to a relatively uninformed attempt to incorporate the Rushdie affair itself as an unsatisfactory coda to a history dominated by the desire to protect and nurture Christianity. This, I suggest, would constitute an even greater example of condescending Orientalism. It is my earnest hope that the history I describe and analyse will provide a context in which future studies of multi-cultural blasphemy in Britain may be placed.

*   *   *

There are some matters of reference and usage of which the reader should also be aware before proceeding further. The laws of blasphemy have altered during the chronological span covered by this book and a precise nomenclature at any given time would be both time consuming to explain and would produce pressure upon space in which more interesting matters may be explored. In some instances a generally understood 'law' as some would describe it does not exist so that the matter is, in these instances, in the hands of those who administer and try cases at Common Law. Whilst significant alterations in the law are of course discussed where they are pertinent I use the non-exclusive phrases 'the blasphemy laws', 'the laws of blasphemy', 'the laws against blasphemy' or occasionally simply 'blasphemy'. I hope that the reader will forgive this inconsistent shorthand but the decision was taken to preserve readability rather than pedantic repetition.

Whilst the title of the book and occasionally the material inside refers to 'Blasphemy in Britain' there is an ambiguity at work here. Quite obviously the legal systems of both England and Scotland, as well as the legal and administrative structure which evolved in Northern Ireland, differed markedly from each other during this period, and indeed the legacy in this area left to all three illuminates this. However the reference to Britain is intended to indicate the clash of blasphemy and blasphemous impulses with moral concerns, motivations and cultural phenomena that are common to Britain as a whole. Whilst the law may, for example, have been different in Scotland there was a concern about the nature, scope and policing of morality, albeit tinged with significant local characteristics, which it shared with England. Also meaningful communication between local systems of justice and the Home Office were a constant of the situation in Scotland. Likewise the extension of the Carlile agitation north of the Border has consequences for the situation outlined in England. Nonetheless this does not mean that the peculiarities of Scottish law are neglected altogether and where necessary and relevant these are mentioned in the text.

*   *   *

This book is divided into two sections and the first of these – Chapters 1 and 2 – provide both background and theoretical grounding in areas pertinent to the second section. Chapter 1 sketches the origins of modern blasphemy from its existence in medieval England through its ambivalent status in the early modern period when the relationship between church and state was in the process of close critical examination and negotiation. This chapter concludes with an outline of the law and cultural climate from which our more detailed study of the modern period can begin. The second chapter, 'Blasphemy and Theory', is an attempt to evaluate a range of theories which have entered the realm of cultural history during the last 20 years. The motivation behind this task has been to assess their contribution, or potential contribution, to the study of the history of blasphemy. The need to do so, as the chapter will outline, is also occasioned by the application of forms of theory to the subject by a number of recent writers. Whilst I remain profoundly sceptical over the utility of these various theories it is hoped that the treatment of them has been fair and even-handed. Potentially valuable insights are highlighted, as are areas where the author considers that the application of theory clouds or distorts central issues. There is no intention to simplistically confront theory in any malicious manner and I hope that readers more enthusiastic about the various bodies of theory discussed will take what they can from the analysis on offer. For readers less versed in this area, or less enthusiastic about it, the chapter should provide a useful introduction to what is being, and will be said by others in the future as they endeavour to take the subject along this road. Ultimately the reader must assess the usefulness of these theories alongside the material and interpretations outlined and discussed in the second section.

The second section of the book is ostensibly the consideration of a number of blasphemous episodes in their context. This involves an examination of the legal status of the crime in the society which witnessed the episode in question and the importance of each case for the cultural history of the offence of blasphemy. However there is also consideration of the arguments, motives and achievements of the blasphemers concerned and a chapter structure organised around their individual 'cases' hopefully reflects this. The third chapter considers the situation during the first 40 years of the nineteenth century and investigates the significance of the cases against the works of Paine, Carlile, William Hone, Southwell, Holyoake and others. Chapter 4 offers a more detailed picture of the cases against George William Foote and his contemporaries in the early 1880s. This is for several reasons which will become obvious to the reader, most pertinent of which is the fact that the Foote case represented the intrusion of the issue of blasphemy into the world of mass media, mass audiences and mass reading publics. As such, government and the newly influential phenomenon of public opinion were made to listen to what Foote was saying and writing in a wider context than just simply analysing the actions which placed him and his compatriots in court.

The treatment of the cases against Boulter, Stewart, Gott and Pack in the subsequent chapter is dealt with in a similar manner. As in Chapter 4, the cases against these men illuminate a different range of societal concerns at work in the actions of those accused, the actions of the authorities and the wider forum of public opinion. Chapter 6 examines the case for the repeal of the laws of blasphemy in the period 1912–1938. The lessons learned from this latter chapter intend to indicate, at least partially, why reform or abolition of the laws against blasphemy has proved so difficult. Whilst at times some blasphemers and their freethinking supporters suggested that reform was possible the evidence of this chapter indicates that significant interests expressed an opinion that the *status quo* should be maintained. These opinions ranged from informed knowledge of the potential repercussion of such action, through to simple lack of political will to act. Chapter 7 investigates a particular episode in 1938 in which a number of the facets discussed in previous chapters came together in a potentially explosive incident. Temporarily heightened concerns for the moral welfare of the country were linked to attempts to redefine its Christian character in the face of a deteriorating international situation. When such concerns were latched onto by the extreme right of British politics the result was an attempt to extend the blasphemy laws which not only undermined a century of what might be called the philosophical 'case-law' of toleration for religious minorities but sought to recapture earlier ground conceded. There is a warning here that progress in the direction of toleration has by no means been a constant within British society and the chapter also highlights the dangers inherent in a bland unthinking assumption that to extend the laws of blasphemy would result in an equalisation of protection for all who are religious.

The penultimate chapter (Chapter 8) investigates the *Gay News* case of 1977 and the significant change in the law which was a central part of this judgment. A particular feature of this chapter is an examination of how far the case actually represented a clear attempt by some sections of Christianity to recolonise the religious laws of the country 'from below'. The conclusion attempts to summarise the main implications of this study in relation to the current status of the law. This task was aided (and to an extent complicated) by the resolution of the case against Nigel Wingrove in the European Court of Human Rights which occurred during the writing of this book. In a real sense the law as outlined in the *Gay News* case is directly invoked and reapplied to this case and it displays in graphic detail the unsatisfactory legacy that this case left society to grapple with. Whilst I am no philosopher, still less a lawyer, the book nevertheless concludes with some suggestions as to how the phenomenon of blasphemy may be tackled by contemporary society. The danger is that the specialist reader will want to review the arguments still further and, whilst some contemporary reading is alluded to, the wisdom of a historian pronouncing upon the subject may be questioned. My answer would be to suggest that the debate should be continued in this generation to, at the very least, avoid future generations having to live with a law they are ignorant of or do not understand. This history deserves to be known because it not only created our present – it is, in cultural, legal and political senses, still a part of our present.

Notes

1. Bailey, S. H., D. J. Harris, and B. L. Jones (1995), *Civil Liberties: Cases and Materials*, London: Butterworths, p. 592.
2. Bradney, A. (1993), *Religions, Rights and Laws*, London: Leicester University Press, p. 83.
3. Nokes, G. D. (1928), *A History of the Crime of Blasphemy*, pp. 107–9.
4. Stephen, James Fitzjames, 'The Law on Blasphemy and Blasphemous Libel', *Fortnightly Review*, March 1884, 289–318. Stephen's view provides one of the most accessible ways of considering this. He seems to suggest that the Christian religion is considered part and parcel of the law of the land and that protection comes to Anglicanism because it is the church then established by that law.
5. Foxe, John (1563), *Acts and Monuments*, London.
6. Foote, G. W. (1886), *Prisoner for Blasphemy*, London; Foote, G. W. (1889), *Defence of Free Speech, being a three hours' address to the jury in the court of Queen's Bench before Lord Coleridge, on April 24, 1883*, London; Hetherington, Henry (1840), *A full report of the trial of Henry Hetherington: on an indictment for blasphemy, before Lord Denman and a special jury, at the Court of Queen's Bench, Westminster, on Tuesday, December 8th 1840*, London; Holyoake, George Jacob (1850), *The Last Trial for Alleged Atheism in England. A Fragment of an Autobiography*, London; Holyoake, George Jacob (1857), *The Case of Thomas Pooley, the Cornish Well Sinker*, London: Holyoake and Company; Holyoake, George Jacob (1864), *The Suppressed Lecture, at Cheltenham*, London; Holyoake, G. J. (1844), *The Scotch Trials. The Trial of Thomas Paterson for Blasphemy, Before the High Court of Justiciary, Edinburgh, with The Whole of his Bold and Effective Defence, also The Trials of Thomas Finlay and Miss Matilda Roalfe (for Blasphemy), In the Sheriff's Court. With notes and a special dissertation on Blasphemy Prosecutions in General by the Secretary of the 'Anti-Persecution Union'*, London & Edinburgh; Hone, William (1817), *The first trial of William Hone, on an ex-officio information*, 2nd ed. [Issued as part of *The three trials of William Hone*], London; Hone, William (1817), *The second trial of William Hone, on an ex-officio information*. [Issued as part of *The three trials of William Hone*], London; Hone, William (1818), *The third trial of William Hone, on an ex-officio information*. [Issued as part of The three trials of William Hone], London; Hone, William (1818), *The three trials of William Hone, for publishing three parodies*, London; Hone, William (1818), *Trial by jury and liberty of the press. The proceedings at the public meeting ... at the City of London tavern, for the purpose of enabling William Hone to surmount the difficulties in which he has been placed*, London.
7. Bradlaugh-Bonner, Hypatia (1934), *Penalties Upon Opinion*, London: Watts & Co; Calder-Marshall, Arthur (1972), *Lewd, Blasphemous and Obscene*, London: Hutchinson; Lawton, David (1993), *Blasphemy*, London: Harvester Wheatsheaf; Levy, Leonard W. (1981), *Treason against God: A History of the offense of blasphemy*, New York; Levy, Leonard W. (1993), *Blasphemy: Verbal Offense Against the Sacred from Moses to Salman Rushdie*, New York: Knopf; Said, Edward (1994), *Culture and Imperialism*, London: Vintage; Said, Edward (1995), *Orientalism*, London: Penguin; Walter, Nicholas (1977), *Blasphemy in Britain: The Practice and*

Punishment of Blasphemy, and the Trial of 'Gay News', London; Walter, Nicholas (1990), *Blasphemy Ancient and Modern*, London: Rationalist Press Association; Webster, Richard (1990), *A Brief History of Blasphemy: Liberalism, Censorship and 'The Satanic Verses'*, Southwold.

PART ONE

CHAPTER ONE

The Law of Blasphemy in Britain: Origins and Development

The law of blasphemy, perhaps our last meaningful contact with medieval and early modern conceptions of morality and society, has from earliest times been used to prevent attacks upon the sacred religious doctrines and artifacts of particular religious beliefs. More specifically many religions have more often than not been assured of, and have accepted, the protection of the state in which they flourish and have thus enforced religious conformity upon its citizens. This exclusivity of protection simultaneously created by definition the offences of both blasphemy (profaning and denying the truth and value of an established religion) and heresy (which was considered to be theological or doctrinal deviation from the established religion). Here the relationship between religion and the state should not merely be considered to be the secular protecting the sacred but a symbiotic one in which the legitimacy of the state was upheld by explicit and frequent reference to sacred doctrine. The negative side of this relationship was that attacks upon such sacred doctrine became automatically attacks upon the sovereignty and civic peace of the state. This desire to protect the state from the encroachment of toleration and the danger that this could be construed as weakness was generally the reason for the punishment of heretics and blasphemers. This is in part an explanation of why offences against divine authority are considered significant secular offences within human society rather than being left merely to the sanction of supernatural retribution. Moreover the desire to protect the blasphemer from the physical consequences of his action introduced at an early stage an at least putative concept of public order as an important civil consequence of the offence.[1]

The Mosaic law understood the crime of blasphemy to be 'showing disrespect for God, doubting his powers, even disobeying his commandments',[2] but nonetheless maintained that the notion of verbal abuse of God or misusing his name was the paramount offence. This aspect of the rabbinical law of the Talmud represented a line which Christendom rapidly deviated from in its desire to protect sacred doctrine and belief.[3]

A clue to the development of the Christian definition of the offence lies in the fact that rabbinical law had no actual conception of heresy.

This was a term which began to replace blasphemy as the supreme sin in Christian circles as the Greek influence upon the early church waned. Despite this the conflation of religious and political deviation persisted in Roman law where it constituted a capital offence for threatening the sovereignty of the state.[4] Heresy encompassed early Christendom's vision of the variety of offences against religion and God and became the primary offence to which all other nuances of transgression could be appended.[5] The increasing interchangeability of the terms blasphemy and heresy was more than just a confused elision of the concepts.[6] As Christian theologians sought to define and prescribe orthodoxy in the face of challenges from Arianism, Gnosticism and other divergent beliefs the concept of heresy completely covered the notion of deviation from orthodoxy.[7] As such, blasphemers became merely a particularly specious, contemptible (and probably to contemporaries faintly bizarre) form of heresy in which denial, profanity and levity substituted themselves for the serious doctrinal deviations advanced by other heretics.

The definition of heretics as antithetical to existing authority placed them effectively outside the polity. Those outside this closed system were to be the object of pity or crusade (in this case the jew, infidel and pagan) or – more pertinent to the heretic – to be punished or restored to this 'closed system'.[8] The structural integrity of this system, its opportunity for action and the supremacy of orthodoxy is demonstrated by Lambert's exposition of an early eleventh-century example of heresy in the West, emanating from Orléans, which involved a number of clergy. In particular the source for the story contains some interesting insights into the early medieval construction of heresy and the operation of the ecclesiastical polity as a closed system. The chronicler Paul, a monk of St Père de Chartres, concluded instinctively that those in the story who were guilty of heresy were diabolically inspired and these are described in the same terms as those suffering from physical or psychological sickness to clearly indicate their deviation from normal society. The culmination of the story involves the Bishop of Beauvais investigating the precise theological errors of the heretics involved and showing himself 'quite uninterested in explaining how the heretical ideas had reached the guilty men', which, as Lambert suggests, are 'precisely the questions which intrigue the modern historian'. The system was safe and self-regulating since the heresy could be explained as emanating from the devil, rendering the source and conduit of the apparent evil as of little or no consequence.[9]

The construction of the heretic as outside society very quickly became the construction of a stereo or archetype which often did much to implicate the transgressor in his own folly.[10] The heretic in the medieval period was often described as displaying a surfeit of pride which led to his or her apostasy. Similarly any display of piety, a characteristic clearly inherent in any searching for religious truth, was clearly a form of deception.[11] Likewise the heretic's estrangement from true learning by way of autodidact strategies was assumed to be a part of the cultural baggage of the offence as well as a cloak for loose or libertine lifestyles. In short, a host of interlocking and interdependent accusations served to signal the heretic as an outsider who threatened the peace and prosperity of the community through disrupting the central tenets of spirituality and government which, canon law argued, were necessary to its survival.[12] It has also been suggested that rulers with a penchant for administrative and governmental innovation were also more likely to consider the detection and prosecution of heretics as a means of justifying and consolidating their forms of power – even to the extent that heresy prosecutions might profitably be seen as a function of growing literacy.[13] Society's creation of outsiders has also been analysed, however, in terms of heresy constituting an outlet for errant tendencies and beliefs in a society with no such internal and institutionalised outlets.[14] More often than not this alternative way of life which came to be regarded as heresy forged itself as a mirror image of the established church-preaching and practising poverty whilst speaking out against the church's endowments, simony and indulgences. This clearly marked such people as representative of an alternative way of life.[15]

The identification of heresy with blasphemy must also be made for some not so obvious reasons that reach beyond the conflation of the two offences throughout the Middle Ages.[16] Whilst some historians of heresy have woven a modern interpretation upon the pronouncements of Wycliffe,[17] some literary scholars have challenged this view suggesting a distinct concept of blasphemy was present in medieval pastoral and didactic literature.[18] The importance of considering heresy, and Lollardy in particular, as significant for the history of blasphemy turns around the introduction of a new legal apparatus for combating heresy which was to form the basis of subsequent law in the area of religious prescription and tolerance.[19] Indeed, the role of religious authority in defining and using 'a power process in which Truth is authorised and anathematised … for dealing with the dangers (moral, intellectual, political) which threaten it' has been underrated.[20] The introduction of the statute *De heretico comburendo* in 1401 marked a significant change in the attitude of secular authority to matters of religious orthodoxy. The final sanction in cases brought under the statute henceforth lay with the secular authority and effectively made heresy a crime punishable by burning at the stake. The state and secular authorities henceforth became 'executioner' as much as 'policeman'.[21]

Such modifications brought England into line with the rest of the Christian West and increasingly linked the offence with treason and sedition which became self-fulfilling prophecy as Lollardy took on a revolutionary political edge arguing for the use of the vernacular and greater lay participation in the liturgy.[22] Indeed determined use of the vernacular by defendents in Lollard heresy trials was a significant defiance of the letter and apparatus of religious conformity.[23] Moreover the ecclesiastical authorities' willingness to indulge in a popular war of words with Lollard theology suggests how successful the latter were at challenging religious governance and authority.[24] *De heretico comburendo* itself may have been introduced as a measure to ensure clerical support for the usurper Henry IV by drawing closer links between the interests of church and state.[25] Indeed, Hypatia Bradlaugh-Bonner could not resist reiterating the story that this statute was passed through the Lords without reference to the Commons – an interpretation which served to undermine the level of popular assent involved and the statute's ultimate credibility.[26]

The link between blasphemy and heresy also had an enduring cultural history for those who were later to be accused of blasphemy and those who were to write against it. Whilst Hypatia Bradlaugh-Bonner identified a number of victims of religious persecution in the thirteenth century, even she was prepared to admit that these were in no sense related to the concerted policy against heresy that was later to take shape. Victims included an Albigensian in 1210 and a Deacon who is described as having apostised to Judaism in 1222.[27] To these writers *De heretico comburendo* thus effectively enshrined the policy whereby heresy and blasphemy became related elements in a history of religious (in)tolerance. Such an approach by sympathetic authors was often necessary to display blasphemers as culturally beyond the advanced guard of modernising theological opinion. Likewise the oppressive nature of state control of religion was also displayed by the law's opponents as having a long history with regular attacks upon opinion construed as anti-Christian.[28] Indeed the creation of this pantheon of perceived injustice had the advantage of illuminating the suffering of individuals for opinions which later became accepted by the state or were even appropriated by it and used in subsequent trials against other defendants. Likewise the perceived antiquity of the laws had considerable dynamic resonance for nineteenth-century English society and its twin cultural obsessions of modernisation and civilisation.

The Statute of *De heretico comburendo* was strengthened by a statute of 1414 which enhanced the clerical control over the offence,[29] a phenomenon which must have itself caused considerable irritation to Lollard opinions concerning the secular power of ecclesiastics. Nokes is clear that the role of Common Law officers was restricted to minor functions which he saw as analogous to the modern role of 'committing' magistrates who investigated individual cases with the view to providing evidence for the arrest of accused persons. At no stage was any offence related to unorthodox religious opinion tried in a court of Common Law.[30]

The persecution of Lollardy from the end of the fourteenth century onwards was evidence enough to Bradlaugh-Bonner that it was the reality of unorthodox opinion that was here being punished. To demonstrate this she drew her readers' attention to 38 individuals executed under the 1414 statute and other individuals including Oldcastle, William Taylor, Thomas Bagley and Richard Wyche. Similarly the trials of over 100 people in Suffolk during a three-year period between 1428 and 1431 were cited.[31] This account drew heavily upon John Foxe's *Acts and Memorials* and this book was instrumental not simply in publicising the heroism of its subjects but also for rewriting the coherence of their collective history. Lambert suggests that this treatment of the Lollards not only signposted them as forerunners and sacrificial victims for the Reformation but also as important examples of independent spirituality. Their deviation from accepted ecclesiastical authority had been precipitated by their collective access to the scriptures in the vernacular which proved instrumental in the solidarity of the Reformation.[32]

The situation of the laws against blasphemy and heresy at this time and their clearly ideological dimension is well summed up by the words of Lambert:

> While so much else changed in the sixteenth century, the medieval concept of heresy and the overriding duty to repress it by force remained in being. Definitions of orthodoxy changed profoundly, but both Catholics and Protestants were agreed in asserting its importance and in using the power of the State to impose their versions on the recalcitrant. Friar John Forest was burned under Henry VIII for fidelity to the medieval doctrine of the papacy; Calvin's Geneva declared itself the legitimate heir to the authority of the now discredited medieval Church by burning Cervetus for his anti-Trinitarian views; ... The Christian Church in the East as well as the West was the heir to the assumptions of the pagan Roman Empire and of the whole ancient world, of the duty of the ruler to enforce right belief, and, with some hesitation, its leaders came to act on those assumptions. Nonetheless, repression of wrongful belief in the West came during the Middle Ages to take on a dynamic quality which it did not have in the East.[33]

*   *   *

The reign of Henry VIII marked a new phase in the linkage between offences against the ideological elements of religion and their connection with treasonable opinion and activity. An Act of 1533 modernised the Act of 1414 by restricting its definition and application whilst enhancing the machinery for its prosecution of the more sharply defined offence. The involvement of clerics in the machinery of this statute was reconfirmed yet the power of the King was foregrounded in the 1533 Act's close relationship with the Act of Supremacy's statutory spiritual jurisdiction.[34] The legal power of medieval religion did not, in this instance, pass away with the break with Rome but was streamlined and transfered to secular government. A further statute in 1547 protected the sacrament from 'any contemptuouse wordes or by anny wordes of depravinge dispisinge or reviling' to be tried at quarter sessions with penalties of imprisonment for offenders. Likewise another statute of the following year served to protect the Book of Common Prayer from 'derogation, depraving or despising'. Both statutes protected the Protestant liturgy and, as such, were victims of the Marian persecution only to be revived in the reign of Elizabeth.[35] The later Elizabethan period saw at least some attempt to modernise the law in this area with the repeal of some of the older statutes against heresy under 1 Eliz. c. 1 s. 6. This same act also gave commissioners the power to enquire into certain offences previously within the ecclesiastical realm of jurisdiction.

Scotland's blasphemy law up to this point evolved in a manner analogous to the situation in England, with ecclesiastical jurisdiction shading into a developing lay and common law interest in the offence. As in England, statutory jurisdiction over the offence began with the Reformation with an Act of 1551 (reinforced in 1581) which provided punishments for the Common Law crime dependent upon social standing.[36]

The Reformation throughout Europe also had profound implications for the alteration of attitudes towards non-orthodox religious beliefs. The differing protestant theologies offered by both Luther and Calvin had considerable impact upon the development of blasphemy as a uniquely modern and uniquely specific offence. Luther himself had long preached against the evil of judicial proceedings against heresy and moreover found himself cast in this mould by the attacks of Catholic theologians. Thus the use of the term heresy became uncomfortable for Luther and he began to use the term 'blasphemy' as a substitute, using it against other protestant theologies as well as against Judaism. Such a position allowed Luther to countenance the punishment of Anabaptists who were clearly beyond the pale but it also produced an offence and charge which he himself could use against the Catholic Church. Similarly, Calvin took to using the term blasphemy and here some of the connotations of the offence that were to become commonplace in England in the succeeding three centuries are present. Under Calvin's administrative control of Geneva the offence was broken down into components of ascending seriousness ranging from swearing by the name of Christ, taking trivial oaths, engaging in impious incantations and, most serious of all, dishonouring God. The elements of profanity, mocking, contumely and scoff which characterise later prosecutions are all here and it is interesting that Levy adds as a coda to this list the suggestion that false doctrine, previously regarded as heresy, was added to this list by Calvin as a component of dishonour.[37]

Although the Reformation produced a revitalisation of theology it was also a period which enabled new conceptions of the relationship between religious and secular government to be negotiated. It was effectively a period during which the legal power vested in the religious establishment became more closely allied and in some cases annexed by the State. Indeed this new relationship gave many of these forms of jurisdiction a new lease of life. Historians have long commented how the increased involvement of educated and enthusiastic laymen was instrumental in the spread and vehemence of witchcraft prosecutions during the same period. However, there was also a sense in which the concept of the godly commonwealth which was shared across the protestant world gave the State the responsibility for policing and enforcing moral conformity.

Nonetheless it is also possible to oversimplify the extent of this shift of emphasis in jurisdiction during the Reformation as well as the replacement of heresy by proceedings for blasphemy. Bradlaugh-Bonner noted that the last victims of the heresy laws in England, Matthew Legate and Edward Wightman, were burned in the reign of James I. Whilst this was the last burning for heresy in England it was also clear that the examination of both of the defendants and the indictments against them once more contained the interleaved identification of blasphemy as a form of heresy. Likewise the laws relating to religious opinion in England, whilst increasingly governed by statute, had nonetheless by no means been secularised in terms of legal procedure and jurisdiction. Nokes suggests that the dominion of ecclesiastical lawyers over the crimes against religion remained unchallenged well into the seventeeth century. The executions of Legate and Wightman constituted the high watermark of the heresy/blasphemy conflation which persuaded Cranmer, as early as 1553, to produce a coherent statement of the ecclesiastical laws of England which, for the first time, sought to distinguish blasphemy from heresy.[38]

The reign of Charles I brought a new wave of organised prosecution under William Laud. Using the Court of Star Chamber and the Court of

High Commission for Ecclesiastical Causes Laud gained a reputation for zealous and arbitrary rule, particularly since the Court of Star Chamber effectively had discretionary power over any matter in which it chose to adjudicate. Despite this Laud was not involved in prosecutions for blasphemy, preferring to proceed on other charges.[39] Interestingly the link between sedition against the monarch and attacks upon the church of which the monarch was head surfaced in the case of Thomas Atwood who was fined and imprisoned for denouncing the quality of preaching. Nokes points out that this case illuminates the consideration of the occasion for a breach of the peace was intrinsic to the actual words being spoken. Since there was no proof that the King's Bench regarded seditious words and breach of the peace as two seperate offences on this occasion the natural conclusion was that the law assumed one proceeded from the other.[40]

The fall of Laud and the disintegration of his ecclesiastical forms of jurisdiction in 1641 left blasphemy as an offence in an interesting limbo which was to prove troublesome by the middle of the decade. The cases brought against Paul Best and John Biddle between 1645 and 1647 illuminated the gaps precipitated by the abolition of clerical jurisdiction. The first of these, Best, was a Socinian whose whole range of opinions – but chiefly anti-Trinitarian ones – were condemned by the Westminster Assembly and recommended for further investigation by a special committee. After imprisonment, the burning of his works by the public hangman and a stream of accusations which confirmed his opinions as blasphemous Best was quietly released. This state of affairs was occasioned by the removal of the ecclesiastical jurisdiction to try cases concerning religious opinion, a situation confirmed by the opinion of Common lawyers that they had no power to assume such jurisdiction.[41]

Similarly John Biddle, sometimes referred to as the father of English Unitarianism, also suffered imprisonment and the public burning of his works. Biddle's attempts at his own defence, however, were noteworthy since they included the release of an underground printing of one of his tracts, the provocatively anti-Trinitarian *Twelve Arguments drawn out of the Scriptures: Wherein the commonly received Opinion touching the Deity of the Holy Spirit is clearly and fully refuted*. The resulting publicity and that which stemmed from the move to publicly burn a subsequent tract was an important catalyst for a renewed attempt on the part of Parliament to regain the jurisdiction lost in the early years of the decade.[42] The late 1640s witnessed the passing of a number of statutes that represented the reacquisition of the lapsed powers.[43] Alongside an ordinance which sought to combat the menace of unlicensed printed matter the main attack was constituted by the Blasphemy Act of 1648. This prescribed the death penalty for denying the Trinity, the

Resurrection and the Day of Judgement. The act also contained statutory protection for several Calvinist ideas in that the doctrine of free-will, general salvation, prayer for redemption of sins and the divine command of the sacraments of communion and baptism all took on the mantle of heresy. Such provisions effectively attacked doctrines ranging from Arminianism to Baptism.[44]

Although some of these powers were superseded by an ordinance of 1650 this did little more than clarify jurisdictional matters. Single justices and heads of Corporations could imprison for periods of six months upon the discovery of certain blasphemies and errors. A second offence involved trial by Justices of Assize and of Gaol Delivery and sentences of banishment with felony status conferred upon those returning from this sentence.[45] Whereas the laws of 1648 had been intended to combat Socinian doctrines it is likely that this later ordinance was intended to be used against Ranter and other Antinomian doctrines.[46]

Whilst the Commonwealth later in 1650 ushered in an era of religious toleration for protestant beliefs[47] not covered by the two preceding acts, the country was rocked by the proceedings against the Quaker leader and quasi-prophet James Naylor. (Bradlaugh-Bonner characteristically chose to call him a 'religious madman' while Nicolas Walter has described it as 'the most notorious religious case of the century'.[48] Naylor, who had attempted to enter Bristol in a Christ-like manner, was arrested for this act although it was simply the last in a long line of brushes with the law for forms of blasphemous preaching which involved warrants being issued in Westmoreland, Lancaster and a spell languishing in Derby prison. Naylor was eventually brought before the House of Commons and once more this raised the thorny question of parliamentary jurisdiction over the case. The Best and Biddle cases had been unsatisfactory since imprisonment had been used as a hybrid detention and punishment primarily to avoid the issue of jurisdiction. The Naylor case elicited hot debate in the Commons about whether it could be tried and punishment decided at all. Levy notes that the issue at stake was whether toleration of the beliefs and active spread of Quakerism should be countenanced. In the event a range of opinion emerged from those who thought the death penalty too harsh through to those who wanted Naylor executed by hanging, drawing and quartering or by the biblically-prescribed method of stoning.[49] In assessing the true context of this reaction we should remember Christopher Hill's suggestion that the millenarian atmosphere of the 1650s meant that the Quakers represented a more dangerous political threat than their subsequently written history would allow.[50] In the event a parliamentary vote narrowly spared Naylor the death penalty although he was sentenced to be whipped through Westminster, pilloried, branded, bored through the tongue and to be detained indefinitely.

Although the case itself and its sentence was extraordinary in its immediate impact it also represented a milestone for future interpretations of the law. Lord Commissioner Bulstrode Whitelocke investigated the original hebrew texts of Leviticus and concluded that the death penalty was not justified by Mosaic law since the notion of blasphemy contained therein required direct misuse of the name of God.[51] It was this line of thinking which surely persuaded Whitelocke, whilst giving judgment, to make a distinction between blasphemy and heresy. The first he considered to be 'the reviling or cursing the name of God or of our neighbour' whilst the latter was the expression of erroneous opinion.[52] Perhaps this judgment could be seen to be sounding the death knell of the conception of heresy as punishable by process of law, although theoretically anti-Trinitarian doctrines remained punishable well into the eighteenth century and technically until the Trinity Act of 1813. Some were also to argue – mischievously – that such opinions were proscribed well beyond this legislation.

The interregnum also had considerable effects upon the development of the crime of blasphemy in Scotland. Although there had been an earlier statute of 1621 which made the holding of atheistical opinions a capital offence it was a statute of 1649 which formally created a statutory offence of blasphemy. This carried statutory punishments for the persistent and wilful denial of the deity which were reconfirmed at the Restoration in 1661.[53] The Restoration in England, however, saw a partial reversal of the trends that had taken root under the Commonwealth. Nokes readily admitted that 1660 marked the start of a period under which the Common Law came to preside over the offence.[54] Similarly the Commonwealth reliance upon Old Testament precedent declined taking with it, for the moment, a Mosaic-inspired interpretation of blasphemy. The Restoration returned the legal system to its condition in 1640 although significantly there was no attempt to re-establish the court of Star Chamber which had vied with the ecclesiastical courts for jurisdiction over these matters. Alongside this attempt to remove the Commonwealth from the statute book there were measures which extended a variety of degrees of toleration to religious minorities who did not threaten the peaceful government of the kingdom.

The first blasphemy case to appear in the Restoration period was the prosecution of Sir Charles Sedley in 1663. This case receives significant coverage in Kenny, Levy and Lawton but curiously not in Bradlaugh-Bonner.[55] Sir Charles Sedley was accused of preaching blasphemously after a number of public acts of libertineage including defecating in the street and, according to Pepys, 'acting all the postures of lust and buggery that could be imagined'. This was followed by the preaching of a blasphemous sermon while naked and further lewd acts with a wine glass which served to parody the communion.[56] Lawton argues the case was important as a discourse which derives power from notions of inversion associated with witchcraft, libertineage and motifs that would later be used by de Sade. However, what is interesting from the legal point of view was the considerable disruption that Sedley's actions had upon the public peace since the inn from which he disported himself was attacked by a mob enraged by his actions. The offence under which he was tried was 'obscenity' or 'indecency'. In finding Sedley guilty the court of King's Bench at once recognised the right of the Common Law to try the defendent rather than the Ecclesiastical Court, as well as acknowledging that the offence of 'indecency' could legally be considered to be derogatory of Christianity. The importance of this precedent enabled local judges to intervene now in matters of blasphemy as they had earlier done with heresy. St John Robilliard concludes that this was effectively the first Common Law prosecution for blasphemy, beginning his chapter relating to the legal history of blasphemy from this case.[57]

The most sensational and ultimately important incident which followed the Restoration was the case of John Taylor in 1675. The magistrates of Guildford took fright when the extent of Taylor's opinions was aired graphically before them. Taylor claimed in quasi-prophetic language that he was sent by God as Christ's younger brother although there were also claims such as 'Christ was a whoremaster' and the use of the phrase 'God damn', which clearly entered the blasphemous area of contumelious language, potentially providing evidence of disturbance of the peace.[58] Taylor was initially concluded to be insane and handed over to the keeper of Bedlam who was instructed to administer forms of beneficial correction. The acceptance of Taylor's unbalanced state of mind by subsequent historians has lately been qualified. Levy suggests that some of his pronouncements – particularly the attempt to qualify the 'Christ is a whoremaster' rhetoric – referred to Christ's mastery of the popish whore of Babylon and constituted an established and generally accepted mode of puritan speech.[59] Lawton takes this line of analysis a stage further, suggesting that the case was a contest of language leading to definitions of what was orthodox and acceptable and what was proscribed. In this instance Taylor's 'Christ is a whoremaster' can be linked to the Ranter ideas that would not have been out of place emanating from Lawrence Clarkson.[60]

Certainly these interpretations are informative since they shed light upon the rapidly diversifying world of religious pluralism (Lawton suggests the word subculture) in Restoration England. As suggested, the possibility of linking Taylor's pronouncements, however tenuously, to the works of Ranters, Muggletonians and other marginal sects, reinforces the view that some extreme forms of deviance from religious conformity threatened the safety of government. Lawton infers that to accept entirely at face value the account of Taylor as an insane man is to miss this important link to a wider subcultural dimension. This is a valuable insight which suggests that a broadly-based protestant religious conformity was increasingly being viewed as central to the Restoration settlement and the basic principles of tolerant yet firm government it sought to embody.

Taylor's case eventually came to the Court of King's Bench where it was heard before Lord Chief Justice Sir Matthew Hale. Despite Taylor's defence that his words had been misinterpreted he was nonetheless swiftly convicted and in his speech passing sentence upon Taylor, Justice Hale pronounced further upon the law. His interpretation was to have a long life and prove very influential into the next two centuries. Hale's speech to the prisoner Taylor effectively demonstrated that Christianity was not only a central underpinning of the laws of the land as they were generally accepted but that, perhaps more importantly for the later history of the offence, attacks upon its integrity constituted an attack upon government, society and morality simultaneously.

Nokes gives two versions, derived from the recognised authorities Ventris and Keble, of the report of Hale's words. The first of these is widely quoted:

> And Hale said, that such kind of wicked blasphemous words were not only an offence to God and Religion, but a crime against the Laws, State and Government, and therefore punishable in this Court. For to say, Religion is a Cheat, is to dissolve all those Obligations whereby the civil societies are preserved, and that Christianity is a parcel of the Laws of England; and therefore to reproach the Christian religion is to speak in subversion of the law.[61]

The second account, whilst obviously containing the substance of the first also has some interesting differences of phrase and emphasis. The passage begins with what must be seen as the complete assumption of power to deal with this matter by the Common Law.[62] This second account, however, also introduced the concept of contumelious words as well as a judgment upon the iniquity of Taylor's assertion that the Protestant Religion was fiction since it dissolved 'all obligation to Government by Oaths'.[63] This statement intended to represent (since it placed religion at the base of all subsequent English Law) the last word on the matter but went significantly further in its attack upon atheism. Cromartie also suggests that this pronouncement importantly embodied Hale's personal denial of the validity of atheism which saw it as 'not really a speculative belief, but a depraving tendency that afflicted fallen man'. Such attitudes were also seen by Hale as an attempt to dissolve the sanctions of natural law.[64]

The Hale judgment was taken to be central to the treatment of cases of blasphemy down to the Foote case in 1883 and the subsequent rescinding of this view by Justice John Duke Coleridge. Bradlaugh-Bonner described the Hale judgment as 'the law which has affected us most during the past two hundred years' and this is scarcely an overstatement. Many subsequent liberal and secularist commentators have sought to unravel the meaning and intention of the Hale judgement from a variety of perspectives. Bradlaugh-Bonner and other interested secularist commentators have quickly pointed out that Hale's creation of a new law emanated from a man who was also responsible for the conviction and execution of women accused of witchcraft. This labelled his dictum as immediately suspect or more cogently identified it with an age of perceived barbarism. The legal impossibility of witchcraft, achieved merely 50 or so years after the Taylor case, served further to highlight the anachronism which blasphemy appeared to represent in this instance. However a more modern reading of this case by Jim Sharpe has emphasised the evidence for Hale's scepticism about the reality of witchcraft and that this particular trial in 1662 shows Hale's thoroughness in the use of court procedures before passing the case onto the jury for a verdict rather than anything resembling barbaric malice.[65] Sharpe also notes that Hale's interpretation of the laws against witchcraft saw them as viable because they were approved by scripture and that all civilised countries enacted such laws.[66] This interpretation of the origin and justification of the law, it could be argued, is a close relative of the 'part and parcel' argument which he advanced in relation to blasphemy. The reiteration of the Hale judgment into the nineteenth century allowed Bradlaugh-Bonner to excuse Hale on the grounds of uncivilised ignorance whilst railing against the more modern judges who had no such excuses for their pronouncements or actions.[67]

More incisive criticism came from others who questioned the wisdom and intention of the Hale judgment. Aspland was prepared to believe that the doctrine was vague in the extreme and almost incapable of interpretation in a meaningful manner.[68] Writing in 1878, W. A. Hunter, the Professor of Jurisprudence at University College London described the judgment as a legal conundrum. Whilst describing that Christianity was the law of the land Hunter asserted that Hale at no point explained why it should be considered to be above criticism. Focusing upon the precise wording of the judgment Hunter's critique suggested

> What follows is a glaring non-sequitur. If Christianity is part of the law, that is one excellent reason why it may lawfully be spoken against; for no judge has ever yet gone the length of saying that the

laws of England are not merely, like the laws of the Medes and Persians, exempt from change, but that they are above criticism.[69]

Levy suggests that Hale's real meaning in asserting that Christianity was 'parcel of the laws of England' had been misconstrued in that his intention was to sanction the Common Law jurisdiction over what could have been regarded as an ecclesiastical case. But equally Levy points out that the effect of this was to take the matter beyond reasonable bounds, since for Hale's argument to be justified some proof of the widespread dissemination of Taylor's ideas and doctrines should have been the measure of whether a threat to government and the laws of England existed.[70] Other interpretations in this instance focus upon the authorities which Justice Hale chose to rely upon. Courtney Kenny suggested in 1922 that Hale's reliance upon Finch's *Common Law*, the widely-used contemporary manual, contained an important mistranslation in which the words 'ancient writing', a proof required for Canon Law to be shown to be a part of Common Law, was mistranslated by Finch from the original source – an error compounded by subsequent editions of Blackstone.[71] This anomaly had first been spotted by Thomas Jefferson during the debates on the framing of religious laws in Virginia in 1785.

Nokes also devotes considerable space to a discussion of the Hale judgment and the mistranslation theory of Jefferson and Kenny. Whilst admitting the possibility of mistranslation Nokes argued that this did not alter the material validity of the Hale doctrine which, he argued, did not rest solely upon Finch. Nokes was also prepared to assert that the Hale judgment had come to represent the widely-accepted belief and practice of contemporary lawyers and judges. He answered the twin accusations that Hale created a new law as well as assuming the power of jurisdiction to the Common Law without cause. Nokes argued that Hale's consideration of Taylor's actions as constituting a criminal offence was neither new nor surprising to the seventeenth century. The power of the Common Law to expand organically had never been in question and had never been successfully challenged. Moreover, he suggested that the history of Common Law misdemeanours could be summarised as 'largely the history of the assumption by the Common Law courts of jurisdiction over offences which at one time they did not recognise'.[72] However Nokes, with customary understatement, betrayed the chinks of light that the early twentieth century had shed upon this arbitrary extension of jurisdiction:

> ... it may be remarked that it is not surprising if the Common Law fails to command the respect of those who find that its vaunted facility for expansion amounts, upon the criminal side, to nothing less than the capacity to alter the rules after its opponent has played his cards.[73]

Extending the accusation that the Hale judgment was meaningless Nokes saw the 'part and parcel' statement as grammatically transparent and moreover asserted that the 1841 Report of Her Majesty's Commissioners on Criminal Law attempted to modernise the expression of the Hale dictum. Although Nokes does not mention this it is also of note that no attempt was made by this Commission to alter or tamper with the law as it stood. The Commission saw Hale's expression as intending to mean that the securities of the legal system as well as the laws themselves were reflective of the Christian religion and the texts upon which it is based. Nokes was, nonetheless, perceptive enough to note that this was a modern attempt to justify an older pronouncement and that the context of the original should not be forgotten.

The assumption which Nokes propounded was that Hale's judgment to all intents and purposes was theoretically true in the seventeenth century. Citing works of constitutional theory Nokes outlined the symbiotic relationship between Church and State, suggesting that if the church was integrated into the state as such theory suggested then Christianity would legitimately have been regarded by contemporary opinion as the law of the land. In support of this Nokes cited the denial of civil rights to infidels, which reinforced that the ecclesiastical interest constituted the prime part of the government of England and that a number of Common Law cases were clearly instituted to punish attacks upon the Established Church. Moreover the recourse to the Bible as an authority where no statute and no case-law existed was also a material consideration. Certainly the example of the denial of rights to infidels would have been seen by modern commentators sympathetic to this cause as a matter of self-fulfilling prophecy emanating from this judgment rather than any clear means of justifying its existence in the first place. Nokes further asserted that attacks upon sacred institutions were at the very least criminal, despite the fact that the existence and defence of these institutions may not have been explicitly part of the law. Covered within Nokes's definition were such institutions as the monarchy and both houses of parliament.

In some respects Nokes's legal treatise had to shoulder burdens not carried by the critiques of the law offered by commentators such as Bradlaugh-Bonner, Kenny and subsequent historians. Whilst opponents of the law and its practice had merely to point to its inadequacies and reiterate its apparent anachronisms Nokes, however, was preoccupied with a legal historian's need to justify and explain the enduring interpretation and nature of the law. In this respect Nokes's treatise is undoubtedly dry and passionless and his interpretation of the Hale doctrine emerges as particularly sketchy. The twin notions of the blasphemy law conceived as a protector of morality within society and any sense that tolerance and progress may have made the notions he was discussing less obvious than he emphatically professed them to be is absent.[74] Whatever the justice or validity of the Hale judgment the fact that it became central to the history of blasphemy from its inception was irrefutable. Lawton argues that the Hale judgment effectively made the laws of England directly protective of Holy scripture and scriptural prescription to a degree which continental Europe would never envisage and America would actively reject.[75]

Hale's judgment was, however, followed in the closing years of the seventeenth century by the Act of 9 & 10 William III c. 32 (an Act for the more effectual suppressing of Blasphemy and Profaneness). This made it a criminal offence to maintain in writing or speech polytheism, denial of the Trinity, the truth of the Christian religion or the divine authority of the scriptures provided the accused was a Christian apostate.[76] The last of these provisions was intended to acknowledge the religious rights of the Jews in England, a fact which Bradlaugh-Bonner noted was a demonstration of cynical expediency yet ironically it protected the tiny number of atheists brought up in the unfaith.[77] Punishments were progressive, ranging from disablement from office upon a first offence to three years imprisonment. A particular feature of this act was that each subsequent avowal of the opinions prosecuted would constitute a further offence even if this occurred in private. Moreover the statute enshrined the conception that the 'matter' of the pronouncement was central to the offence since even reverent expression of it constituted no defence whatever. This statute was mirrored by a similar statute in Scotland which established progressive punishments, considerably beyond those in England, for the persistent denial of God or the Trinity. The persistence was intrinsic to the offence since, after punishments of public atonement and imprisonment, the death penalty was enacted upon a third offence. It was this statute and the earlier ones which were used to punish the unfortunate Thomas Aikenhead, an Edinburgh student executed in 1697, who persisted in a denial of the deity, the incarnation and the Trinity. Many accounts suggest that the law in this instance was applied viciously, relying upon circumstantial evidence for a conviction and public persistence of his views were also, even to contemporaries in doubt. Even an attempt to abjure appears to have been ignored.[78]

Unlike in Scotland the English statute was never used but nonetheless acted as an important spur to those who argued for repeal of the laws. It amounted to a statutory recognition that the Christian religion was to be favoured and most degrees of doubt, even reverently expressed, were potentially at risk from prosecution. What was not clearly understood by those who framed the legislation was that the subsequent history of religious toleration would make it a spur to freedom of opinion.

Bradlaugh-Bonner probably overstated the case when she called the provisions of the statute a 'sword of Damocles over the head of any heretic who has seceded from the Christian faith' but equally her account of her father Charles Bradlaugh's fruitless attempt to have this apparently moribund statute repealed, many years after his own struggle to enter parliament had been accepted by the Commons, should not pass unnoticed.

The supremacy of the 'matter' indicted for prosecution was reiterated by Nokes who advanced a number of precedents from the late seventeenth and early eighteenth century to justify this view. In particular, drawing upon the example of sedition, Nokes attempted to show that contemporary lawyers and commentators themselves were satisfied what the offence entailed, thus according to Nokes the same was true of blasphemy. Likewise the similarity in the two offences persisted since the words used need not necessarily be aimed directly at doctrines or institutions which the law sought to defend. A trial in 1710 established the criminality of an individual who wrote applying the word 'person' to the deity – yet without any intention to vilify Christianity or call into question the doctrine of the Trinity. In citing the trial of Peter Annet and others Nokes came to the conclusion that denial of intention to attack nor the expression of such attack in the form of reasoned argument would establish any defence in Common Law.[79]

The Hale judgment was frequently invoked in cases into the nineteenth century and was present in the indictments against Jacob Ilive in 1756 and also against Peter Annet in 1763. The cases against these two individuals in some sense brings us to the close of this preliminary exploration of the origins of the modern blasphemy laws. Not only did these cases reiterate the law as it was established under Hale but the culture from which both sprung was emphatically sceptical and their reliance upon ideas in embryo signposted the way to deism and beyond. Moreover, the end of the eighteenth century marked a period of innovation in the way the offence was perceived. Macdonell noted that Chubb or Toland were more likely to be bombarded with hostile tracts than face prosecution.[80] Henceforth the history of the offence was to be rather different.

*   *   *

Hale's judgement was effectively accepted by the judiciary throughout the first three-quarters of the nineteenth century. Whilst it seems possible that the increasing gaps between major blasphemy trials (or related series of trials) – roughly one per generation during this period – could be shown to be evidence that the crime was considered less important, it was equally the case that each generation revived it. Moreover the experience of administering the law was thereby diluted with the notable exception of the Pooley and Foote cases. John Duke Coleridge served as prosecuting counsel in the first of these in the 1850s and as Judge in the last case against Foote to be heard. In this case Coleridge delivered his landmark summing up which declared that Christianity should no longer be considered to be parcel of the law of the land. Similarly he moved the emphasis from legal interest in the 'matter' spoken as blasphemy to the 'manner' in which it was spoken. The shift of emphasis to the 'manner' constituted a recognition that the Established Church and, arguably, Christianity as a whole could no longer be accepted as above, beyond or capable of being legally defended from criticism.

With minor modifications the Coleridge dictum remained the conventional judicial interpretation of the blasphemy laws into our own time. Indeed, it will be argued below that this inherent liberalisation of the laws served to convince some that the law had evolved into one sympathetic to acceptable forms of religious pluralism. Others saw it as ensuring the survival, in an unsatisfactorily partisan form, of bad and iniquitous laws. The Coleridge dictum could reasonably have been expected to become the last word on the subject of blasphemy. After all, the philosophy behind it did recognise modern trends towards enlightenment-inspired liberal dissent and away from the Judeo Christian origins of western society. However the result of the final appeal in the *Gay News* case of 1977 cast doubt upon the survival of the Coleridge dictum. The Law Lords rejected the defences which had been operative under Coleridge of the need to prove the likelihood that such blasphemies could occasion a breach of the peace and also the need for the prosecution to prove a deliberate intention to attack Christianity. The refusal to admit these two defences has arguably left the interpretation of the blasphemy laws once more reliant upon the Hale judgment – that publication and dissemination of blasphemies constitutes the offence in its entirety against which, without considerable ingenuity, there appears to be little defence.

So far this book may have appeared at times to be steering a chronological and progressive course through the legal history of offences against religion. The hostile reactions to the apparent logic of the Coleridge dictum and the *Gay News* case comes as a sharp reminder that progress and apparent modernisation have at best a limited place in discussion of this area. A tendency in the foregoing text has been the portrayal of authority at the heart of the blasphemy debate. It should be remembered that the law applied to and protected the beliefs of individuals in latter years in place of institutions in former years. Thus the following chapters hope to show a chronological lineage of the actions and motivations of those who entered the debate from a variety of perspectives. Individuals blasphemed, mounted prosecutions and found their beliefs challenged or their religion brought into disrepute by such prosecutions. Moreover individuals ranging from central figures like Thomas Paine and Mary Whitehouse to individuals who wrote to the Home Office created and articulated aspirations regarding 'their' religion. Only recently has the power and articulacy of religion 'from below', and the strategy and tactics that it uses to periodically revitalise itself, been recognised by sociologists and historians. An identification that this phenomenon has influenced the provision of laws to protect religion in modern times will provide an important companion to the reader of the following pages.

Notes

1. Levy, Leonard W. (1993), *Blasphemy: Verbal Offense Against the Sacred from Moses to Salman Rushdie*, New York: Knopf, p. 3.
2. Ibid., p. 10.
3. Ibid., pp. 13–14.
4. Lambert, Malcolm (1992), *Medieval Heresy: Popular movements from the Gregorian reform to the Reformation*, Oxford: Blackwell, p. 11 Leff, Gordon (1967), *Heresy in the Later Middle Ages; The Relation of Heterodoxy to Dissent c.1250–1450, Volume II*, New York: Manchester University Press.
5. Leonard Levy notes that Tertullian's third century 'Prescription Against Heretics' advanced the notion that heresy was the speaking and spreading of false doctrines which rapidly came to mean that the terms blasphemy and heresy were interchangeable. Levy, op. cit.
6. Smith, F. Lagard (1990), *Blasphemy and the Battle for Faith*, London: Hodder & Stoughton, p. 40.
7. Moore, R. I. (1987), *The Formation of a Persecuting Society*, Oxford: Blackwell, pp. 11–12.
8. Leff, op. cit. pp. 1–2.
9. Lambert, op. cit., p. 13; Moore op. cit., pp. 8–9 and 13.
10. Asad, T. (1986), 'Medieval heresy: an anthropological view', *Social History*, xi: pp. 345–62.
11. Leff, op. cit., p. 12.
12. Lambert, op. cit., p. 4.
13. Moore, op. cit., pp. 135–6.
14. Leff, op. cit., p. 47.
15. Ibid., p. 10.
16. Levy, op. cit., p. 81 and Nokes, G. D. (1928), *A History of the Crime of Blasphemy*, London: Sweet & Maxwell, p. 2.
17. See Leff, op. cit. for an analysis of Wycliffe's 24 articles of which one arguing for the religious to be subordinated to secular government was expressed as 'God should obey the Devil'. Leff suggests this can be regarded as blasphemous purely through its mode of profane expression. This is

nonetheless a modern view which downplays doctrinal unorthodoxy in favour of the investigation of the manner of the statement. See also the more conventional conflation of blasphemy as a word interchangeable with heresy in the case of Thomas Bilney burned for blasphemies which identified him as a Lutheran. See also Levy, Leonard W. (1993), *Blasphemy: Verbal Offense Against the Sacred from Moses to Salman Rushdie*, New York: Knopf, p. 83.

18. Craun, Edwin D. (1983), '"*Inordinata Locutio*": Blasphemy in pastoral literature', *Traditio*, 39: pp. 135–62.

19. See Asad, T. (1986), 'Medieval heresy: an anthropological view', *Social History*, xi: pp. 345–62 for a suggestion that heresy and heretics should be given greater credit for attempting to change society rather than being manifestations of various theories of social and economic dislocation.

20. Ibid., p. 356.

21. Leff, Gordon (1967), *Heresy in the Later Middle Ages; The Relation of Heterodoxy to Dissent c.1250–1450*, volume I, New York: Manchester University Press, p. 596.

22. Lambert, op. cit., pp. 238 & 266.

23. Aston, M. E. (1993), *Faith and Fire: Popular and Unpopular Religion, 1350–1600*, Cambridge: Hambledon Press, pp. 43–4.

24. Ibid., pp. 73–93.

25. Lambert, op. cit., p. 261.

26. Bradlaugh-Bonner, op. cit., p. 8.

27. Ibid., p. 5.

28. But see also Walter, Nicholas (1990), *Blasphemy Ancient and Modern*, London: Rationalist Press Association, p. 25 for the suggestion that blasphemy was already clearly present in some cases tried under *de heretico comburendo*.

29. Bradlaugh-Bonner, op. cit., p. 9; Nokes, op. cit., p. 3.

30. Nokes, op. cit., pp. 4–5.

31. Bradlaugh-Bonner, op. cit., p. 10.

32. Lambert, op. cit., pp. 377 and 380.

33. Ibid., p. 395.

34. Nokes, op. cit., pp. 6–7.

35. Bradlaugh-Bonner, op. cit., p. 13; ibid., pp. 7 and 123–4.

36. Maher, G. (1977), 'Blasphemy in Scots Law', *Scots Law Times*, 257–60, p. 257.

37. Bradlaugh, Charles (1870), *Heresy, Its Utility and Morality: A Plea and a Justification*, London: Austin & Co., pp. 10–13 and Levy, op. cit., pp. 60–62.

38. Bradlaugh-Bonner op. cit., p. 16–17; Levy, op. cit., pp. 96–100; Nokes, op. cit., pp. 12–15.

39. Levy, op. cit., pp. 108–9.

40. Nokes, op. cit., p. 21–7. Nicolas Walter suggests that the Atwood case constitutes the first recognisably modern blasphemy case in England. Walter, Nicolas (1990), *Blasphemy Ancient and Modern*, London: Rationalist Press Association, p. 31.

41. Levy, op. cit., p. 112–17.

42. The Biddle case is discussed at length in Levy, ibid., p. 116–35. There are also references to it in Bradlaugh-Bonner, op. cit., p. 18 and Henriques, Ursula (1961), *Religious Toleration in England 1787–1833*, London: Routledge, p. 10.

43. However see Nokes, op. cit., pp. 36–8 for an account of how both Houses of Parliament summarily assumed these powers of jurisdiction.
44. Levy, op. cit., pp. 120–21.
45. Nokes, op. cit., pp. 37–40.
46. Walter, Nicholas (1990), *Blasphemy Ancient and Modern*, London: Rationalist Press Association, p. 27.
47. See Davis, J. C. (1992), 'Religion and the Struggle for freedom in the English Revolution', *Historical Journal*, 35 (3): pp. 507-30 for an alternative analysis of the roots and importance of religious toleration.
48. Bradlaugh-Bonner op. cit., p. 18; Walter, op. cit., p. 27.
49. Levy, op. cit., pp. 178–204.
50. Hill, Christopher (1972), *The World Turned Upside Down*, London: Penguin; Hill, Christopher (1996), *Liberty Against the Law*, London: Penguin.
51. Levy, op. cit., p. 199.
52. Bradlaugh-Bonner, op. cit., p. 19.
53. Maher, op. cit., p. 258; The Viscount Dunedin, John L. Wark, and A. C. Black (1928), *Encyclopaedia of the Laws of Scotland*, Edinburgh: W. Green and Son, p. 165.
54. Nokes, op. cit., p. 42.
55. Kenny, Courtney (1922), 'The Evolution of the Law of Blasphemy', *Cambridge Law Journal*, 1: p. 127–42, p. 129; Lawton, op. cit., pp. 23–6; Levy, op. cit., pp. 213–15.
56. Lawton, op. cit., p. 28.
57. Robilliard, St John A. (1984), *Religion and the Law*, Manchester: Manchester University Press, p. 25.
58. However Lawton suggests that central to the content of Taylor's pronouncements was an implicit anti-trinitarianism. Lawton, op. cit., p. 27.
59. Levy, op. cit., p. 220.
60. Lawton, op cit., p. 27–8.
61. Levy, op. cit., p. 221; Nokes, op. cit., p. 48.
62. Cromartie, Alan (1995), *Sir Matthew Hale 1609–1676: Law, Religion and Natural Philosophy*, Cambridge: CUP, p. 175.
63. Nokes, op. cit., pp. 48–9.
64. Cromartie, op. cit., p. 175.
65. Sharpe, James (1996), *Instruments of Darkness: Witchcraft in England 1550–1750*, London: Penguin, pp. 225–6.
66. Ibid., p. 226; Cromartie, op. cit., p. 238.
67. Bradlaugh-Bonner, op. cit., p. 30–32.
68. Aspland, L. M. (1884), *The Law of Blasphemy: a candid examination of the views of Mr. Justice Stephen*, London, p. 7.
69. Hunter, W. A. (1878), The Past and Present of the Heresy Laws. A lecture delivered before the Sunday Lecture Society on Sunday afternoon, 1 December, 1878, London, p. 12.
70. Levy, op. cit., p. 221–2.
71. Kenny, op. cit., p. 130–131.
72. Nokes, op. cit., p. 50.
73. Ibid.
74. Ibid., p. 50–61.
75. Lawton, op. cit., p. 110.
76. Kenny, op. cit., p. 132.

77. Bradlaugh-Bonner, op. cit., p. 25.
78. Maher, op. cit., p. 258.
79. Nokes, op. cit., p. 73–5.
80. Macdonell, John (1883), 'Blasphemy and the Common Law', *Fortnightly Review*, new series, June 1883, 776–89, p. 784.

CHAPTER TWO

Blasphemy and Theory

It has been impossible to work in humanities research over the last 20 years without encountering the concept of theory. Whilst contemporary definitions of theory cover a multitude of approaches and perspectives, as far as historical research is concerned their common thread is a rejection of the primacy of empirical research. This rejection itself has ranged from the search for historical evidence which does not lend itself to empirical forms of analysis, right through to versions of post-modernist history which portray the search for the empirically-grounded analysis as both invalid and illusory. Some also attack what they perceive to be an undesirable quest for objectivity amongst historians. The aspirations of some of these attempts to 'revitalise' dry, unambitious history have led them to produce radical critiques of existing canons and historical methodology. These critiques have by no means carried all before them and resistance varies from those suspicious of a history floating free from empirical sources to a more forthright questioning of the professional motives of theorists and an identification of their position as indicative of a smug relativism that befits the morally impoverished last quarter of the twentieth century.[1]

In particular such methodologies, which owe their lineage to investigation in social science, increasingly attempt to colonise historical research with questions pertaining to social relations and the possession and exercise of power. They strive to produce a history which strongly emphasises the social reality of power relations and the investigation of everyday struggles, thoughts and strategies. Almost diametrically opposed to this tendency is a similar effort of colonisation undertaken by certain branches of literary theory which seek to emphasise the total dominance of language and, by implication, texts and textuality. For many of these theorists the meaning of texts multiplies with their readership and history becomes the totality of these multifarious 'discourses'. As such this approach effectively scorns most historical traditions of empiricism and undermines the conception of an historian's goal and object: the production and dissemination of what is seen as historical truth.

It is clearly not the purpose of this chapter (or book) to debate the merits and demerits of the potentially fruitful exchange (or colonialism) of these various approaches but to engage with them in an area of historical investigation where they might claim they provide essential tools of analysis. Blasphemy, after all, contains elements within its history which could be said to provide rich raw material for the application of a range of theories emanating from sociological, literary and philosophical traditions. Blasphemy in the hands of sociologists could potentially become an area for the investigation of modes of social relations and their conduct. Likewise the incidence of and response to blasphemy by a given society can shed important light upon the ideas of positivist and functionalist sociologists who seek to use these to justify their assumptions concerning the rise and development of modern societies.

However, blasphemy is also emphatically about language and texts. Indeed, some arguments suggest that its rejuvenated existence as a species of linguistic expression owes much to the late modern cultural interest in the 'linguistic turn' and competing contests for metanarratives.[2] The basic premise behind the offence in all cultures has been the use (or rather abuse) of language to impugn the existence, nature or power of sacred beings, items or texts themselves. The temptation to investigate the use of language is inevitable and thus provides a potential area for devotees of linguistic theory. In this sense blasphemy becomes the generation of texts; to blaspheme, to attack that blasphemy, to defend the blasphemy and to simply comment upon it – all of these constitute texts for such investigation. These texts themselves are then subjected to multiple readings which reproduce themselves as discourses about the fundamental first questions of civilisation's relationship with a supreme being, as well as notions of justice, injustice and cultural freedom. The various arenas in which blasphemy itself is aired also provide the opportunity for discourses to further multiply as agencies such as the law, the media, popular and established religion and government bring a variety of interests to bear upon the subject.

Cultural theorists also have a vested interest in the investigation of blasphemy. It provides a series of very stark and uncompromising ways of defining what is acceptable and what constitutes cultural delinquency in society at various historical junctures. In cultural terms it systematically creates and recreates systems of 'otherness' and casts individuals as 'other'.

Lastly it should not be forgotten that some elements of sociological theory which have a more obviously empirical slant have an interest in blasphemy as an institution. The branches of sociology concerned with the function of religion and the growth of the secular state clearly are interested in what a history of blasphemy can say about the role of these institutions in modern society. The proponents and opponents of the secularisation thesis thus would seek some answers to their questions in the utterances and pronouncements of blasphemers, their opponents and the array of government and legal opinion at all stages ready to pronounce the sudden death or rude health of religious sensibilities.

Ultimately the attempt made here to engage critically with precisely how elements of theory can be applied and misapplied to the history of blasphemy is a response to this range of methodological approaches. However, more importantly, an attempt to engage with the paradigms of blasphemy and 'theory' is also inspired by David Lawton's book *Blasphemy* which attempts to argue for a multi-layered and widely nuanced reading of blasphemy that has an applicability way beyond a simple legal history of the subject. Lawton proposes a more universal definition by which the phenomenon is used to marginalise specific groups within society and a wider world order by recreating them as 'other' – in his words a way of 'demonising difference'.[3] Lawton's task is both brave and ambitious and deserves to be applauded – yet there is a sense in which it should not be considered either definitive or to lay claim to have fully investigated the historical context of a particularly opaque and misunderstood offence.

The reader may already have detected an air of scepticism about the approaches that will be discussed. The rest of this chapter continues to be sceptical of most of the ways in which blasphemy could be considered through the looking glass of theory. But it should be remembered that scepticism does not equal unqualified distrust, nor does it constitute outright ingratitude for the new light which such approaches have to offer the subject. If the reader views this chapter simply as a brute struggle between empiricism and theory with a foregone conclusion then this will be a great pity. An engagement involves serious consideration of the virtues of a position before attempting to expose the vices. As such, elements of the different theories considered survive as potential tools of analysis and may even be used to enrich the approach adopted here. These elements will, I hope, provide a useful starting point in the debate for subsequent scholars who are more enamoured of specific forms of theory than this historian.

Postmodern Turns

Postmodern approaches to historical studies have proliferated considerably in recent years alongside the scope of their relative ambition. Some advocates of the variety of postmodern approaches have indeed tried to throw the gauntlet down to the profession by suggesting that what they see as a peculiarly British petty obsession with empiricism has failed to address the problems of writing history in a postmodern world.

As such the widespread use of postmodern approaches grounded in sociology and linguistics have had considerable impact upon historians who increasingly are being asked to acknowledge, or define, the type of history they write in relation to these theoretical developments.[4]

Whilst any definition of postmodern approaches to history would be at best selective there are certain characteristics and paradigms which stand out as needing critical outline and engagement. Postmodern history stems from a perception that ideas and institutions that have serviced and justified western society since the enlightenment are in crisis. The observed enfeeblement of political and other rationalistically conceived ideologies such as marxism and positivism – the latter in its broadest sense – have been accompanied by a revival of supposedly anti-modern (or postmodern) tendencies. These include the denial of the benevolence of the empirically based social and natural sciences and the revival of religious fundamentalism. Attendant upon this marginalisation of so-called metatheories of society and historical development, so postmodern approaches assert, has been a blurring of the boundaries between disciplines and the discredit of their goals in favour of a recognition that they are 'interlaced with rhetoric and power' so that 'the very meaning of knowledge is changed'.[5] Attempts to recognise the implications of this power were inherent in the work of Foucault but some postmodern attempts to create a so-called human studies that deconstructs and traces genealogies that investigate the relations between power and knowledge and their producers and consumers has been seen as preserving the spirit of the enlightenment.[6] Paradoxically some postmodern approaches have also sought to undermine the primacy of enlightenment thought, seeing it as western, male, heterosexual and produced by dominant castes or classes.

In its approach to historical studies postmodernism denies the search for a chronological and theoretical standpoint for the commencement of historical investigation. This simultaneously denies the validity of history as a chronologically distinct past and also calls into question the desire for a factually definitive account of an epoch, or in the case of social history, object or subject of study.[7] The dichotomies between fact and fiction and other bi-polar stable concepts such as masculine and feminine, science and literary knowledge, prejudice and reason are destabilised and blurred. Thus a central predisposition of postmodern history is to produce a range of investigations of the different narratives disclosed by the decentering of so-called truth. It is these multiple narratives which postmodern approaches suggest enables the charting of dispositions of power and rebellion within individual contexts.

One accusation against such an approach has been that it introduces a spurious democratic relativism which steadfastly refuses to judge the value, importance or influence of one narrative over another so that the means and the form transcend the ends and the meaning. In part some postmodern theorists such as Renato Rosaldo have attempted to answer this with a manifesto which suggests that the way forward for social critics is to quarry their own communities for standards of morality and behaviour. This also is seen as having the benefit of placing such critics within their communities and an answer to the accusation of a spurious relativism is to point a similarly accusing finger at the redundant and impossible concept of the empirically detached observer or chronicler.[8]

One of the best attempts to write history with postmodern preoccupations has been Judith Walkowitz's attempt to recreate the multiple discourses which coalesced around the phenomenon of the Whitechapel murders.[9] This book has added relevance to the investigation of blasphemy since its subject also examines a classic case of the politics of transgression, of disadvantaged groups seeking to gain access to public space and of multiplying narratives of permissiveness versus moral retrenchment. Like the blasphemers considered in this book, the characters in the Walkowitz work also reach for contemporary forms and narratives to give themselves voices with which to express positions, experiences and desires. Inherent within this structure is a denial of the preoccupation of conventional forms of historical investigation which would see the Whitechapel murders as a 'case' which is in need of investigation and solution. Instead the Whitechapel murders 'forced a range of constituencies to take sides and to assert their presence in a heterogeneous public sphere ... these narratives reverberated in courtrooms, learned journals, drawing rooms, street corners, and in the correspondence columns of the daily press'.[10] Such an approach was considered by the author as necessary since

> ...it has had to depart from a traditional historical narrative to convey the dynamics of metropolitan life as a series of multiple and simultaneous cultural contests and exchanges across a wide social spectrum. It has resisted, for example providing narrative closure to some chapters, or organising its historical account in terms of fixed gender and class polarities.[11]

Similarly the Walkowitz book demonstrates a preoccupation with 'the operation of power in a Foucauldian sense, as a dispersed and decentred force'.[12] The range of discourses that she identified with such contests for power emanated from literary and social commentators to encompass '... religious self-doubt, social unrest, radical challenges to liberalism and science, anxiety of imperial and national decline, as well as an imaginative confrontation with the defamiliarised world of consumer culture'.[13]

Drawing upon the work of Stallybrass and White, Walkowitz argues that the narratives of sexual danger which she encountered created a low 'other' which constituted 'an eroticised constituent of its own fantasy life' which made what was socially ostracised symbolically central.[14] Whilst Walkowitz's identification of this fantasy life as erotic is linked to her subject of female transgression it nonetheless provides a useful way of seeing blasphemy and blasphemers as a potentially malignant component of their opponents' narrative displacing hidden doubts and desires. Walkowitz's pertinent examination of salvationism in the context of the colonisation of space allows her working women to speak to a range of audiences in a range of voices appropriate to the context. Certainly this provides (as G. W. Foote himself realised) an interesting counterpoint to the work of blasphemers.[15] Foote himself was also particularly adept at the construction of narratives and the advancement of these into new areas of public space. However, they frequently took on the mantle of what some postmodern analysts would see as a highly charged inversion of norms. This conception of history comes to resemble a description of attempts to gain control of sites where discourses are produced.[16]

In particular Foote's flirtation with melodrama bears comparison with Walkowitz's exposition of W. T. Stead's use of melodrama as a mechanism which 'allowed the weak to speak out and gain agency in their own defense'. Melodrama was an extremely malleable cultural form with a variety of potential meanings and scenarios. Foote's own class dialogue about the rough exponent of blasphemy can be painted as bearing direct comparison since, in the case of Foote, personalised oppression identified the state with corrupt power.[17] Likewise Walkowitz's identification of the fears, or in her explanation narratives, related to both pornography and the metropolitan fear of the consequences of international terrorism also has cogency alongside blasphemy. Walkowitz's work even contains a reference to the double standard or privileged nature of some narratives at the expense of others. Charles Bradlaugh complained that Stead's crusading journalism was left alone whilst he had been prosecuted. Nonetheless Stead was accused of democratising pornography just as Foote was over blasphemy.[18]

City of Dreadful Delight's explicitly postmodern approach downplays the importance of chronology in favour of an assertion that the production, display and working out of some narratives transcend their historical context. Hence the narratives of sexual danger which were a product of the Whitechapel murders are again rehearsed in the context of the Yorkshire ripper murders. As such this could be seen as an attempt to realise the postmodernists' objective of scouring their own community for standards of moral behaviour with which to judge their own and past societies.

Overall Judith Walkowitz's book provides an impressive example of what postmodern approaches can achieve. A series of events are made to yield up their meaning by an intensive analysis of context and the motives and actions of individuals are usefully made to voice the concerns of a particular historical moment about a particular historical problem. What makes the book so valuable is its notion of the importance of the event and indeed the need to explain such an event's deeper significance. However it should be remembered that some attempts to posit broader, arguably more universalist, postmodern explanations of entire historical phenomena have been less careful with examining context. Indeed the conclusions essentially offered by Walkowitz are that the narratives subsequently created around the various 'rippers' have made it necessary to put them 'back' into context.

There are, nonetheless, other areas where postmodern concerns with narrative can shed some light on the larger problems related to the consideration of blasphemy as a discourse and perhaps it might be fruitful to examine these also. Linda Colley's construction of a British hegemonic Protestant constitution sheds considerable light on why early nineteenth-century infidels and blasphemers can be seen explicitly as 'other'.[19] Drawing their ideology partly from France they represented a tripartite attack upon elements that were essential to the Colley definition of Britishness. They were republican and they were atheist (or anti-clerical in the cases of Carlile and Hone). Through their forms of expression and culture they represented, in the shape of Robert Wedderburn and Robert Taylor, an attack upon the morally improving version of Christian society so prevalent in the first third of the nineteenth century.

Whilst it would obviously be going too far to state that this interpretation of blasphemy is influenced by the belief that structures inform and create themselves through the medium of language it is possible to argue that notions of language, and in particular the means by which narrative organises the responses of individuals, can constitute a powerful tool of analysis. In this respect blasphemy contains appeals to, and attacks upon, the power of narrative in various forms. Blasphemers are inspired by narratives of martyrdom starting from John Foxe leading through John Toland to Thomas Paine and Richard Carlile and onwards to the supreme exploitation of this form – G. W. Foote in the *Freethinker* case and its aftermath. Blasphemers also argue that the power of biblical narrative should be broken and that this is explicitly their historic mission. Narratives of Christianity as truthful or untrustworthy, moral or immoral, useful or useless are ostensibly central arenas of struggle and all secularist campaigns can be interpreted as reflective of this. Indeed, even their strategy of lampoon, satire and burlesque associated with some radical journalism represented efforts in this direction. Newspaper columns entitled 'Acid Drops', 'Profane

Jokes', cartoons and the mock historical voice of the *Jerusalem Star* were all methods of substituting the broad mischievous grins of blasphemy for the stern faces of Christianity. This in itself could turn directly into a contest for the control of biblical language. Foote's numerous portrayals of himself and cartoon portrayals of biblical scenes relied upon the inherent textual absurdities and occasionally upon childhood mishearings. If these could be repeated often enough the theory was that their sanctity and religious content would lapse.[20]

However, it seems likely that in order to indicate the existence of 'structured discourse' (or even Foucault's discourse of 'right') in which blasphemy takes a leading part it becomes necessary to construct an authoritarian cultural project. Such a project might be seen as class- or perhaps culturally specific with aims and objectives motivated by precise concerns at specific historical junctures. But can this really be sustained since attempts to do so must face some tough questions? If there was such a project, who constituted the establishment in this context? Who was involved in the formulation of such a project? What areas did it seek to regulate and how was this implemented – through brute social control or forms of hegemony? Or is it perhaps easier to postulate merely a series of unrelated responses at particular moments? In which case the notion of an overarching structure appears discredited.

There is a considerable number of other potential problems with embracing a large topic like blasphemy under the umbrella of a postmodern approach roaming free across chronological and subject boundaries which blur or become malleable. In this area David Lawton's study of blasphemy cannot avoid a tendency to produce what amounts to a universal history, conveyed through the use of the simple title *Blasphemy*. Whilst Lawton's book amounts to one way in which blasphemy can be 'read', his approach and the approach of postmodern studies to such problems potentially obscure more avenues of investigation than they illuminate.

Postmodernism removes objective absolutes from the realm of judgement and critical practice. In this the so-called objective systems of religion, the law, blasphemy, and morality are destabilised and divested of meaning to become merely discourses. Thus the history of blasphemy from a postmodern perspective becomes the history of changing discourses of blasphemy. This in itself can be very pedestrian since, as I hope I have already demonstrated, the most enduring discourse/narrative that has been hitherto centred around blasphemy is that of martyrology. Examination of the case, the trial and accusation discourses is capable of glossing over other discourses and other events. Moreover blasphemy becomes defined for what it is only upon objective decisions by real individuals connected with governments, legal apparatus and with pressure groups and opinion-forming bodies. Whilst I would emphatically argue that there is a culture of potential blasphemy or a reservoir of texts and examples to be drawn upon, the problems arise when individual blasphemers are asked by postmodern theorists to construct a discourse they have no control over. Whilst they may have cultural, religious and moralistic agendas through entering into the discourse they have these transformed for them by the objective reality of the law. This also, however, indicates another worrying – wider – tendency that afflicts postmodern analysis but has particular limits in the discussion of blasphemy. So often in postmodern analyses are texts and discourses 'destabilised', 'altered' or 'rendered ironic' that it is possible to believe that engaging with forms of the establishment on its own ground with its own weapons constitutes the only form of resistance available. Whilst this is possibly an exaggeration, postmodernists must at least work much harder to provide a model for how countercultures arise and give themselves meaning. When the *Freethinker* asked 'What shall I do to be damned?' it was doing considerably more than simply inverting John Bunyan. Blasphemers attacked the Bible but through their actions and the publicity of their beliefs they indicated that there was a positive moral dimension to their struggle. Moreover it is precisely in this area of activity that some postmodernists claim to offer significant advances upon the world created by empiricists. The so-called impartiality of the empiricist is attacked as unworthy and unsatisfactory.[21] Clearly this is a misrepresentation of the whole field of historical studies that has had its concerned and ideologically motivated historians, from Gibbon to E. P. Thompson and even to David Irving, long before postmodernists arrived on the scene.

Indeed the whole question of blasphemy as a fruitful area for discourse and linguistic analysis has already been called into question by some theorists. A postmodern history of texts and discourses sits uneasily with a history of blasphemy which dictates that ideas and arguments have a social reality and objectively quantifiable social effects. Those who were imprisoned, those who currently suffer for this crime in various ways would shake their heads ruefully at the potential concept of the 'death of the blasphemer' which has a shuddering resonance in modern civilisation. It is no coincidence that Bryan Palmer's assault upon postmodern approaches actually begins with the example of the Rushdie case to demonstrate that texts have authentic effects for their readers and translators and that specific readings can quite literally be imposed upon the work and its readership by objective action. As he suggests the Rushdie case constituted a very real circumstance in which '… it would have been rather outlandish to argue that there is nothing outside of the text and that authors do not exist'.[22] David Bowen, who witnessed the reaction of Bradford to the publication of the *Satanic Verses*, similarly reiterates the point consistently that in a socially powerful sense 'books represent ideas'. Likewise he suggests that the experience and real context that individuals bring to their reading have substantial, concrete effects. Those who were supposed to respond to the subtlety of Rushdie's *Satanic Verses* were, according to Bowen, required to have a nuanced appreciation of the recent history of the English novel alongside a more than passing acquaintanceship with German, French and South American Spanish literature. That individuals did not possess this capacity further indicated that there was a real world of interpretation outside of the text for which 'the creation of discourse' is a profoundly inadequate term.[23]

Postmodern analysis also runs into problems as an approach to the history of blasphemy because it argues for competing narratives with none of these narratives necessarily attaining dominance or even pre-eminence. However the nature of blasphemy is that it is an open conflict that reaches emphatic conclusions. A victor and a vanquished are both necessary – these constitute a type of closure that postmodernists would find glib, artificial and unacceptable.[24] Either errant opinions are punished and destroyed or they dilute and destabilise the object of their ridicule. From here it would be tempting to see the battle as comprising action solely in the courtroom. In truth this is only one theatre of war alongside public opinion and the battles for access to media as well as other public spheres. Postmodernists also argue that narratives fragment and reproduce themselves so that the best historical writing displays this multiplication in action, cataloguing its products and describing the conflict that results from this. The application of this approach to blasphemy raises problems since it is not where narratives multiply; rather, it is a structured anchor point for those who pin moral and sometimes national decline upon unwelcome and unbidden forms of (anti) social behaviour – indeed a place where narratives contract. What is particularly noticeable is the terms complainants against blasphemy use, drawing upon a consistent and often rehearsed litany of complaints which takes in moral decline, the perceived effect of such works upon lower classes and impressionable societal groups, the special role and blessing conveyed upon a godly nation and other comforting and established rhetorics of reference.

The postmodernist argument that social critics should look for standards of behaviour located within their own communities would, in the case of blasphemy, be contradictory. The modern world finds itself living with a standard of behaviour that has not been validated by that world, nor has it been the subject of revision or serious discussion. The search for standards of behaviour would, in a postmodern sense, merely produce a series of conflicting narratives about the abhorrent other, or otherwise nature of the blasphemer. Thus such a call in the postmodern paradigm for contemporary morality and individual communities, or the collective community, to provide answers to the questions posed by the blasphemer, his or her blasphemy, and its reception would fail.

The analysis in David Lawton's *Blasphemy* comes from a blend of postmodern and structuralist critiques drawing on work from Foucault and Bataille but most importantly from Roland Barthes. Lawton draws on structuralism to describe blasphemy as an area where power relations within society are played out within 'an exchange transaction'. Blasphemy is a place, for Lawton, where languages and texts are theorised and tested. He makes a distinction – which informs much of his analysis – that blasphemy is form whereas heresy is pure content. This last suggestion would appear to have little relevance in English blasphemy trials where precisely such simple analyses are rendered unworkable by the shifting emphasis between the 'matter' used in the work or utterance and the 'manner' in which it is used.

In the nineteenth century any suggestion that blasphemy is purely form is taken to its limits, wherein that which is blasphemy becomes simply that which is selected by public opinion for prosecution. Lawton might argue, however, that he is perhaps more interested in the difference between orthodoxy and dissidence. Thus he is prepared to consider the work of Freud as a discourse which is capable of being defined as dissident and hence potentially as blasphemy. Similarly in one of his chapters he takes the episode of the Gulf War as an example of how the modern world still produces carnivalesque representations of 'otherness'. Using an American television wrestling programme in which an Iraqi stereotypical figure is humiliated, scourged and vilified, Lawton demonstrates the notion of entrenched cultural attitudes as precursors and an inspiration to those who would proscribe and persecute. Lawton's prose in this chapter is powerful but leads to a climax that only just avoids being overly conscious of its own textuality.[25]

There sometimes appears little sense of context, no sense of progression and indeed very little sense of historical change in Lawton's work. In fairness Lawton would be the first to argue that he has not written a history of blasphemy but has sought to concentrate on the importance of textuality rather than be absorbed in the creation of context and historical change. Whilst this is perhaps understandable – even commendable – there are a number of implications inherent in Lawton's treatment of the subject which require further discussion.

Firstly his depiction of blasphemy as an exchange medium, where language and linguistic (mis)understanding take pride of place, effectively robs the phenomenon of concrete existence. Blasphemy does have a legal, cultural and social history as does orthodoxy and these change in response to historical circumstances. One particular problem which arises from Lawton's treatment is the perpetual presentation of the blasphemer as victim. In some respects this is inherent in Lawton's approach – within any structuralist critique we are all victims of overarching structures but blasphemers are far more so than most. Whilst his comparison of the respective improprieties of Sussanah Fowles, the lower-class visionary, and Sir Charles Sedley as the upper-class rake illuminates the class differential in the treatment of blasphemers they remain victims of structures which are manipulated against them. Fowles becomes an unfortunate victim of condescension whilst Sedley appears simply as a libertine whose outrageous behaviour takes him beyond the bounds of acceptable practice and morality. Similarly the choice of Menocchio from the *Cheese and the Worms* has problems associated with it. Ginzburg's primary intention in the book was to assert that Menocchio's creation of an alternative cosmology comprised a blend of specific reading, folkloric tradition and myriad observations of friulian peasant life showed how cultural mentalities can be created by diverse influences. The use of Menocchio again reinforces the blasphemer as victim analogy with the mentality and cosmology of a friulian miller pitched against the might of the papal inquisition with predictable results. Perhaps more importantly still blasphemy was a component of only the second case against Menocchio and the rest of Ginzburg's book indicates that he had serious religious heretical beliefs and that levity made only a fleetingly episodic appearance in his personality.[26]

In concentrating upon the structures that create blasphemy, Lawton effectively robs all protagonists coming under the umbrella of blasphemy of any rational choice and responsibility. This objection to such treatment can take two forms: firstly, those who choose to implement prosecutions and the penalties which follow their success respond to a range of personal feelings and concrete public order and morality concerns. Often the context–historical, cultural, religious and political – is crucial to an understanding of why particular blasphemy episodes occurred. Secondly, the rather brutal portrayal of blasphemer as victim robbed of power throughout the proceedings seems to deny blasphemers access to language and counter arguments or even alternative discourses which are constructed and added to by successive blasphemers. Although Lawton's choice of blasphemer precludes him from discussing some of these areas his portrayal of blasphemy effectively robs blasphemers themselves of any coherent ideology. Those who were prosecuted for blasphemy, from the eighteenth century onwards, did undertake other activities which marked them out as creators of an anti-Christian counterculture.[27]

Perhaps the most intriguing comment from Lawton which reveals his preoccupations with a victimological framework is the suggestion in his introduction that all the blasphemers he encountered never needed anything more than help.[28] As such they emerge as unfortunates, victims and sacrifices to structural societal frameworks which oppress and limit. Whilst one can certainly see examples such as Thomas Pooley or Lawton's use of Sussanah Fowles, where the portrayal of a simple or handicapped individual is the correct one, the portrayal of blasphemer as powerless victim is certainly not the whole story. One wonders just how far Richard Carlile, George William Foote or Dennis Lemon would react to this suggestion.

Whilst postmodernism appears useful in unpacking the many-sided importance of specific historical events as far as its applicability to chronologically wider-ranging historical problems and investigations it would appear to leave much unexplored and unanswered.

Foucauldian Analysis

Although perhaps not quite as revered as it once was, the canon of philosophical and studies in society undertaken and communicated by Michel Foucault until his death in 1984 constitutes an enormously influential collection of insights. It would be a mistake to use words such as ideology or theory in connection with Foucault since he himself persisted in refusing to be limited by the notion of ideologically entrenched positions and even his favourite mode of communication – the interview – constituted an opportunity for reflection and contradiction. Indeed, one of the most recent books to consider an aspect of Foucauldian theory described his way of working and communicating his thoughts as 'resistant and capricious'.[29]

In the area of historical studies Foucault's aim was to de-discipline the subject since in his view it constituted a needless and unnecessary set of limitations.[30] His lead has been taken by many who have followed the raw material of his investigations in areas such as medicine, sexuality and the social construction of insanity. Others have sought to produce Foucauldian readings of specific historical events and epochs such as the French Revolution.[31]

Foucault attempted to show how previous studies of opaque areas like sexuality, forms of madness and deviancy assumed power within the relationships of these situations as unproblematic. An example of how this was related by Foucault to real historical situations is furnished by one of the central arguments of his three-volume *History of Sexuality*. Its analysis of forms of repression and the construction of transgression provides a particularly pertinent introduction to the relationship of this set of insights to the subject of blasphemy. The relationship of individuals to their sexuality, according to Foucault, has been the subject of a developed form of policing which had its origins in the medieval period. The evolution of Catholic penance after the Council of Trent began a 'painstaking review of the sexual act' which dwelt on knowledge and detail of its significance.[32] Foucault argues that the introduction of discussion of sexuality in the medieval period emphasised the temptations of the flesh and the theme of penance and the necessity of confession. The development of this effectively turned the West into a confessing society which itself created an environment of listening and evaluation. In other words, such confession took place within a power relationship where an authority 'requires confession'.[33] This, he argues, was broken by the arrival of exclusive areas of discursiveness in the form of psychiatry, psychology, medicine, biology and ethics. The 'Age of Reason' thus did not usher in censorship but a growing 'incitement to discourse'.[34] The appearance of concern about sexual matters was not evidence of them straining at the bounds of the acceptable (and achieving occasional liberation) but rather evidence that they were increasingly the subject of surveillance. The development of apparatus for observation, interrogation and investigation thus constituted a machinery of incitement.[35]

Attempts to appropriate elements of Foucauldian thought for historians and analysts of the phenomenon of blasphemy must centre around these tendencies that cluster about his work as well as some more specific subjects of investigation. One of the primary elements that characterises the Foucauldian vision is an inherent mistrust of the notion of progress. In this denial of progress is an implicit attack upon the positivism that underlies versions of both bourgeois liberalism and Marxism. Foucault effectively denied the contention that the positivist enlightenment ushered in more reasonable and humane ways in which members of society play out their relationships. From this point onwards it becomes clear that one of his main interests was how power is constituted as a philosophical and, for our purposes, an historical phenomena. What is significant is that Foucault did his best to suggest that attempts to locate power within institutions and their control of this power was probably illusory.[36] In this respect he did much to suggest that power relationships deserve to be studied in operation at a variety of different locations and junctures.[37] More specifically Foucault's invention of the insane and institutions to police and incarcerate them is particularly important. Foucault's 'birth of the clinic' and 'birth of the prison' attempted to show how logic and rationalism could be tyrannical, with the creation of those who were on the receiving end of these developments as subjects for study and treatment. For him power was present where knowledge was created and subjected to other forms of knowledge.

For historians of blasphemy an engagement with Foucault on these levels would appear to offer some insights. Firstly the outspoken attack upon the benevolence of liberal society would appear to be well-founded. Blasphemers have not found modern societies noticeably less willing or ready to condemn their actions and indeed for blasphemers in Britain, it could be argued, a total process of rational modernisation never took place. Indeed it could be seen to have recently gone into reverse – particularly in the light of legal decisions made in the second half of this century. Foucault's assessment that society moved through phases, or 'epistemes', which he termed sovereignty, surveillance and lastly confinement and correction would appear to justify some readings of blasphemy.[38] The form of government which triumphed in the West by the middle of the medieval period has been characterised by Foucault as '... a strange technology of power treating the vast majority of men as a flock with a few as shepherds'.[39] This conception of 'pastorship' required unquestioning conformity to the central figures and doctrines of authority, a situation which had developed only since classical Greek society. This pastoral power was seen by Foucault as the cause and battleground of a number of medieval heretical episodes such as the Vaudois, the Beghards and the Hussites.[40]

Within this framework of control it was essential that religious conformity be enforced. The transformation into the new conception of government which Foucault termed 'surveillance' would in England be contemporaneous with the conception of blasphemy outlined by the Hale judgment and the legislation enacted by William III, a suggestion with which Lawton would concur.[41] Foucault argues that the new mode of surveillance modelled itself upon the patriarchal structure and relied for its power upon knowledge of its subjects to police and control morality. This process, it could be argued, is contemporaneous with the growing identification of blasphemy with the preservation of the public peace and morality.[42] In fact the Sedley case would provide appropriate material for such a reading. The problem arises with the lingering nature of this concern. A connection between blasphemy, libertineage and immorality does not pass into oblivion with the dawning of Foucault's age of confinement and the invention of institutions of control. In this respect the attitude of authority and some versions of public opinion to the twentieth-century trials of T. W. Stewart and later Dennis Lemon (see below) would appear to sit oddly with the shifting paradigm that the Foucauldians would propose.

As manifestations of the new ethic of confinement Foucault identified through his work, *Discipline and Punish*, the creation of 'delinquency'. The later works – *Madness and Civilisation* and *The Birth of the Clinic* – extended the objectification of what was deemed errant and socially unacceptable. The mad and the insane replaced the leper in the attempt to marginalise the notion of errant existence. Foucault's description of the early asylum contained those who society had effectively marginalised and increasingly objectified – including the blasphemer.[43]

Confinement was designed to govern unreasonable populations and itself produced new forms of knowledge which advanced the objectifying characteristics of the institutions of confinement and the constitution of the mad and insane.[44] In consideration of how to categorise the 'mad', Foucault notes a dread of unreason which may also be pertinent in relation to blasphemy. In this sense a Foucauldian analysis of repression would see the treatment of apostasy as analogous to the soviet regime's treatment of political opposition as insanity.[45] The desire to objectify the patient could be seen to apply potentially to the blasphemer. Just as Foucault saw the patient as subtracted from the calculation of the physician so the law could be interpreted as seeking to objectify the blasphemer by subtracting him and his special circumstances from the crime of blasphemy itself. Again the cases of Fowles, Taylor and Pooley are instructive – Lawton himself cited the Fowles case as demonstrating Foucault's 'logic of censorship'.[46] It could be argued that the most modern conception of the case-law of the crime of blasphemous libel contains within it 'a logic of censorship' which denies legitimation to any form of expert defence against an accusation of publishing blasphemous material. This tendency perhaps reached its zenith in the refusal to consider expert evidence in the *Gay News* case of 1977/78.

In some respects this can represent the ultimate objectification of the offence becoming a crime of pure content devoid of subjectivity. However this particular analysis can fall foul of the fact that the intervening period of laxity or subjectivity which surrounds the Coleridge judgment would not fit into an orthodox Foucauldian chronology as used for the birth of the clinic and the prison. The Coleridge judgment – with its emphasis on the 'manner' rather than the 'matter' involved in the crime – did introduce a significant element of subjectivity into the power relations of the offence. Whilst this might constitute a form of surveillance it also nonetheless enshrines consideration of the individual circumstances of the blasphemous offence and the attitude of the individual blasphemer. Moreover Foucault's development of surveillance is founded upon a realisation that European forms of law eschewed the accusatorial system in favour of inquisitive forms of justice that required the operation of a whole machinery of investigation.[47] This conception of change fails to explain the unique situation in England where accusatorial justice survived unscathed – a circumstance long regarded by historians as a significant reason for the absence of widespread witchcraft prosecutions. By the same token a more detailed study of blasphemy in Scotland may see it fit an orthodox Foucauldian model more readily since its system of justice was, until the nineteenth century, closer to the European model. Whilst the chronology may nonetheless fail to produce an exact fit Foucauldians would attempt to point to different contexts providing a different set of power relations for which chronological continuity is entirely unnecessary. Moreover, according to Foucault, surveillance entailed the skilful and precise calculation of penalties for specific crimes so that each only just exceeded the advantage of committing the crime. Such an analysis would patently not apply to the offence of blasphemy where many arguments address the anomaly that in this area punishments seem somewhat arbitrary and that the crime does not have a widespread socially acknowledged existence for such punishment to constitute a deterrent. Time and again the message of commentators on both sides in English and Scottish cases is that there is a vast difference between the guilt of defendants and conceptions of how they should be punished – a dichotomy for which Foucauldians would have to account. Moreover the fact that it has an incredible rate of recidivism also mitigates against this view.

The Foucauldian conception of power as dissipated and in varying degrees of flux also has important resonances for historians of blasphemy. Whilst Foucault demonstrated ambivalence to the use of discourse analysis as a tool his thought has nonetheless been linked inextricably with this phenomenon. In particular a 'discourse of right' was seen as informing governments and legal apparatus from the Middle Ages onwards. Most importantly, Foucault's analysis examined 'how subjugation at an on-going level actually works not at the practice or possession of power or conscious intention'.[48] As such this appears to say that a history of blasphemy should not simply follow the power of institutions but would also accept that power was dispersed to all protagonists and that each episode could perhaps benefit from the application of what anthropologists term 'thick description' and Foucauldians term 'archaeology of knowledge and power'. Such investigations would, for a Foucauldian, potentially unpick the complexities of the Pooley, Foote and Gott cases to analyse the interplay of power between protagonists. However the desire of Foucauldians to assist the powerless against the powerful would equally come up with some surprising analyses of the Islamic Revolution and the Salman Rushdie case. In these instances those in the West, with access to the media and the influence it gives, could be accused of objectifying the notion of religious belief. In this sense Foucauldian ideas were torn in two ways by these events. Confronted by this objectification Foucault applauded the action of the powerless in resorting to street protest. Foucault dismissed the Western left's adverse reaction to the Iranian revolution as failing to accept that a revolution always began with the tools to hand. This contained a clear implication that the Iranian revolution was the start of a process which (at the time of writing) may eventually have produced what orthodox Western perceptions would recognize as a revolution. He also argued that the materialism of such critiques of the revolution failed to see it as the 'spirit of a world without spirit'. In other words the embrace of Islamic cultural presuppositions which acted as an antidote to the regime of the Shah was seen by Foucault as an astonishingly unified search for a renewed subjectivity.[49] However the apparent defence of earlier forms of surveillance that this constituted, which should have been absent from any remotely Foucauldian episteme, must equally have been perplexing to Foucault and devotees of his earlier work. Furthermore, the suggestion that the Islamic Revolution was a search for subjectivity (a phenomenon associated elsewhere in Foucault with the rise of the self) fits uneasily with a religious outlook which foregrounds collectivist revelation and solutions in opposition to what is seen as the poverty of Western individualistic outlooks.[50]

An essential part of Foucault's philosophy which emerged as cogently in his activism as much as in his writings and interviews was his insistence upon the existence, and necessity, of forms of resistance and counter-expression. He did not simply accept uncritically the triumph of confinement and spoke out against the creation of the gulag and the treatment of soviet mental patients.[51] A constant theme surrounding this conception of power was that it cannot exist without resistance and from this point onwards Foucault's formulations take on a new optimism from a range of forms of dissidence.[52] He suggests that

> If power is dispersed in a multiplicity of networks, resistance can only be realised through a series of localised strategies ... in effect, that we must no longer analyse modern politics as a congealed and essentialized conflict between master and rebel, but rather as a dispersed and indefinite field of power relations or strategies of domination.[53]

From this point Foucault's practical suggestion encompassed the desire to extend identity and the expression of new forms of life that did not equate with existing forms of institutions. In short the antidote was to realise the quest to become a subject again.[54] Once again the notions of resistance and the search for identities outside structures implicate blasphemers as possessors of a particularly developed form of resistance and perhaps also as victims of 'subjugated knowledge'. They could be described as having attained new ways of being through a blunt and determined expression of resistance against what Foucault would regard as the power structure with the greatest genealogy and longevity of all! Emphasising this struggle at a personal level, Foucault identified the difference between homosexuality and 'being gay' as an exploration and creation of subjectivity and as such it may equally be applied retrospectively in the case of blasphemy and blasphemers. A Foucauldian might argue that for someone like G. W. Foote, atheism was not enough without the sobriquet blasphemer. Indeed the two subjectivities and the often-remarked closeness of religion and sexual morality could be said to meet in the homoerotic religious exploration of Kirkup's poem 'The Love that Dares to Speak its Name' – the publication in question during the *Gay News* prosecution.

However, there remain drawbacks beyond those already expressed to an acceptance of a Foucauldian interpretation of blasphemy. It remains, as critics have often remarked, an event-free historiography which imposes epochs or 'epistemes' upon large swathes of human history. This drawback is inherent in this periodisation model despite the fact that it can accommodate conflicting facts, ideas and observations within co-existing epistemes where more conventional rationalist teleologies (such as Marxism, or probably more pertinent to this enquiry, secularisation theory) might struggle to explain their survival or resurgence. Despite Foucault's claims to the contrary[55] there is an implicit denial of the importance of empirical investigation of the event or of individual human agency to affect the course of history. As we have already noticed, Foucault's chronology of 'epistemes' fits more than uneasily with the history of blasphemy in Britain. Whilst Foucault tries to convince much of Western European culture that it is living a lie through its bourgeois liberal chimera, blasphemers would deny that this modern transformation, for better or worse, has in fact occurred. They would (perhaps legitimately) ask when the State's surrender of 'pastorship' or the end of primitive early modern forms of 'surveillance' inherited from the seventeenth century will finally happen. Moreover Foucault's birth of the clinic/prison relied upon the systematic production of knowledge and the objectification of the inmate in a kind of trap of rationalism. From this creation of rationalist knowledge it would be necessary, in Foucauldian terms, to posit the retreat or eclipse of the subjectifying qualities of revealed religion. Not only is it possible to suggest that the complete eclipse of religion as a source of power has not happened but it would not be wholly fatuous to suggest that blasphemers, through their creation of resistance, would have preferred infinitely to have been imprisoned by rationalism. The evidence presented elsewhere in this book would also suggest that whilst power contains resistance the willingness of individuals to take power in order to give it back to represssive yet revered institutions should also not be forgotten. Blasphemers have at all times been on the receiving end of public and professional opinion which has not fought shy of using the courts, and worse, to defend a variety of sacred institutions.

Whilst Foucault's chronology would appear to be unconvincing in relation to blasphemy the historian of this subject should be grateful for the reminder that his work leaves to other historians and social scientists of the way that power creates resistance. This lends a more nuanced defence for the suggestion often encountered in the literature of this area that orthodoxy always needs and tends to create forms of apostasy, blasphemy and heresy.

Edward Said and Orientalism

The recent work of Edward Said to suggest how western society has created the orient as an alien 'other' has shed important light upon the construction of Victorian attitudes to race, empire and power.[56] Broadly speaking his perceptions have been described as producing a quasi-historical cultural phenomenon which '... became the literary means of creating a stereotypical and mythic East through which European rule could be more readily asserted'.[57] Additionally Said suggests an important strand of Victorian and, arguably, later western thought has been an explicit attempt to situate the orient and Orientalism as a series of exotic sites for fantasy and speculation as well as a clear antithesis of western manners and attitudes. The theories associated with Said have been a major force in the creation of post-colonial studies which have sought to investigate the cultural legacy of imperial attitudes and the history of how discourses subjected and colonised races and individuals from societies deemed to be less civilised. In this respect Said's creation of the orient (and to an extent a wider 'other') contains interesting suggestions in relation to any British history of blasphemy. Said's work indeed provided a blueprint for how some have seen the Salman Rushdie case and arguably a critique of British imperial policies relating to religious tolerance.[58]

The regular advocacy of the so-called Indian Code solution to the blasphemy law of late Victorian England is one such area of interest. Such a solution, proposed by James Fitzjames Stephen, several atheist campaigners and a small devoted following in the Home Office, would have altered the law so that all attacks upon religious images artefacts and beliefs would be punishable by imprisonment. Whilst this would have posed a legal solution there was a discernible distaste for such a measure occasionally exhibited by the Home Office. On one level the Indian Code was a method by which India was effectively 'governed' and in this context the imperial preservation of 'order' outshone the discussion of intra-religious antagonism.[59] In this instance the Indian Code itself could be said to have had a dual identity – conceivably a facet of imperialism to the governed but equally an expedient forced upon them by the governors. But such attitudes could be more polarised still since some Home Office opinion opposed the Indian Code solution by curtly dismissing the suggestion that protection should be extended to religions other than Christianity represented elsewhere within the empire. Moreover the very conception of a colonial governing authority imposing a system which argues for a relativism and tolerance which would be intolerable at home must appear – to many eyes – to be a symptom of cultural imperialism. However such a reading, which would see this as a piece of Orientalism in action, assumes that the rejection of the Indian Code solution was wholly motivated by occidental distaste. In effect the relativism adopted by such a solution was deemed primarily to have considerable implications for the legal definition of what precisely constituted religion which legislators fought to avoid at all costs (see Chapter 6 below).

Orientalism is not the only mode of exclusion[60] – nor should we be led to think that the eastern and western cultures and modes of expression, particularly in the religious sphere, are themselves nearly so unified and homogenous as supposed. Ira Lapidus has suggested that to categorise 'Islam' as one all-embracing system which linked Church inexorably with State in a form of permanent revolution is historically innacurate.[61] Lapidus points to a diversity of systems and likewise we should also remember that the 'West' and its imperial mission is certainly no more homogenous and monolithic. Moreover forms of modernising liberalism constituted resistance to what is often portrayed as an exclusively pro-imperial outlook. Hypatia Bradlaugh-Bonner was one among several secularists who continually railed against the lack of respect shown by Christianity towards other eastern religions – in particular citing the Missionary exhibition of 1911 as a clear example of such exploitation.[62]

In contemporary times, the Salman Rushdie affair produced a violent cultural encounter in which Saidian ideas could perhaps provide insight. Orthodox Saidian theories produce an analysis which would see the Salman Rushdie affair as providing further evidence of the West's ability to marginalise and demonise the East – a view with which Said himself is extremely uncomfortable. Such an analysis further emphasises the fact that Orientalism is an ongoing project. There is more than a passing acknowledgement of this in the work of Richard Webster, Neal

Robinson and others in their discussions of the West's dismissal of the claims of Islam against Rushdie.[63] As such these and other critics argue that Said's description of Orientalism lives in the twentieth-century totemic defence of western liberal conceptions of free speech and a free press in the face of what is deemed to be both irrationally primitive and anti-modern. However the use of Saidian Orientalism and its terms of reference do little to assist in understanding the complexities of the Salman Rushdie affair which requires, amongst other things, a nuanced understanding of different forms of Islam, different forms of free speech, the intellectual development of the author and the history of blasphemy in England. None of this can be accommodated in a theory which relies on such inflexible polarities as orient and occident.

In some senses liberal rationalism is itself on trial in Said's analysis, occasionally with mistaken results. For example Said's critique of the philologist Ernest Renan's biblical criticism (which was popular with western secularists and freethinkers) associates his view of the semitic languages as primitive with a form of Orientalism. This seems to largely ignore the motivation of rationalist system builders to escape Judeo-Christian forms of social and intellectual organisation. Said in this context perhaps mistakenly links the biblical criticism of early rationalists with a form of Orientalism. Devotees of the orientalist thesis see this also at work in modern western cultural exchanges with the East. In a sense Renan's own outlook and criticism of Semitic and Islamic culture have been identified – wrongly – as attacks upon the East when they are more likely to be attacks upon the special claims of revealed religion. It is indeed such attacks upon forms of tribalism that characterised the great pan-European liberal project of the nineteenth century. Arguably the longevity of such liberal traditions as free speech, the developing free press and an enhanced respect for the identity and rights of the individual are precisely those qualities which have led to the widespread dissemination and even popular acceptance of many of the central tenets of the 'Orientalism' thesis. None of this could have been achieved in the West under a system as closed as Saidians argue was dominant.

However, the problem of Orientalism being advanced as another post-modern style discourse once again invites the clear accusation that this analysis is another form of unhelpful, uncritical relativism. The essence of the Orientalism critique is a western institutionalisation of uncritical monolithic cultural guilt encouraged by post-colonial theory, which worryingly occurs almost in a historical vacuum. There is a clear indication in this analysis that colonial history could have been different and that it would have been possible to develop a discourse about the orient which did not exoticise it. To accept such a view at face value is to accept a history which denies the importance of underlying economic social and cultural forces which made the versions of colonialism possible and, if you believe Marxists, inevitable. It is to ascribe motives and single-minded control of a one-dimensional unilaterally agreed colonial cultural project. Increasingly this single cultural imperative and 'discourse' behind imperialism has become untenable in the hands of Said's critics. Writers like MacKenzie have striven with some success to suggest the East/West cultural encounter has been symbiotic, productive of change in both Orient and Occident as well as splintering into numerous views and discourses rather than the tiresome binary opposites that Saidian theory relies upon.[64] Likewise some legal commentators have suggested that Stephen's work on the Indian Code was a masterful bridging of the gap between East and West that has significantly stood the test of time.[65] Indeed, some aspects of the Rushdie case illustrate that Saidian definitions of what constitutes East and West are simplistic, naive and unhelpful to the advance of knowledge and understanding. David Bowen's portrayal of Bradford, both before and after the publication of the *Satanic Verses*, emphasises that a part of multi-cultural Britain was drawn almost unbidden into the affair by decisions taken in only one part of the islamic world. Similarly attitudes and responses from this community were not as uniform as Saidians would expect. Bowen's sympathetic and humane analysis of what was required at the time was not an unhelpful descent into a polarised orientalist discourse but rather 'vigilance in fostering mutual understanding and cross-cultural maturity'.[66] Likewise the British muslim plea for protection from blasphemy was based substantially upon the conception that a group of naturalised and proud British citizens were being denied civil rights.[67]

Specifically in the study of an area like blasphemy it is equally untenable to construct an overweening and conspiratorial cultural project which systematically seeks to destroy religious unorthodoxy, atheism or irreligion either in Britain or in any colonial situation. Moreover an acquaintanceship with Home Office papers and the opinions of civil servants and Home Secretaries over the last century suggests that the dominant theme in the area of blasphemy is not cultural control but bureaucratic confusion and ignorance. The chronological logic of a Saidian view, as proposed by Webster, is that western liberalism and its defence of the concept of free speech is merely a later, arguably less tolerant, chapter in the process of creating the orient as 'other' and uncivilised. However whilst Orientalism invites the western world, quite rightly for most of the time, to feel shame about aspects of its past imperialism there is also a partial failure to recognise that the West's own process of modernisation has enabled it to confront the sins of its own past.[68] Whilst an attack upon western liberalism is used to argue that the West is up to its old orientalist tricks, proponents of the Orientalism thesis remain silent on how oriental cultures will confront and interact with social, religious and economic change – phenomena that cannot wholly be blamed upon the West. Perhaps here more than anywhere else Saidians betray their failure to engage with historical contexts and betray the worst faults of the cultural/area studies approach which Orientalism embodies. It is significant that MacKenzie chose to highlight this leading drawback in the Saidian approach. Even Said himself, in the closing pages of *Orientalism* and perhaps later developed in *Culture and Imperialism* (to his considerable credit), suggests that much of the way forward relies upon the discipline-specific work of historians, anthropologists and geographers rather than relying on the unhistorical assumptions of area studies phenomena like Orientalism. This comment is particularly revealing since it tends to suggest that postmodern-style attacks upon the boundaries between subjects, according to Said, are likely to imbue such subjects with a series of partisan and potentially prejudiced viewpoints.[69] It is surely Said's greatest hope that he has uncovered a phenomenon from the past and not provided a crude tool for perpetuating misunderstanding.

Moreover Orientalism as a thesis at times, curiously, appears to place the non-European world in a position of indiscriminate passive reception. Whilst this is also at the very least questionable in historical terms, it contains an implication that all that have really altered are the cultural presuppositions and forms of western economic imperialism. Thus Said's own argument that the oil crisis signalled the triumph of westernising tendencies within the East increasingly seems outdated.[70] The economic power which came to many Arab states produced not simply westernising influences and lifestyles but also religio-cultural forms of resistance to these which have moved from defence to forms of resistance. In this respect these forms of resistance have gone rather further than exoticising the 'other', and instead have gone as far as to demonise it. Whilst the West apologises and is belatedly becoming tolerant and receptive to world cultures some branches of eastern thought are anxiously extending their spheres of influence whilst frequently closing off the channels of cultural discussion. The West must accept its role in the process of imperialism yet this should be used as an opportunity to transcend the human evils that have been perpetrated in the name of imperialism and exclusionist racial/ethnic self-images. Yet recognising that these evils occurred is not an excuse for the recommencement and conduct of cultural wars by another name.

Secularisation Theory

The positivist assumptions of secularisation theory have in recent years been faced by challenges which generally have taken two forms. Firstly, historians such as Robin Gill and Calum Brown, have cast doubt upon the notion of a religious golden age where adherence and the acceptance of religious belief was at an optimum level. Secondly, arguments also consider whether religion suffered from a simple over-supply of outlets particularly during the nineteenth century. Additionally some philosophers, such as Gilles Keppel, have posited a rejuvenated religiosity in the Muslim, Catholic and evangelical world which has succeeded in discrediting secular, positivistic versions of society and human development. What is a distinctive feature of the philosophical investigation of this phenomenon is that it has been observed to be happening almost exclusively 'from below'.[71] That is to say, earlier pictures of religion and religious culture as a series of ideologies imposed by elites in the name of morality and conformity are rejected in favour of one in which renewed religiosity stems from the populace and remains defiantly indigenous to it. This quest for a 'new' morality – from salvationism to modern evangelism – is particularly pertinent to the way the offence of blasphemy works at a cultural level.

Rather than suggest that elite religion shows that it is still powerful through blasphemy prosecutions, it may be more plausible to consider that religion has an ability to influence those in power as a rallying cry, at specific moments, which calls for proceedings against that blasphemy. This constitutes a modification of the secularisation thesis which posits that only certain circumstances make religion important rather than arguing for the long-term health or deterioration of the scale and scope of religiosity.

Gilles Keppel in *The Revenge of God* describes blasphemy and apostasy as forms of 'escape' from Islam and in this respect this analogy can be linked to the situation of blasphemers in Victorian England where it was also a culturally pioneering step. Keppel uses the 'from below' and 'from above' typology in connection with Islamisation which can also be used for those in the past who saw themselves consciously involved in the process of secularisation. In this respect the 'from above' typology tends to fit the Bradlaugh model which sought to alter legislation whilst 'from below' fits blasphemers like Foote and Gott who sought to undermine cultural preconceptions. Within this model these blasphemers also view religion in the same way since Foote continually stressed the difference between polite and impolite forms of Christianity – one was tolerable, the other unacceptably vulgar – hence Foote's personal crusade against the Salvation Army. The 'from below' and 'from above' typology has further historical relevance when we consider that Foote and his later compatriots complained that free-thought itself was forced to accept only artificial versions of its own critique. Polite doubt couched in scientific terms and sold in expensive editions was permissible whilst full scale cheap and cheerful (in the widest senses of those words) irreligious material was always more liable to be prosecuted by the courts.

In some respects putting to one side secularisation as a concept enables the concerns of secularists to make a lot more sense. Indeed, fear of religious 're-colonisation' is what maintains militancy in these circles arguably into the contemporary period. Previous analyses have tended to see blasphemers simply as individuals who press a case beyond the pale. This view describes these cases and individuals as beyond social acceptability because they are prosecuted and end up in the courts. Too often, however, such a view is linked to the original concept of secularisation. If we accept the contention that society has become more secular, that religion and religious forms are taking less and less part in the construction of the modern state and modern consciousness then blasphemers have an almost predetermined role merely as precursors, trailblazers, martyrs and a whole host of other dismissive unhistorical labels.

If we reject this model thereby putting aside secularisation in its various versions then blasphemers can no longer be dismissed or pigeon-holed as unhistorically slightly ahead of their time. The reassessment of secularisation as by no means an inexorable social fact and process thus sheds new light upon the views of blasphemers. They can now emerge as representatives of a minority lifestyle and belief who frequently express serious concerns that religious authority can be in flux rather than decline. Matthew Arnold's Dover Beach metaphor of religion as an ebbing tide through the eyes of blasphemers contains within it, as the twentieth century progresses, the capacity to turn and come in again. Thus blasphemers can now be seen not simply as awkward intransigents forcing society to come to terms with an advanced guard of rational, free speech libertarianism. They are seeking to defend beliefs, lifestyles and modes of thought that have, to varying degrees, entered the realm of tolerance and the status of acceptability. This tolerance is thus not an absolute and at certain historical moments has in fact appeared to be very amorphous indeed. Such tolerance, of course, can itself be withdrawn owing to a number of changes in circumstances, one of which is a periodically enhanced profile for religious explanations of human development.

Most particularly the importance of religious and moral movements 'from below' appreciate as religion itself takes a smaller role in the governance of the state. This can, however, appear to be a partnership in the case of blasphemy. Certainly Coleridge's judgment in the Foote case was important in establishing that Christianity was 'no longer part and parcel of the law of the land' but the blasphemy laws (as the offence of blasphemous libel) remained intact as a component of the Common Law. In its way this was the ultimate concession to organic public opinion – that it would regulate the acceptance or rejection of certain beliefs and attitudes. Moreover the Home Office argued that the law was an excellent example of how Common Law solutions could evolve over time to adapt to changing circumstances. In this way judge-made law could also, at least theoretically, remain highly responsive to public opinion.

An offence like blasphemy can thus emerge as a litmus test of how far society will tolerate heterodox views. If an overarching history of 'official attitudes' to religion can ever be written, even here a modernising history of growing enlightenment is difficult to sustain if blasphemy is considered as a part of the equation. The attitude of some Home Secretaries in particular makes interesting reading in this context. Sir William Harcourt did what he could to forward the prosecution of G. W. Foote, with reckless regard for his own reputation and likewise took action which made Foote's imprisonment more uncomfortable than it need have been. Harcourt's immediate successors refused to prosecute but Home Office papers repeatedly indicate that this was a matter of expediency rather than the exercise of a more enlightened attitude.

The first two decades of the twentieth century saw the laws used once again to circumscribe the activities of public speakers who were considered dangerous. By the third decade of the twentieth century arguments to repeal the blasphemy laws had been rehearsed but nonetheless had come to nothing. Individual Home Secretaries were, during the period, surprisingly reticent about accepting a simple alteration in the laws that would allow the offence to be a part of public order legislation. Whilst conciliatory words are spoken to Chapman Cohen and others the offences remain on the statute book. Meanwhile, although opinion is softening on the matter of heterodox views this is to notions of private opinion and to an elite conception of wider freedom of the press. Whilst an intellectual philosophical culture is becoming attuned to, and more tolerant of, the ideas for which blasphemy is frequently only the vehicle this does not equate either with acceptance from the official or the popular mind. As such, to secularists and even the mildly sceptical, statutory blasphemy is a potential weapon that can be activated at any time. If this sounds far fetched then a glance at Chapter 7 will show that blasphemers in Britain in the 1930s found themselves faced by a vibrant undercurrent of Christianity 'from below'. This not simply objected to their right of assembly but constructed a discourse in which the imperial Protestant state was being systematically undermined and arguably dismantled by people who did not share a consensual view of British society and destiny. Indeed this particular period shows evidence of widespread fear that this very consensus was unravelling.

*   *   *

This has been an eclectic and perhaps exhausting tour through the theoretical conceptions that, in various ways, congregate around the subject of blasphemy in Britain. I hope it has been possible to demonstrate engagement as well as scepticism in evaluating these various approaches. As I stated at the start of this chapter this has not been a wholesale attempt to downgrade or dismiss utterly the theoretical approaches to this and other historical topics. However, we still do not know enough about the raw material of blasphemy and its prosecution and it is the investigation of this to which the second part of this book is devoted.

Notes

1.   There is already a vast literature on this subject and the following list provides only an indication of the work involved in this area. The works are also biased towards the arguments that have been advanced for a reappraisal of modern British History. Eagleton, Terry (1996), *The Illusions of Postmodernism*, Oxford: Blackwell; Eley, Geoff and Keith Nield (1995), 'Starting over: the present, the post-modern and the moment of social history', *Social History*, 20 (3): pp. 355–64; Evans, Richard (1997), *In Defence of History*, London: Granta Books; Jenkins, Keith (1991), *Re-Thinking History*, London: Routledge; Joyce, Patrick (1991), *Visions of the People*, Cambridge: CUP; Joyce, Patrick (1993), 'The imaginary discontents of social history: a note of response to Mayfield and Thorne, and Lawrence and Taylor', *Social History*, 18 (1): pp. 81–5; Joyce, Patrick (1995), 'The end of social history?', *Social History*, 20 (1): pp. 73–91; Kirk, Neville (1995), 'History, language, ideas and postmodernism: a materialist view', *History*, 20: pp. 222–40; Mayfield, David and Susan Thorne (1992), 'Social History and its discontents', *Social History*, 17 (2): pp. 165–88; Palmer, Bryan D. (1990), *Descent into Discourse: The Reification of Language and the Writing of Social History*, Philadelphia: Temple University Press; Spiegel, Gabrielle (1990), 'History, historicism, and the social logic of the text', *Speculum*, 65 (1): pp. 59–86; Spiegel, Gabrielle (1992), 'History and postmodernism', *Past and Present*, 135: pp. 194–208; Veeser, H. Aram (1989), 'Introduction', in H. Aram Veeser (ed.), *The New Historicism*, London: Routledge; Vernon, James (1994), 'Who's afraid of the "linguistic turn"? The Politics of social history and its discontents', *Social History*, 19: pp. 81–97.

2. Unsworth, Clive (1995), 'Blasphemy, Cultural Divergence and Legal Relativism', *Modern Law Review*, 58 (5): pp. 658–77, p. 674

3. Lawton, David (1993), *Blasphemy*, London: Harvester Wheatsheaf, p. 202.

4. The postmodern debate was essentially begun by a series of works which aimed at reassessing the nature and purpose of late twentieth-century culture. These have since become the standard introduction to the subject and readers wishing to engage in this debate in more depth than there is space for here should consult the following. Lyotard, Jean-François (1992), *The Postmodern Condition: A Report on Knowledge*, Manchester: Manchester University Press; Harvey, David (1989), *The Condition of Postmodernity*, Oxford: Blackwell; White, Hayden (1987a), *Metahistory: The Historical Imagination in Nineteenth-Century Europe*, Baltimore; and White, Hayden (1987b), *Tropics of Discourse*, Baltimore; Connor, Stephen (1991), *Postmodernist Culture*, Oxford: Blackwell. The following account clearly does not ignore the work of these writers but has opted to discuss in more detail some more contemporary outlines and statements regarding the general postmodern position which often also have the advantage of implicitly acknowledging these older works. As such, it is hoped that these can be viewed as in some sense as a summation of the main characteristics of the various postmodern positions. The exposition of two 'worked' examples from the books of Judith Walkowitz and Carlo Ginzburg serves to demonstrate some of the ideals of postmodern analysis applied to history in action as well as suggesting that both these works have discourses and approaches to their respective subjects which could be (and have been) used to approach the subject of blasphemy. Moreoever the reference to the types of study these works embody is intended to mirror and engage with the approach pioneered by David Lawton.

5. Seidman, Steven (1994), 'Introduction', in Steven Seidman (ed.), *The Postmodern Turn*, pp. 1–23, Cambridge: CUP.

6. Ibid., p. 5.

7. Eagleton, op. cit., p. 50.

8. Seidman, op. cit., p. 13.

9. Walkowitz, Judith (1992), *City of Dreadful Delight: Narratives of Sexual Danger in Nineteenth-Century London*, London: Virago.

10. Ibid., p 5-6.

11. Ibid., p. 10.

12. Ibid., p. 8.

13. Ibid., p. 17.

14. Ibid., p. 20, Stallybrass, Peter and Allon White (1986), *The Politics and Poetics of Transgression*, Ithica and London: Cornell University Press.

15. Walkowitz, op. cit., p. 74.

16. Stallybrass and White, op. cit., pp. 18 and 80.

17. Walkowitz, op. cit., pp. 86 and 93–4. See below, Chapter 4.

18. Ibid., p. 124.

19. Colley, Linda (1992), *Britons: Forging the Nation*, London: Yale University Press.

20. Marsh, Joss Lutz (1991), '"Bibliolatry" and "Bible Smashing": G. W. Foote, George Meredith, and the heretic trope of the book', *Victorian Studies*, 34 (3): pp. 315–36.

21. Veeser, H. Aram (1989), 'Introduction', in H. Aram Veeser (ed.), *The New Historicism*, London: Routledge.

22. Palmer, op. cit., pp. xii–xii.
23. Bowen, David G. (1992) (ed.), *The Satanic Verses: Bradford Responds*, Bradford, p. 15.
24. Eagleton, op. cit., p. 67.
25. Lawton, op. cit., pp. 191–201.
26. Ginzburg, Carlo (1976), *The Cheese and the Worms*, London: RKP, pp. 102–5.
27. See Epstein, James (1994), *Radical Expression: Political Language, Ritual, and Symbol in England, 1790–1850*, Oxford: OUP; McCalman, I. D. (1975), 'Popular Radicalism and Free-Thought in Early Nineteenth Century England: A Study of Richard Carlile and His Followers, 1815–32', M.A., Australian National University; McCalman, I. D. (1984), 'Unrespectable Radicalism: Infidels and Pornography in Early Nineteenth Century London Movement', *Past and Present*, 104: pp. 74–110; McCalman, I. D. (1993), *Radical Underworld: Prophets, Revolutionaries, and Pornographers in London, 1795–1840*; Royle, E. (1971), *Radical Politics 1790–1900, Religion and Unbelief*; Royle, E. (1974), *Victorian Infidels*, Manchester; Royle, E. (1980), *Radicals, Secularists and Republicans: Popular Freethought in Britain, 1866–1915*, Manchester; Wood, Marcus (1994), *Radical Satire and Print Culture 1790–1822*, Oxford: Clarendon Press.
28. Lawton, op. cit., p. 202.
29. Visker, Rudi (1995), *Michel Foucault: Genealogy as Critique*, London: Verso, p. 1.
30. Goldstein, Jan (1994) (ed.) *Foucault and the Writing of History*, Oxford: Blackwell, p. 3.
31. Baker, Keith Michael (1994), 'A Foucauldian French Revolution?', in Jan Goldstein (ed.), *Foucault and the Writing of History*, Oxford: Blackwell, pp. 187–205.
32. Foucault, Michel (1976), *The History of Sexuality: Introduction*, London: Penguin, pp. 18–19.
33. Ibid., p. 59.
34. Ibid., p. 33.
35. Ibid., p 58.
36. Foucault, Michel (1990), 'Politics and Reason', in Lawrence D. Kritzman (ed.), *Michel Foucault; Politics, Philosophy, Culture Interviews and Other Writings 1977–1984*, London: Routledge, pp. 57–85, esp. p. 83.
37. Foucault, Michel (1980), 'Truth and Power', in Colin Gordon (ed.), *Power/Knowledge: Selected Interviews and Other Writings 1972–1977*, Brighton: Harvester, p. 122.
38. Ibid., p. 121.
39. Foucault, *Politics and Reason*, p. 63.
40. Ibid., p. 72.
41. Lawton, op. cit., p. 85.
42. Foucault, *Truth and Power*, p. 121.
43. See Foucault, Michel (1965), *Madness and Civilisation: A History of Insanity in the Age of Reason*, New York: Vintage Books. It is interesting to note that some accounts of the Taylor case (see below) involve descriptions of the blood content of the hymns sung at this chapel as clear indications of the madness of the blasphemer. See Cutner, H. (n.d.), *Robert Taylor (1784–1844). The Devils Chaplain*, London: G. W. Foote & Co.
44. Smart, Barry (1985), *Michel Foucault*, London: Routledge, p. 26.
45. Ibid., p. 21.

46. Lawton, op. cit. p. 21.
47. Foucault, Michel (1976), *The History of Sexuality: Introduction*, London: Penguin, p. 58.
48. Smart, op. cit. pp. 73 and 78.
49. Foucault, Michel (1990a), 'Iran: The Spirit of a World Without Spirit', in *Michel Foucault: Politics, Philosophy, Culture. Interviews and Other Writings 1977–84*, edited and with an introduction by Lawrence D. Kritzman, London: Routledge. See also 'The Ethics of the Concern of the Self as a Practice of Freedom', in Foucault, Michel (1997), *Essential Works, Volume I: Ethics*, London: Penguin. In this latter piece, Foucault reasserted that forms of power (of which fundamentalist religion might be considered an example) were not monolithic and should be viewed as constantly in flux. He also suggested that they also did not deny the possibility of freedom. The search for what he called 'the attainment of a certain mode of being' or subjectivity might legitimately use 'spirituality' as a vehicle for achieving this.
50. Webster, Richard (1990), *A Brief History of Blasphemy: Liberalism, Censorship and 'The Satanic Verses'*, Southwold: The Orwell Press, pp. 28–31 and 58–60. Webster suggests that the West's development of the individual conscience and the creation of a 'Bible within' has no counterpart in Islamic theology. However, the rest of Webster's work portrays portions of Western Liberalism as monolithic, dictatorial and intransigent in a manner which would clearly interest foucauldians.
51. Foucault, Michel (1990a), 'On Power', in Lawrence D. Kritzman (ed.), *Michel Foucault: Politics, Philosophy, Culture. Interviews and Other Writings 1977–1984*, London: Routledge, pp. 96–109, esp. p. 98; Kritzman, Lawrence D. (1990), 'Introduction', in Lawrence D. Kritzman (ed.), *Michel Foucault: Politics, Philosophy, Culture. Interviews and Other Writings 1977–1984*, London: Routledge, pp. ix–xxv, esp. p. ix.
52. Foucault, *Politics and Reason*, p. 83.
53. Foucault quoted in Kritzman, op. cit., pp. xv and xvi.
54. Ibid., p. xvii.
55. Foucault, *Truth and Power*, p. 113.
56. Said, Edward (1995), *Orientalism*, London: Penguin.
57. MacKenzie, John M. (1995), *Orientalism: History, Theory and the Arts*, Manchester: MUP, p. xii.
58. Sardar, Ziauddin and Merryl Wyn Davies (1990), *Distorted Imagination: Lessons from the Rushdie Affair*, London: Grey Seal.
59. Colaiaco, J. (1983), *James Fitzjames Stephen and the Crisis of Victorian Thought*, pp. 100–104.
60. Stallybrass and White, op. cit., p. 5.
61. Lapidus, Ira M. (1996), 'State and Religion in Islamic Societies', *Past and Present*, 151: pp. 3–27.
62. Bradlaugh-Bonner, Hypatia (1934), *Penalties Upon Opinion*, London: Watts & Co., p. 135.
63. Ahsan, M. and A. Kidwai (1991) (ed.), *Sacrilege versus Civility – Muslim Perspectives on 'The Satanic Verses' Affair*, 2nd edn, Leicester: The Islamic Foundation; Kabbani, Rana (1989), *Letter to Christendom*, London: Virago; Omer, Mutaharunnisa (1989), *The Holy Prophet and the Satanic Slander*, Madras: The Women's Islamic Social and Educational Service Trust; Robinson, Neal (1992), 'Reflections on the Rushdie Affair – 18 April

1989', in David G. Bowen (ed.), *The Satanic Verses: Bradford Responds*, 33–44, Bradford; Sardar, Ziauddin and Merryl Wyn Davies (1990), *Distorted Imagination: Lessons from the Rushdie Affair*, London: Grey Seal; Webster, Richard (1990), *A Brief History of Blasphemy: Liberalism, Censorship and 'The Satanic Verses'*, Southwold.

64. MacKenzie, op. cit.

65. Radzinowicz, L. (1957), *Sir James Fitzjames Stephen 1829–1894*, p. 14. But see also Colaiaco, J., op. cit., pp. 111–13, 116–17 for a paraphrase of Stephen's contemporary opinions which could be construed as Orientalist.

66. Bowen, op. cit., p. 12.

67. Ahsan and Kidwai, pp. 341–50, 385–6.

68. Eagleton, Terry (1996), *The Illusions of Postmodernism*, Oxford: Blackwell, p. 125.

69. Said, Edward (1994), *Culture and Imperialism*, London: Vintage; Said, Edward (1995), *Orientalism*, London: Penguin, p. 326.

70. Said, Orientalism, p. 324.

71. Brown, Callum (1991), 'Secularisation: A Theory in Danger?', *Scottish Economic and Social History*, (II): pp. 52–8; Brown, Callum G. (1988), 'Did urbanization secularize Britain?' *Urban History Yearbook*: pp. 1–14; Bruce, Steve (1992) (ed.), *Religion and Modernisation, Sociologists and Historians Debate the Secularisation Thesis*, Oxford: Clarendon Press; Keppel, Gilles (1994), *The Revenge of God*, Cambridge: Polity Press.

CHAPTER THREE

Thomas Paine, William Hone and the Carlile Agitation: The Creation of a Modern Blasphemous Rhetoric

The contributions of freethinkers from the period of the late eighteenth and early nineteenth century to the history of blasphemy and radicalism are immense. Whilst many appear as advocates of attack being the best mode of defence individuals also found themselves in court due to the increased interest taken by a number of groups in the phenomenon of blasphemy as a possible means of controlling errant opinion in a range of spheres. Nonetheless the actions of blasphemers did have the effect of allowing deistical and increasingly atheistical views to emerge finally from the shadows of both active and nominal Christianity.

The relationship between Christianity and the state itself was in some degree of flux during this period. Methodism had been a substantial challenge to this relationship but from the late eighteenth century onwards some branches of Anglican evangelical thought were working to rejuvenate it. This branch of religious thought became increasingly concerned with the debilitating effects of economic and social destitution upon the moral makeup of the lower orders and considered the redefinition of social discipline to be an important domain of activity. This widespread current of belief was to be one of the influential interest groups which stimulated the Society for the Suppression of Vice in the first years of the nineteenth century. A related development which was just as influential in the Society was the influx of loyalism which sought to protect society from the implications of Jacobin teaching in all areas of life.[1] Wilberforce, one of the Society's leading lights, demonstrated how these two lines of thought could be interwoven since he was convinced that the enemies of the British Constitution were also the enemies of religion.[2] In a sense the Society was a logical consequence of the law's operation during this period since it provided an important bridge between government wishes and public opinion. The composition of the Society was predominantly urban and prosperous middle class and is reminiscent of that involved in the formation of other metropolitan and provincial prosecution societies. As such it might be useful to view the Society as a symptom of bourgeois consciousness and its increasing identification with the state and its power. As a private organisation the Vice Society could initiate prosecutions and allow the government to retain a discrete distance from the actual prosecution. Nonetheless it is clear that the Society did, on occasions, act with governmental approval and information, yet on others the government itself was to be embarrassed by its apparent ineptitude.

Thomas Paine's encounters with blasphemy were on his terms clearly an accident, yet no consideration of the subject and one of its underlying themes, the creation of a blasphemous culture, can exist without him. It would be difficult to attempt an evaluation of Paine's contribution to secularist and freethought ideas when much has already been written by so many. For our purposes, however, there remain a number of themes that need highlighting. So much has been said about the impact of Paine's *Rights of Man*, particularly in England, that the impact of Paine's *Age of Reason* has to an extent been overshadowed.[3] A confluence of both these areas of investigation is provided by the historical investigations and personality of Edward Thompson. The study of Paine's emphatically political writing occupied Thompson's early years whilst his last, posthumously published, work examined the challenges to religious authority which created the milieu in which the ideas of Paine, Blake and other deists and antinomians flourished.[4] Thompson has suggested – rightly – that the rejection of religious authority is too readily identified purely with a rationalist deism. His investigation of popular antinomian survivals in the London of the 1790s, and of Blake in particular, indicates the existence of a fierce brand of freethinking Christianity. This challenged tyrannical religious authority and the disciplined jurisdiction over religious thought that it attempted to exercise. Thompson even cites Blake's introduction to Jerusalem as condemning the notion of religion seeking vengeance for sin and for imposing strict doctrinally rigid readings of the Bible.[5] In a clear detachment from a state church and from imposed religious authority, this belief circulated in London from the 1790s onwards and clearly had an influence on later religious freethinkers such as Robert Wedderburn and Robert Taylor.[6] Likewise the manner in which established religious authority subverted a traditional and uncomplicated Christianity influenced individuals like William Hone.

However, deist rejection of religious authority was influenced largely by Thomas Paine's *Age of Reason*. This work, like much of Blake's thought, opposed tyrannical readings of the Bible and externally imposed doctrinal conformity but went further by condemning attempts to convert Jews, Muslims and Huguenots.[7] Suggesting that the creation of an established church encouraged persecution Paine, like Blake, saw the enforcement of conformity as potentially blasphemous since it presumed to know the will of God.[8] Paine thus reached a libertarian view of religious belief by denying external authority in matters of religious doctrine. He argued that religious toleration required individuals to diminish the importance of their own religious belief in order to accommodate those of others. To further undermine closed and seemingly unshakeable biblical literalism he also condemned large sections of the creation story and other sections of the Bible as constituting a collection of myths.[9] Thus the *Age of Reason* offended implicitly in two areas. It contained actual blasphemous attacks upon the Bible as well as constituting a manifesto for the wholesale rejection of religious authority. As Keane puts it

> Ecclesiastical and spiritual matters once clothed in reverent silence now found themselves dragged into the public sphere and, stripped naked, forced to answer tough questions. The sheer diversity of points and counterpoints, questions and answers, undoubtedly deepened the sense of desacralized controversy.[10]

This blend of serious biblical and doctrinal criticism which identified contemporary religious authority with forms of malignant power was to be stunningly popular throughout the first third of the nineteenth century.[11] The book was, like Paine's earlier works, an instant success largely on the back of its timing. Frank Prochaska has suggested that the *Age of Reason* elicited rapid action from the government supported by the Society for the Suppression of Vice since 'what began as just another confrontation between Moses and Copernicus in a French prison became a confrontation between Robespierre and Pitt in England'.[12] But the contents of the work would probably have influenced deists and secularists in any case. Hypatia Bradlaugh-Bonner recognised that the actions taken against Paine and his publishers marked the opening of the modern history of the offence and in a sense the implicit plea for religious toleration contained within the *Age of Reason* is echoed in most subsequent secularist arguments surrounding the offence.[13] The *Age of Reason* constituted what the prosecuting counsel Thomas Erskine would call an attack upon the hope of an afterlife filled with compensations for the poor – sentiments that the Society for the Suppression of Vice would have echoed.[14] Thus government was constrained to act, ably if erratically supported by some elements of popular loyalism, since the work threatened to undermine both religion *per se* and the social system which had previously been guarantor and beneficiary of established religion and political stability.[15] This perhaps mirrors the line of thinking and the reactions to it that Sir Matthew Hale had anticipated.

In 1797 the government moved against a London bookseller, Thomas Williams, who was found guilty of selling a copy of the *Age of Reason*.

In court Thomas Erskine, who had earlier defended Paine himself against sedition, advocated a – for the time – liberal attitude to freedom of the press declaring that it had 'led to all the blessings both of religion and government'.[16] Yet Erskine was nonetheless prepared to consider that the *Age of Reason* went too far. Despite his apparent libertarianism Erskine's attack on the work was surprisingly traditional and still reliant on Hale since it insisted on reverence for the scriptures as a component of law. For him there was a world of difference between criticism and outright denial. The latter would inevitably unravel the state and result in 'insolence and disobedience'.[17]

Whilst Erskine appeared to accept the legal right to criticise Christianity, what is perhaps more evident is the creeping introduction of a perceived distinction between 'matter' and 'manner' which was to have eventual importance.[18] This aspect was echoed by the defence counsel Steward Kydd who worked hard to promote Paine's apparently respectable and honest motives in writing the book – namely to attack the dechristianisation programme in France and to promote a deist view of the universe. Kydd challenged Erskine to 'find a single passage in the whole of the book inconsistent with the most chaste, the most correct system of morals'.[19] Moreover he emphasised that Paine's attacks were openly premeditated, even suggesting that the intellectually honest would react in a similar way when confronted by biblical absurdities and debaucheries.[20] Whilst it seemed as though Paine and his ideas themselves were on trial the defendant Thomas Williams was clearly pushed into selling the *Age of Reason* by his destitution. After being persuaded to visit the defendant's family who were in a sick and wretched condition, Erskine petitioned the Society for the Suppression of Vice to plead for a commutation of any sentence. When this was refused by a meeting of the Society Erskine indignantly severed any connection with its dealings and refused the fee offered for his services – a fact noted with obvious relish by Bradlaugh-Bonner.[21]

Williams himself was fined £1000 and sentenced to a year in prison and in the course of the judgment of the court Justice Ashhurst noted that Paine's works were attacks upon Christianity, which by this stage could legally be defined as being a part and parcel of the laws of the land. The works thus had a tendency 'to destroy all civil obligations, the solemnity of oaths, and to strip the law "of one of its principal sanctions – the dread of future punishments"'.[22] Paine himself replied with an attack upon the use in this case of the Special Jury system which originally had been composed of merchants overseeing disputes in the world of commerce. Paine saw this as a cynical ploy to co-opt and use middle-class metropolitan opinion that had also been the mainstay of the Vice Society's subscription list.[23]

The culturally defined link between Christianity and the law of the Land was confirmed 14 years later when Daniel Isaac Eaton was prosecuted, again by the Vice Society, for selling a self-penned third part of the *Age of Reason*. Whilst the assertion that Christ was an impostor went further than Paine the descriptions of Christianity as comprised of myth, the attacks upon established religion and the Bible as treasonable and blasphemous to God were certainly in line with the original *Age of Reason*. The judge, Lord Ellenborough, stated in his summing up that religion clearly depended upon the doctrines of which it was comprised and once more made a clear assertion that the 'matter' used was the fundamental test in determining blasphemy as an offence. Eaton's sentence was eighteen months imprisonment and regular appearances in the pillory which elicited demonstrations of sympathy from the public at large.[24] The fundamentals of the legal judgment in the Eaton case were re-enacted a few years later when Justice Bayley asserted that James Williams's parody of the Athanasian Creed would undermine the 'sacred ordinances of the church' and moreover would 'fill the minds more especially of the lower orders with light and trivial matters when they ought to be devoted to the service and adoration of God'.[25]

The Eaton case had also gained sympathy from Percy Bysshe Shelley who denounced the prosecution and wrote craving wider tolerance for the notion of artistic free speech and expression.[26] This process, however, was also reflected in early nineteenth-century attempts to extend religious toleration to other denominations. Although relief from disabilities for Catholics and Nonconformists had to wait another two decades the fundamental basis of their belief did not contradict the central tenets and doctrines of established religion as the anti-trinitarianism of Unitarianism had done. Leonard Levy noted that William Smith's campaign to promulgate legal recognition of Unitarianism which resulted in the passing of the Trinity Act of 1813 would have extended recognition to the views of Deists and even atheists but these provisions were compromised in order to provide for the safe passage of the bill. This act, at least in theory, removed the component of anti-trinitarianism from the offence of blasphemy and effectively closed the door finally upon the pursuit of medieval heresy. Nonetheless a striking feature of the offence beyond this date was the way in which such components had an incredible cultural longevity. Whilst the professedly religious would clearly escape legal and cultural censure it was still the case that outright attacks upon the doctrine of the Trinity were still attacks upon the fundamental tenets of the Anglican religion, as stated in the Thirty-Nine Articles, and other texts.[27]

The political repression of the years after the end of the Napoleonic Wars linked deism and infidelity with forms of sedition.[28] The use of blasphemous libel as a charge against the seditious press was construed by government to be the most effective method of dealing with the problem. Many commentators have noted that the association of radicalism with French jacobinism was instrumental in persuading many individual radicals to frame their critiques in resolutely loyalist constitutionalist language and idioms.[29] In some respects this analysis of radicalism partly explains the position which blasphemy retained in the minds of both radicals and the authorities during this period. As far as the authorities were concerned blasphemous libel, as has already been suggested, was a useful method of attacking radicals which was more likely to elicit convictions from sympathetic juries.[30] The atheistic and anti-clerical associations that went with the offence of blasphemy were also deemed to indicate foreign 'other' ideologies in the public mind. The eventual success of this tactic, particularly in relation to the later trials of Richard Carlile, was emphasised by the fact that Carlile and his shopmen and women realised that they had pushed themselves beyond the protection of any constitutionalist and conservative radical rhetoric.

In this respect the William Hone case represents an interesting confluence of ideas and influences.[31] On the one hand Hone drew upon the older constitutionalist rhetorics for his defence yet the case contained some aspects of procedure and defence which were to become established facets of future cases. Likewise the government was to learn much from its humiliation at the hands of Hone and the radical press which later was to be of considerable use against Carlile, Southwell and the next generation of blasphemers.

William Hone was arrested in May 1817 on three charges of blasphemous libel, two of which were also accompanied by charges of seditious libel. These were related to three satirical works – *The Late John Wilke's Catechism*, *The Political Litany* and *The Sinecurists Creed*. Hone was a Christian of an indeterminant sort absorbing elements of Evangelicalism, Catholicism, Methodism and Unitarianism in equal measure – he appears nonetheless to have been anti-clerical without being either an atheist or actively intending his blasphemy. Indeed, if his Unitarianism was as developed as some have suggested then hostility to his view that the Incarnation of Christ was blasphemous, alongside the rejection of his attacks on the Trinity contained in the parodies, constituted clear evidence that toleration was as yet incomplete.[32] Hone also learned to use these parodies of established religious texts as a means to attack forms of corruption and governmental abuse of power. Hone's defence depended largely upon asking the court to scrutinise the content of what he was writing and to set to one side the form in which it was couched. In this respect the government had fallen into a trap of its own making. With a law enshrining the matter as being of primary importance it was thus no surprise when the jury agreed with Hone's assertions that the content of what he had said was purely political.

As Marcus Wood has pointed out, Hone was a particularly unfortunate choice for the government to target since he was acutely aware of the subtlety and power of literary forms, the operation of the blasphemy laws and the idioms of popular journalism and pamphleteering. Hone had blended religious forms with other legal rhetorics in an earlier instance noted by Wood. The anti-Catholic *Trial of Antichrist* constituted a mock trial of the Pope for High Treason which offered evidence from the prosecution from a number of victims of persecution.[33] In this instance the pamphlet would have fallen into the area of loyalist anti-Catholic and anti-French rhetoric but the attempt to blend two forms would be replicated later by Hone. One other important literary genre which Hone had invoked was that of martyrology. This he reached through a contemporary customary familiarity with Foxe's works as well as a studious interest in the works of Leveller pamphleteers and Bunyan.[34] In particular Wood suggests that Hone's use of Lillburne's trial was an attempt to establish the supremacy of the jury in deciding the precise interpretation of the law and justice. Likewise his use and invocation of such a widely-known text as Bunyan perhaps presages Foote's use of biblical misquotations.[35]

Hone's use of Lillburne was also an attempt to appeal to established English constitutional traditions that both Wood and Epstein have investigated in recent studies.[36] For both Wood and Epstein a whole host of genres and forms from advertising literature, through radical dress and toasting customs to trial discourses, were a means of establishing popular consent for, as well as active interest in, forms of radical action. Moreover they were also used with explicitly radical intent to demystify questionable procedures, forms of authority and political practices. As Wood puts it:

> The Labyrinthine language of the legal profession is set against the common sense and colloquial diction of the defendant. The defence and jury are cast as the representatives of a vulnerable state of honesty that is uncalculating and very English, while the law is a dark and degraded lower region which uses obscure ancient and foreign languages and divisive trickery.[37]

Some of these characteristics were to establish precedents which later blasphemy defendants were to use in their own defence. Perhaps this could be said to mark out the case against William Hone as the start of a modern blasphemy and free speech case tradition.[38] Hone's appeal to martyrological literature proved a blueprint for later blasphemers and the element of control upon proceedings which this gave Hone was to prove particularly useful to Foote in the 1880s. The analogy can be taken further since Hone made a point of drawing upon the extensive tradition of publishing the verbatim accounts of radical trials – a genre which at one time occupied William Cobbett.[39] Hone also displayed considerable theatricality in his defence, using images of personal poverty (invoked through his own mock embarrassment), the exploration of the meaning of the courtroom itself, the protracted discussion of the significance of gestures, and the display of stoical ignorance intended to appeal beyond the scope of legal technicalities and to evoke sympathy from a common jury. Moreover, as Olivia Smith points out, Hone's trial was also a trial of the right to use language since the notion of it being used indecently and improperly would have obtained a legal existence had he been convicted.[40] The whole language of argument was also portrayed for an eager public by Hone's own contributions to the vast trial literature of the period. By the end of 1818 each of the accounts of the three trials he endured had gone through multiple editions and the three were collected together and repackaged for an eager public as late as 1876.[41]

What the trial and these accounts of them committed to posterity was a series of lines of argument which were to prove useful to Hone's descendants. These opened the door for the depiction and reality of blasphemous utterance to be considered a self-generating and self-sustaining culture. Marcus Wood has noted how much this trial belongs to the world of post-Napoleonic satirical radicalism. But some of this satire also had the effect of scotching and discrediting the religious and cultural innovations which were also a feature of the immediate post-war period. Just as the post-Napoleonic period witnessed satirical radicalism it also was characterised by loyalist evangelism and Bibliolatry which was to be personified by Hannah More in the 1820s.[42] Hone's parodies attacked these innovations as well as stock religio-political targets which bordered upon the anti-clerical. This suggests that an accusation of blasphemy itself was in part turned from a means by which the authorities could achieve some easy convictions against the radical movement to an opportunity for defendants to use the process of the law to enhance the impact of their writings. The trap which the authorities had fallen into through asserting the 'part and parcel' argument of the blasphemy laws meant that a close examination by judicial process of the content of these writings served to highlight, in a very public sphere, their real and intended targets. Similarly the use of religious forms to attack corruption also served to highlight conceptions of the 'just' law of the land and to have a potentially enhanced effect upon juries as it had done for other radicals such as Robert Wedderburn and Samuel Waddington.[43]

Hone's trials also contained a further line of argument which was, as we shall see, to be an ambiguous intellectual legacy to later blasphemers.

Popular justice was invoked by the appeal of Hone to the unbridled sanctity and trust in the jury system and the sovereignty of trial by intellectual as well as social peers. Hone also cited earlier examples of the use of religious forms to portray political messages which had escaped prosecution. These were to appear in later blasphemy trials as a defence which drew attention to the fact that for the agencies which brought prosecution there was a perceived build-up of offensive incidents and wider offensiveness in society at large. This defence highlighted the paradoxical arbitrariness of the decision to prosecute and the effect it had to seemingly wipe the cultural slate clean each time prosecution was initiated. Moreover, taking a stand at this juncture would theoretically prevent retrospective attempts to legislate earlier established and accepted ideas and idioms out of acceptability.

*　　*　　*

One aspect of Hone's defence which was, arguably, a central reason for his success was his assertion of constitutionalism and his carefully crafted place in a pantheon of traditional English radicalism. This persona and image was, largely through choice, not available to Hone's primary successor Richard Carlile. This in part explains Carlile's own particularly abrasive approach and the comparative success of the government in dealing with his agitation.

Carlile had moved into religious radicalism primarily as a result of his conversion to the ideas of Paine for whom he retained, in various forms, a lifelong regard.[44] Additionally a strong belief in the power of the press common to many during this period was likewise a motivation for Carlile.[45] Whilst Carlile was once thought to have swallowed the whole canon of Paine's ideas almost verbatim more modern views suggest that his own personal views gradually advanced beyond Paine's Deism. Certainly the celebratory tone of Aldred's brief biography suggested that their ideological positions were symbiotically linked as Carlile's brushes with the law constitutied a continuation of Paine's earlier work. Edward Royle likewise saw this natural continuity although Joel Wiener in particular emphasised Carlile's move to outright atheism as indicative of a continuously ongoing journey – an analysis confirmed by David Berman and to a lesser extent Robert Hole.[46] In a later piece Wiener refined the relationship between the two by emphasising Paine's skills as a writer and populariser who wished to avoid brushes with the law, juxtaposed with Carlile's lack of intellectual concreteness or originality. This was nonetheless more than compensated for by a, for the authorities, sometimes unnerving fixity of purpose.[47]

Carlile first came to the attention of the authorities when he became

involved in the production and distribution of William Sherwin's various
newspapers. He even deserves a footnote in the Hone prosecutions for
mischievously producing his own copies of his blasphemous works in
August 1817.[48] After a spell in the King's Bench Prison Carlile's attempt
to forward the cause of radicalism lived in the shadow of the Hone
prosecution and acquittal. What really set Carlile on the road to
notoriety was his decision to republish Paine's *Age of Reason* alongside
an edition of Elihu Palmer's *Principles of Nature*. The government
moved against these in January 1819 and from this point onward
worked largely in tandem with the Society for the Suppression of Vice to
produce a range of public and private indictments which Wiener
estimates approached almost a dozen by September that year.[49] Even
from the earliest court appearances in June 1819 Carlile appeared to be
the antithesis of Hone through his persistent refusal to desist from
further publishing the supposed libels as he began to construct the
reputation for stubbornness which was to prove one of his chief radical
assets. Carlile's role as an eyewitness to the events of Peterloo made him
an even more dangerous adversary for the government since his
published account became almost definitive in radical circles.[50]

When Carlile came to trial on 13 October 1819 the arguments of the
prosecution turned not simply upon the explicit attacks upon scriptural
authority contained in the *Age of Reason* but upon the pernicious
influence which such a widely disseminated text would have upon the
partially educated. As Aldred succinctly put it 'The eyes of all the
country were upon the jury, who had to decide whether Christianity was
a fabulous imposture.'[51] Carlile's own defence was long-winded to say
the least. He managed to read the whole of the *Age of Reason* as a
putative means of extending its publication through newspaper reports –
a tactic which Wiener suggests was unsuccessful. This was followed by a
series of readings from the Bible and the Koran and miscellaneous quotes
from various treatises arguing for toleration. Wiener suggests that this
line of approach dashed hopes for a show trial which would grip the
nation and create a radical hero in the mould of Hone. Whilst the
courtroom was doomed to endure these lengthy readings in silence the
frequent attempts to interrupt Carlile could nonetheless be envisaged as
attempts to interfere with a legitimate defence – however tedious it
appeared to be in practice. Certainly this reading of events survived for
Guy Aldred to reiterate.[52] Whilst Carlile claimed that he was trying to
clear the *Age of Reason* of the calumnies associated with it Wiener
suggests that he had no real alternative. His consistent rejection of legal
advice offered to him by Francis Place and Jeremy Bentham left him with
a one-dimensional defence which he offered to the bitter end. This was
never likely to assist him in resisting the only element which the

prosecution really had to prove – the fact and responsibility for publication of such works and libels. However, the failure of his defence made Carlile realise that his martyrdom was to consist of a lengthy prison term rather than the glory of a victorious show trial.

Despite the comparatively pedestrian nature of Carlile's use of texts he did also proffer some elements of defence which had important resonances outside the courtroom. The frequent attempts at interrupting his lengthy oratory were portrayed as an attack upon the popular notion of a 'fair' trial and the admissibility of a 'fair' defence. Likewise the judge's intervention – which was aimed at preventing the repetition of the supposed blasphemies – had the result, in the popular mind, of placing the Christian religion and its links to the law as manifestly above criticism. Moreover there were some enticing arguments which took the prosecution into interesting territory. Carlile, following Paine, criticised the Bible as an immoral book unfit for the eyes of children in particular and publicised a popular infidel and later secularist discourse about biblical immorality. Likewise he drew upon the standard 'tiberian' argument which questioned the right of human courts to operate jurisdiction on behalf of a God supposedly capable of defending himself. The exercise of this right was further questioned when Carlile suggested that Christianity was malignant since it required persecution to support it.

Carlile also attempted to push at what he thought was an open door for universal toleration when he began to untie the precise nature of the English Constitution in the wake of the Toleration Act's removal of the disabilities upon Unitarians. Carlile suggested that because this appeared to nullify the first of the Thirty-Nine Articles then the argument that Christianity was part and parcel of the law of the land was spurious and effectively annulled. At best the law of the land, he asserted, was based upon a deism and moreover one which could be shown to have embraced the works he was on trial for publishing. The ambivalent status of Unitarians in a country which, by the early nineteenth century, asked for allegiance to a broadly based conception of Christianity which seemed to include the Trinity was an oft-highlighted anomaly which would appear in later defences. In Carlile's case the attempt to draw statute law into the issue actually backfired since investigation of the nature of 9 & 10 William III led to the court reaching the unprecedented conclusion that the statute was intended to strengthen and supplement the Common Law of blasphemous libel.[53] The case also invoked a modernisation motif of progress which would also serve later blasphemers well, although arguably with widely differing results. The apparently enlightened vision of Sir Matthew Hale was once again questioned because of the witch executions. Carlile also painted himself into a radical religious martyrological pantheon which ranged from likening himself to Galileo and Luther to a stark, if melodramatic, attempt to awaken consciences nearer home by invoking the Marian fires of Smithfield.

Despite this heavy-handed rehearsal of an English tradition Carlile's leading mistake was that he had moved outside the orbit of constitutionalist regency radicalism. His doctrines, which had already progressed beyond the marginally acceptable deism of Paine, seemed still more in line with varieties of jacobinism and foreign infidelity.[54] Berman adds further weight to this view by suggesting that Carlile's atheism could be distinguished from that espoused by his predecessors through its explicit attempt to argue for social change in the manner of more modern Marxist analysis. This further cemented the link between atheism and the attitudes of the lower orders.[55] Moreover Carlile's antagonistic approach to religion as a social system led individuals to posit the infidel rejection of supposedly absolute values as creating a dangerous 'kind of moral anomie' which would dissolve respect and repsonsibility.[56] As time went on Carlile's stubbornness, his desire to remain master of his own agitation and his lack of connection to indigenous radicalism was exacerbated when leading figures in this latter movement went to great pains to distance themselves from him.[57] Aldred noted that Samuel Bamford described Carlile as a man 'now enduring the reward of his temerity'.[58]

The verdict of the case was never seriously in doubt once the Attorney-General had answered the distinction between the relief offered to Unitarians and the actions of an individual prepared to scoff openly at religion. Once the proof of publication had been produced then it was clear, as far as the court was concerned, that Carlile's opinions had been intended to be made public with results potentially injurious to the population at large. Once Carlile's appeal (largely on technical grounds) had failed he resigned himself to prison. He had been fined £1500 and asked to offer sureties amounting to £1200 for his behaviour. The refusal of these eventually resulted in him serving an additional sentence of three years.

Carlile was perhaps the first prisoner to systematically make use of his confinement. He returned to his journalism, which he was able to conduct successfully from prison in Dorchester, as well as sharpening his religious, political and philosophical insights.[59] To an extent Carlile's resolve to continue journalistic work was necessary to maintain him in prison but was also indicative of how his plight had highlighted questions of press freedom as he became a figure on the fringe of what was to become the unstamped press agitation.[60] Carlile's wife Jane and his sister Mary Anne Carlile continued publishing his paper the

Republican and within two years both had shared his cell in Dorchester. Jane was convicted for selling the *Age of Reason* whilst Mary-Anne's prosecution, initiated by the Vice Society for the publication of an *Appendix to the Theological Works of Thomas Paine* had, briefly, some notoriety. Her status as a single woman meant that she was liable for a fine, a situation Jane had escaped, whilst the intervention which refused her a complete defence speech resulted in the 'suppressed' elements finding their way into a radical pamphlet.

From this point onwards Carlile amassed around him a large number of individuals willing to promote his ideas and continue the sale of blasphemous and seditious literature. Joel Wiener used a range of military metaphors, describing them as an 'army' and their battle with the authorities as 'the War of the Shopmen'.[61] As Wiener points out, many of these men and women were broadly anti-clerical and demonstrated not only how much Carlile had tapped into an anti-Christian sub-culture but also how much he had demonstrated that radicalism in religion and politics were linked. Indeed Wiener's use of military metaphors have their own echo in Carlile's assertion that the priesthood acted as though they were a standing army. Philosophically Carlile was supported by the growth of a movement of zetetic societies which promulgated free discussion and scientific investigation as well as raising substantial funds for Carlile and the shopmen.

Carlile's 'guerrillas' suffered a series of prosecutions from the Vice Society between 1821 and 1824 which were aimed at breaking the backbone of his agitation as well as preventing the dissemination of his ideas through imprisonment and sporadic confiscation of his literature. Many of those prosecuted, such as James Watson, were to take a further part in later radical journalism and agitation. Although many of these trials fell into an established pattern some defences offered by these shopmen constituted a continuous display of popular conceptions of the law's glaring anomalies advanced in a uniformly defiant manner. William Tunbridge argued that it was an uncivilised system which compelled individuals to acknowledge by law the truth of 'such an indefinable matter', moreover he asserted that the law was intended to protect property and no case could be made for his actions constituting a danger to property.[62] William Campion suggested that rigid definitions of Christianity served to deny allegorical interpretations and effectively made them illegal.[63] James Watson challenged the court to produce proof of injury and intimated how juries were being used as crude tools for censorship which could be extended at any moment.[64] Susannah Wright, following information laid by the Vice Society, used her court appearance to attack laws which were created without the assent of the people and to indulge in old-fashioned anticlericalism which forced the judge to intervene. She continued by lambasting the Vice Society for suppressing free discussion and asserted that the application of law outside statute was a law of 'whim, caprice, and tyranny' operated by juries which she claimed were hand-picked.[65]

The last major crusade against Carlile took place in 1824 when a wave of prosecutions were followed by stock seizures which proved so unpopular that charges of blasphemous libel were less easily commenced. These prosecutions were this time instigated by Peel himself to rescue the situation from the failure of the Vice Society. Whilst this spate of cases elicited convictions against a further six individuals, the Carlile agitation continued unabated.[66] Despite this the 'war of the shopmen' was not the victory which Aldred construed from the cessation of prosecution. Nonetheless the fact was that when the authorities moved next in defence of religion and morality, although retaining a concern with sedition, it was to be against a less obvious target.

The next major case of blasphemy involved the so-called 'Devil's Chaplain' Robert Taylor, who had shared a platform with Richard Carlile at the Rotunda and earlier had been an Anglican curate. Upon encountering *The Age of Reason* and the works of Gibbon, Taylor slid into deism. From this point on opinions regarding Robert Taylor, or as he became known colloquially 'The Devil's Chaplain', tend to differ widely. His first biographer Cutner saw a sort of genius in him whilst Leonard Levy considered him a wayward eccentric and 'a bit of a religious zany'.[67] The clue to this disparity is perhaps illuminated by the contrast with Carlile. The latter's very bookishness has seemed to mark out Taylor's intellectual shifts and inconsistencies as indicative of a second-rate mind and second-rate radicalism. We should remember, however, that Ian McCalman has already warned us of the danger of associating radicalism with coherent and fully considered political programmes and that much underworld radicalism which existed on the ideological, economic and moral margins of society had a consistently episodic nature.[68]

Taylor associated with many of the individuals who constituted the raw material of McCalman's study. In particular Robert Wedderburn's career as blasphemer, dissenting preacher, brothel keeper and brawler represented the centre of an extreme sub-culture of which Taylor could only lurk on the fringes.[69] Whereas Carlile's blasphemy had been of a literary nature Taylor's orations at meetings of his, perversely named, Christian Evidence Society blended forms of street culture with religious sermons. In this respect, alongside Wedderburn's brush with the blasphemy laws, Taylor's pronouncements are indicative of a street culture which had imbibed, discussed and verbalised Christian doctrines and ideas alongside artisan ones.[70] This verbalisation was potentially at odds with the Thirty-Nine Articles yet was not as obviously anti-Christian as proceedings against it might suggest – as often as not individuals like Wedderburn could complain about the quality of Christianity they encountered.[71] In some respects it is no surprise to discover these quasi-products of the antinomian tradition as descendents of those whom Thompson identified with Blake and his millieu.[72] Deism thus was the ideological position which Taylor claimed to adopt yet his appeal to a popular congregation was in the attack upon authority and the underlying implication that there was a pure form of Christianity which had been lost, betrayed or usurped. That such a connection could be made is suggested by one visitor to Robert Taylor's Theobald's Road chapel in the years immediately after his last brush with the law of blasphemy. At this service Taylor declared gin and water to be better than the Blood of Christ and further asserted that Jesus was drunk when he walked on water.[73] Once more this verbalising of Christianity and ribald discussion of doctrine appears to owe as much to fringe conceptions of Christiantity as it does to putative freethought.

The City of London initially moved against Taylor in early 1827 and he appeared before Lord Justice Tenterden. Taylor was prosecuted primarily for a discourse presented at Salter's Hall in which he cast doubt upon scripture and introduced ribald interpretations of biblical texts. Amongst other pronouncements repeated in court he denied the authority of the title page of the New Testament, demanded an eye witness to the confrontation between Christ and the Devil and finished this off with a declaration that Christianity was a 'mischievous fable'.[74] Taylor's defence appeared to be an abortive attempt to establish his respectable credentials as a deist. All this was to no avail and the judge chose to focus upon the clear element of sarcasm that ran through most of Taylor's writings. The jury concurred and Taylor was sentenced to one year in prison and the need to provide £1000 in recognisances. Some elements of the press took note of the case and used it to question why religion was legally protected from criticism.[75] At first Taylor sought to go the way of Carlile and refused to find these recognizances but eventually was persuaded to relent, ironically by Carlile himself.[76] Taylor was less comfortable with the reality of prison and petitioned frequently for his release. When this occurred he toured the provinces in the company of Carlile on what appeared to be an infidel mission.

It seems that despite the discomfort of prison, Taylor's willingness to publicise his opinions flourished unabated and in 1831, soon after the authorities had moved once more against Carlile, he became the centre of attention of the Society for the Suppression of Vice. What is interesting from the passages mentioned is the area where religious and political language could merge in a heady, if wayward and unfocused, critique that nonetheless contained authentic millenarian undertones:

> O awful mystery! O love divine! There you behold the Almighty God arraigned as a felon at the bar of Pontius Pilate ... : the author of nature suffered: the immortal Christ expired: ... the Living God was dead. There was a radical reform in the Kingdom of Heaven; the borough mongers were turned out; the jure-Divino-ship of God himself was no longer respected; "God over all" was put under; "Blessed for evermore" was no more blessed: "Holy, Holy, Holy" was wholly kicked out; "Jehovah's awful throne" was declared vacant; and the provisional government devolved into the hands of that venerable republican, Lieutenant-General Beelzebub.[77]

Taylor's defence here differed in that he attempted to argue that similar language was in constant use and that only his lowly position and circumstances deemed that his pronouncement of them should be equated with blasphemy. Levy suggests that this second trial was deliberately low key to avoid providing Taylor with a platform from which to arraign a wider world. Certainly the conviction caused less of a stir and a clear conclusion to be drawn is that the authorities were but slowly learning effective techniques to combat forms of street blasphemy.

The 1830s were the decade when the voice of radicalism gained a new confidence in the hands of the radical and illegal unstamped press.[78] Many of the papers related to this agitation, such as the *Slap at the Church*, had almost exclusively anti-clerical content. Others produced similar material in passing, largely as a consequence of their reiteration of the paineite message in various forms. In this respect it is no surprise to find the central figure in the agitation – the self-professed freethinker Henry Hetherington – in the courts for blasphemy, though it might surprise the unwary to discover that he also appeared as a plaintive in a blasphemy case related to the publication of out of copyright material.

Between the case against Robert Taylor and the case against Hetherington an intriguing case tried at York produced a verdict which had the effect of spelling out what blasphemers had often argued. The case against a clergyman, Gathercole, arose from his written libel against a Catholic Nunnery. The case against him was thrown out because the law was deemed to protect only the established branch of Christianity 'because it is the form established by law, and is therefore a part of the constitution of the country'.[79]

Hetherington was tried in December 1840 for publishing Haslam's *Letters to the Clergy* which occurred at the instigation of the Bishop of Exeter. The thrust of Hetherington's opinions in this work was that the human race should burn every bible and that it was ' ... a vile compound of filth, blasphemy, and nonsense, as a fraud and a cheat, and as an insult to God'. He also asserted provocatively that 'the human race have been too long gulled with such trash'.[80] The prosecution proved – successfully – that Hetherington had sold the book, a situation facilitated by the fact that he was also named as an agent for its publication.

Hetherington's defence, which he conducted himself, opened customarily by trying to establish his respectable motives. The particular letter indicted, he argued, was being considered out of context and that Haslam's initial letter contained an appeal to the clergy to defend their doctrines. Hetherington, with the experience of the unstamped press behind him and the steadfastness of Carlile a recent memory, suggested that prosecution of the work was innappropriate and counterproductive. Cheekily citing the financial collapse of his own *Poor Man's Guardian* after Lord Lyndhurst declared in court that it was not a newspaper, Hetherington argued that anti-establishment publicity created a readership for such works.[81] Thus for him, in the manner of the unstamped press, freedom of opinion would eventually triumph and a crime like blasphemy seemed to actively encourage recidivism. Hetherington's impassioned defence of free speech, 'a right deemed of pre-eminent importance from time immemorial', is probably the most lucid, entertaining and convincing of the period.

> How, then, can the truth upon the various subjects interesting to human beings, be elicited? Not by letting interested men think for us, but by judging for ourselves – by collecting and examining facts and arguments, and communicating to society the impressions they respectively make on our minds. There is no effectual mode of arriving at truth but by the exercise of the right of free inquiry, and the unrestricted publication of such inquiry.[82]

Nonetheless Hetherington came perilously close to arguing that effectively he was not in control of what he was publishing, a potentially risky assertion in view of what this might provoke the authorities to do. Moreover it served to take the gloss off his arguments for free speech which he quickly moved onto. He attacked the hypocrisy that sought legal control over penny publications but left other, richer, blasphemers unmolested. In effect Hetherington was more on home ground here than he had been during most of the blasphemy case since he had already admitted publication. The jury disagreed with Hetherington's arguments, despite interventions by the judge on his behalf – Justice Denman stated that he had heard Hetherington's defence 'with feelings of great interest, aye, and with sentiments of respect too'.[83] Once proof of the material facts of the case was forthcoming then questions regarding tone, spirit and intention were resolved quickly. When Hetherington appealed against the conviction he tried to claim – unsuccessfully – that *Haslam's*

Letters referred merely to the Old Testament and did not attack the New Testament, deemed to be the wellspring of Christianity. Justice Denman refused to accept such an artificial cleavage between the two and Hetherington was sentenced to a comparatively lenient four months imprisonment.

Hetherington's vendetta against the culturally privileged position of the respectable publishing world took a slightly bizarre turn when he filed a blasphemy suit against Edward Moxon for publishing Shelley's *Queen Mab*. Editions of this work were circulating widely in London since its blasphemous character nullified the law of copyright, making it both economically attractive and easy to produce. Ironically this denial of protection served to ensure that many cheap (and expensive) editions regularly entered the public domain. Moxon was the most respectable publisher in London so the element of revenge and the desire to expose hypocrisy in publishing regulation were clearly uppermost in Hetherington's mind. For once Hetherington thought the boot was on the other foot and undoubtedly would have used an acquittal for widely political purposes since the choice of 'Queen Mab' was also intended to show that all areas of culture, both past and present, were not safe under the blasphemy laws. The eventual conviction of Moxon at least consoled Hetherington in this way although the real effect was to confirm the operation of the laws and to reiterate that yet one more work of anti-religious sentiment was denied access to the wider literary canon. Nonetheless the very fact that a choice of work had been made by Hetherington opened the door for some conceptions that have sustained the law in its current form into the twentieth century – namely that silence around any potentially blasphemous work can be seen as consent. Thus Hetherington did at least reinforce that the public must decide what must be done about publishers, the works they publish and the way that they publish them.

The 1840s saw a string of blasphemy prosecutions in which a number of important infidel radicals connected through both business and ideological ties were indicted for blasphemy. Although this connection was to all intents and purposes a movement related to Owenite infidelity its attacks upon religion were not initially part of a concerted campaign. Three of these individuals – Charles Southwell, George Jacob Holyoake and Thomas Paterson – coalesced around the newspaper the *Oracle of Reason* whose initial editor Southwell was the first of this group to face a charge of blasphemy.

Southwell is almost universally described as impetuous and curiously unaware of the consequences of his own actions. In the fourth issue of the paper he penned an article entitled 'The Jew Book' which dwelt upon the now-established theme of biblical immorality but finished with a suggestion that the Bible was not the product of God but 'the outpourings of some devil'. This resulted in a charge of blasphemy levelled by the Bristol authorities. Levy suggests that Southwell was quite manifestly beyond anything that had been seen previously suggesting that he, most of all, deserved conviction for blasphemy.[84] Certainly central to Southwell's attacks on the Bible was a profound disgust at the doctrines contained within it and Edward Royle correctly reiterates the point that his apostasy on moral grounds could be considered by some not to be a species of atheism at all.[85] By now the impact of lengthy defences was starting to wane and Southwell was not particularly adept at forwarding his case. His attempts to question the definition and indeed existence of the law were ineffective and the judge's summing up closed the door to any potential acquittal with a reiteration of the Hale judgment. Southwell was promptly convicted and sentenced to £100 fine and a year's gaol sentence.

The publication of the *Oracle of Reason* was noteworthy particularly since it drew others into the world of blasphemous discourse, especially those from the rationalist wing of the Owenite movement. Southwell's successor as editor of the *Oracle* was George Jacob Holyoake – at this stage making his first forays into a world that was to prove his life's work. Holyoake had been enraged by the treatment of Southwell despite the monumental and unequivocal nature of his blasphemy in the *Oracle*. In this respect the desire by Holyoake and other Owenite infidels to press forward such an impetuous case suggests the millenarian appeal of Owen's attacks upon Christianity for some who had drawn their own conclusions about its place or otherwise within the universe.

During the course of espousing another facet of the Owenite cause, namely home colonisation, Holyoake travelled to Cheltenham in May 1842 to address a meeting on the subject. After the lecture a local preacher named Maitland asked Holyoake about the role the socialists had assigned to God in the new order. Holyoake's reply was to reiterate his own disbelief and add a piece of almost paineite regency invective by suggesting that the almighty should be placed on half-pay. Whilst Holyoake was later to admit that this remark was inadvisable it crystallised into a moment just how combative and antagonistic some branches of infidel culture actually were. Whilst the question itself may have been prepared with the use of legal restraint in view it is a mistake to see Holyoake as an even partial innocent being led into making a chance remark. Even Holyoake himself could subsequently be equivocal on the subject, sometimes within the same pamphlet. He built his reputation on the martyrdom for the cause which surrounded the Cheltenham episode claiming he had given 'a courageous answer to a cowardly question'; yet he could also suggest that he was 'trepanned' into answering.[86]

His defence, like others before him, ranged around the reiteration of established infidel texts and the usual expression of the class bias of the offence was particularly effective here. Holyoake had spoken at a mechanics institute and had thus addressed an avowedly working class audience. His subsequent detention for this thus seemed even more like the quasi-suppression of free speech which his supporters argued it was. Moreover some of Holyoake's suggestions in his defence could well have provoked doubt in the minds of the public encountering the facts of the case. Holyoake had not actively published his opinions – or at least the precise ones at issue in the case – in a printed and readily available form, the consumption of which could occur beyond moral supervision. This was an important fact, bearing in mind that many previous cases and indeed defences turned around the proven fact of publication. It could thus prove difficult for an outside observer to construe that Holyoake intended a wider attack upon the whole moral underpinning of society. He clearly had a point at his trial when he stated that he had not sought to advance his opinion but merely that his opinion had been actively solicited by others present. He had replied honestly and from this point onwards he considered that his rights of free speech and those of others had been actively infringed. He went further to demonstrate that this was, in his eyes, a legitimate clash of opinions in his assertion that a God could not be insulted in an objective sense and that merely the feelings of some Christians present were offended. The ambivalence of the case led Levy to conclude that the case against Holyoake was against objectionable theological views and that 'mere disbelief constituted blasphemy'.[87] Berman went still further than this by examining Holyoake's own account of a dialogue he had in prison with the chaplain. This contained Holyoake's view that his opinions had been the crime substantially in question allied to a vigorous disbelief and confirmed by the fear of atheism exhibited by the prison chaplain.[88] However this seems to rely on Holyoake's own opinion a little too readily. Of more interest in Berman's analysis was the suggestion that Erskine's summing up, anxious as it was about the effect of Holyoake's words on others, introduced a tentative 'manner'/'matter' dichotomy. This could, at the time, easily be mistaken for an attack upon Holyoake's theological views themselves.

Over 20 years later when Holyoake reflected upon the events at Cheltenham (and a more recent move against him when he visited the town) this aspect was still uppermost in his mind when he formulated a series of important principles at the end of the tract entitled 'The Suppressed Lecture'. His secular principles forged from experience contained the following:

> The free publication of opinion considerately expressed, and the free action of conviction within the limits of respecting the equality of others ... . Criticism conducted in a fair spirit, and in the hope of

reducing differences which divide, and discovering truths which
unite ... . Inculcating the sinlessness of intelligent sincerity as the
incentive of thought and action, and the source of that clear
conscience which replaces apathy, doubt and fear by earnestness,
service, and trust.[89]

The line of thinking which Holyoake alludes to here 20 or so years later
was instrumental in his desire to establish an unshakeable ethic of free
speech and free discusion which, though echoing Mill, contains elements
of the Coleridge dictum in embryo. The belief that these rights should be
protected eventually led to his formulation of the doctrine of Secularism
which effectively provided institutionalised protection for divergent, if
increasingly private opinions.[90]

An earlier manifestation of this belief was Holyoake's Anti-
Persecution Union which was intended to provide protection for infidels
but the organisation nonetheless eagerly took the opportunity of
displaying its even-handedness. A Calvinist, Dr Robert Kalley, had been
imprisoned by the authorities in Madeira for over-zealous attacks upon
elements of the Catholic religion, specifically against the Virgin Mary.[91]
Eventually a subscription was sent and Holyoake himself took great
pride in the fact that the '... Union anxious to prove that they did not
merely talk of equal liberality to Christian and atheist, embraced the first
opportunity of proving it'.[92]

However, the activities of the Union began to centre upon a Scotland still
reeling from the disruption where it was deeply involved in providing
assistance for Holyoake's successors. In June 1843 the authorities moved
against two Edinburgh radical booksellers, Thomas Finlay and Henry
Robinson. Once more the connection between infidel opinions and obscene
immorality was noted in the works confiscated. Whilst it was possible to
buy *The Bible An Improper Book for Youth* from Robinson's Greenside
Street premises the authorities were also more than interested to discover
copies of a Malthusian work, *Man and Woman,* and copies of Cleland's
Fanny Hill. Initially Robinson tried to get around this by suggesting that
some of the material had arrived unsolicited from London whilst other
items were his personal property.[93] The cases against these two men were
postponed on the grounds of Robinson's ill health and this allowed the
authorities to concentrate upon bringing to book a far more dangerous and
resourceful adversary in the shape of Thomas Paterson.

Paterson's shop in West Register Street Edinburgh had begun to offer
a range of works which attracted the interest of the authorities – a
situation aggravated by his use of placards and hired bill posters to
publicise his shop around the city. Amongst the items used in the case
against him was the already familiar work *The Bible An Improper Book
for Youth and Dangerous to the Excited Brain* alongside *Saul a Drama*

in Five Acts translated from Voltaire, The Protestant's Progress from Church of Englandism to Infidelity, A Home Thrust at the Atrocious Trinity as well as copies of the *Oracle*, works by Diderot and Shelley's *Queen Mab*. Paterson never denied selling these but astounded the authorities by his blunt assertion that he did not consider any of the material he offered for sale to be blasphemous.[94]

Paterson's trial retrod the precedents set in the conduct of previous defences. Paterson spent four hours in his defence, citing once again the standard infidel works of criticism and comparative religion. This time, though, the jury were slightly more impressed and he was convicted only on a majority verdict. Despite this equivocal conclusion Paterson received the comparatively draconian sentence of 15 months incarceration under felon status at Perth penitentiary. The nature of this punishment was enough to incense the APU. One correspondent to the *Movement* attacked the Judge's comment that Paterson would have received worse treatment in an English Court and prison system seeing a peculiarly local definition of justice at work. 'I suppose he was dreaming of a new invasion of England, by the covenanters, in the time of Charles.'[95]

By now the actions of the Edinburgh courts were taking their toll and the incarceration of Paterson, Finlay and Robinson left the representation of militant infidelity in the hands of Matilda Roalfe. An ex-Sunday School teacher, Roalfe was driven to take action by the harsh treatment of the others and, after moving from London, continued the sale of the controversial material from premises in Nicolson Street.[96] Almost immediately the ire of local clergymen was aroused and when she returned from her initial arrest her premises were besieged by a local mob which was only dispersed by the intervention of the police. Roalfe had been selling a number of works from these premises including *The Bible an Improper Book, Trinity of Trinities, God Versus Paterson* and a number of editions of the *Oracle of Reason*.[97]

At her trial the purchase of the articles in question was quickly proved but Matilda Roalfe concentrated her defence upon trying to ascertain their effect upon the officers sent by the Procurator Fiscal. In court she managed to expose the fact that only one of them had read the item he had purchased and confessed that its effects upon his moral behaviour and welfare were non-existent. From this point Roalfe argued that she should be exonerated from any malicious motives in publishing the material and tried to demonstrate that from an atheist point of view she was serving her fellow man. The allusion to the right to disseminate infidel opinions appeared to take the case into the realm of civil liberties matters – as she put it: 'Her object was to disseminate truth, and no terrors of authority should prevent her from acting in accordance with the dictates of her own conscience.'[98] Despite being sentenced to 60 days imprisonment, once again as a felon, she defiantly resolved to continue the fight and proposed to recommence selling the works in question when released. However, as Levy points out, the law did not explicitly deny this right, rather it reserved power in matters where attacks upon the state religion were concerned.[99] Certainly it is clear that this rhetoric of free speech was uppermost in APU pronouncements upon the subject. In an open letter to the people of Edinburgh the Scottish Anti-Persecution Union asked:

> We ask is it fitting, is it just, that *any* individual should be denied the right to express what he thinks true; be either bribed or terrified into silence when conscience bids him speak? To freely speak what we think is the most valuable of all human privileges. It is a privilege all demand, and surely it is a privilege for which all should struggle.[100]

Although Matilda Roalfe's place was taken by William Baker the authorities failed to proceed further against the infidels in Edinburgh and the dwindling publicity, despite the strenuous efforts of the APU and the *Movement*, meant that the matter dropped out of sight. The authorities finally realised that Paterson, Roalfe and co. were attempting a deliberate and conscious 'rerun' of the 1820s which it was concluded was best killed by, if not kindness, then at least a more relaxed approach. In some respects the authorities may also have counted upon popular forms of opprobrium to accomplish the extinction of this agitation.

The 1850s saw the issue of blasphemy once more enlivened by the case of Thomas Pooley which attracted considerable radical and liberal interest particularly in London. The Pooley case, whilst not establishing any radical reinterpretation of the law, has been noteworthy for the historiographical interest and interpretations that have clustered around it – inspired largely by the interest of prominent contemporaries. T. H. Buckle alluded to the case and indeed one edition of Mill's *On Liberty* includes a citation of the case as indicative of the fact that tolerance and free speech were not as yet recognised in Britain.[101] Moreover the case was also notable for the participation of Justice Coleridge and his son John Duke Coleridge as prosecuting counsel – the latter eventually to be the Judge responsible for the ground-breaking judgment in the Foote case of 1883. Timothy Toohey suggests that the case itself has been overrated and has really attracted attention because of Buckle's review of Mill which took the opportunity to denounce the activities of the two Coleridges.[102]

Certainly the Pooley case stands as an isolated instance in what historians still see as the relaxed and prosperous 1850s. Whilst it is at least partly appropriate to visualise the Carlile agitation alongside the struggle of the Unstamped and the Edinburgh agitation with the

Owenism that was as much a part of the 1840s as economic distress and Chartism, the Pooley case is different. George Jacob Holyoake realised this when he asserted that the law, with the dormancy of 16 years behind it, looked increasingly anachronistic. Certainly what was of considerable importance in the case was the harshness of the law's operation in imprisoning a patently insane man. Holyoake took considerable interest in the case and seemed to suggest that the very inability of Pooley to compile a coherent argument (his letters to Holyoake are a sorry but occasionally interesting jumble of lucid and not so lucid anti-clericalism) further undermined the benefits to society offered by any blasphemy laws. His letters from prison to Holyoake exemplify this miscellany of belief and prejudice since they contain opinions and pronouncements on everything from the wickedness of the Bible to the moral conduct of the prison chaplain.[103] As Holyoake concluded:

> No one can have sympathy with Pooley's opinions – opinions indeed, he has none – they are delusions. His manner of acting in alluding to his notions is exactly what would bring Freethought into contempt. We will neither justify this or encourage it, but as a poor man harshly dealt with, he is an object of sympathy. He has been treated as a sceptic, and ill treated because he was thought to be a sceptic, and the judge punished him *as such*, and on this ground we protect him.[104]

The case itself was simple enough. Thomas Pooley, a labourer, (according to some a well-sinker) had spent many years in Liskeard, Cornwall, professing a range of folk beliefs that merged at some points with Christianity to produce a hybrid set of eschatalogical beliefs[105] – a situation which historians earlier noted as having been instrumental in producing the early nineteenth century charismatic Joanna Southcott.[106] Holyoake seems to have concluded as much in his assessment of Pooley's thought:

> ... here it must be said that Pooley's caricature of Pantheism, or worship of nature is self-originated. He has not a work on Freethought of any kind in his possession, nor did his wife ever see one.[107]

Pooley had punctuated these beliefs with occasional anti-clerical outbursts which often took the form of graffiti chalked in prominent places in the area – most notably the waspish attack upon his locality: 'Duloe stinks with the monster Christ's bible – blasphemy – T Pooley.'[108] Although Pooley was never caught in the act he was eventually charged with four counts of blasphemy, the first two related to the appearance of writings on various gates. His unbalanced mind was clearly implicated in the third count when he made chance remarks to the constable denouncing Christ as 'the forerunner of all theft and whoredom' which Holyoake characterised as 'the language of retaliation'.[109]

At his trial, however, Pooley complicated matters by conducting a sporadically lucid defence although his unbalanced mind, at other times, was plain to see. The verdict went against Pooley and he was sentenced to a total of one year and nine months although his state of mind deteriorated rapidly while in confinement and he was admitted to the local asylum. Holyoake's own pamphlet on the case was a clear attempt to gain clemency for Pooley and to have him discharged to better care. In one sense Pooley was obviously a danger to the Freethought movement and it was in Holyoake's interest to demonstrate the former's insanity and to maintain a clear distance from him in education, manner and intention. Despite this Timothy Toohey has argued that Holyoake drastically overcompensated for this in his attacks upon the actions of the two Coleridges involved in the case. Toohey suggests that the established view – initiated by Holyoake and filtered to the public through the works of Mill and Buckle – wrongly sees the two judges as inflexible and heartless monsters. In his focus he suggests that such a view ignores their careers as a whole, ignores the fact that Pooley still represented a threat to the public peace and the fact that the elder Coleridge chose the more liberal interpretation of the law of blasphemy as outlined by Starkie.[110]

Whilst the extent to which Pooley displayed obvious symptoms of insanity is clearly a matter for speculation the judgement that he represented a threat to the public peace seems fanciful. Whilst Coleridge may have used an apparently more liberal definition of the law which required an investigation of intent the effect of the sentence, whatever its origins, had demonstrably the same effect on the law's reputation. The law thus seemed ridiculous, unnecessarily draconian and impractical. The isolation of the Pooley case itself further tended to emphasise this and in some respects from the perspective of 1860 suggested that the repeal and end of such a law was just around the corner.[111]

This is an appropriate place to end our preliminary survey of the blasphemy law. From this point on the case studies contained in this book belong to the age of burgeoning mass media and the late Victorian concerns about the reaction of potential audiences to all forms of cultural production. A mass age made blasphemers at once more powerful, more dangerous and more odd. No longer were they denizens of radical mass movements but they were individuals who posed more questions to society than each generation discovered and rediscovered it was prepared for. Just as the question of blasphemy never went away, secular culture and the blasphemers it made continually fought to be recognised as members of a society to which they wished to contribute. The refusal of society to allow this pluralism to flourish in exactly the way they expected is perhaps the coda that readers of this work will most readily take away with them.

Notes

1.   Roberts, M. J. D. (1984), 'Making Victorian Morals? The Society for the Suppression of Vice and its Critics 1802–1886', *Historical Studies*, xxi: 157–73, pp. 159–60.
2.   Roberts, M. J. D. (1992), 'Blasphemy, obscenity and the courts: contours of tolerance in nineteenth-century England', in Paul Hyland and Neil Sammells (eds), *Writing and Censorship in Britain*, London: Routledge, pp. 141–53, esp. p. 145.
3.   Prochaska, Franklyn K. (1972), 'Thomas Paine's "The Age of Reason" Revisited', *Journal of the History of Ideas*, (33): pp. 561–76.
4.   Thompson, E. P. (1963), *The Making of the English Working Class*, London: Penguin. Thompson, E.P. (1993), *Witness Against the Beast: William Blake and the Moral Law*, Cambridge: Cambridge University Press.
5.   Thompson, *Witness*, pp. 61–2.
6.   McCalman, 'Unrespectable Radicalism: Infidels and Pornography in Early Nineteenth-Century London Movement', *Past and Present* (104): 74–110; McCalman, *Radical Underworld: Prophets, Revolutionaries and Pornographers in London, 1795–1840*, Oxford, Clarendon Press.
7.   Keane, John (1995), *Tom Paine: A Political Life*, London: Bloomsbury, p. 395.
8.   Kirk, Linda (1987), 'Thomas Paine: a Child of the Enlightenment?', *Bulletin of the Society for the Study of Labour History*, 52 (3): 3–8, p. 8.
9.   Ayer, A. J. (1988), *Thomas Paine*, London: Faber and Faber, pp. 142–43; Claeys, Gregory (1987), 'Paine's Agrarian Justice (1796) and the secularisation of natural jurisprudence', *Bulletin of the Society for the Study of Labour History*, 52 (3): 21–31, p. 27; Wiener, Joel H. (1988), 'Collaborators of a sort: Thomas Paine and Richard Carlile', in Ian Dyck (ed.), *Citizen of the World*, New York: St Martin's Press, pp. 104–28, esp. pp. 117–18.
10.   Keane, op. cit., p. 397.
11.   Wiener, op. cit., p. 117.
12.   Keane, op. cit., p. 396; Prochaska, op. cit., p. 576.
13.   Bradlaugh-Bonner, op. cit., p. 38.
14.   Roberts, *Blasphemy, Obscenity and the Courts*, p. 142.
15.   Booth, Alan (1983), 'Popular loyalism and public violence in the north-west of England, 1790-1800', *Social History*, 8: pp. 295–314.
16.   Howell's State Trials (1797), 'Proceedings against Thomas Williams for Publishing Paine's "Age of Reason"', 653–720, 26, p. 661.
17.   Ibid., p. 664.
18.   Ibid., pp. 671–95.
19.   Ibid., p. 681.
20.   Clifford, Brendan (1993), *Blasphemous Reason: The 1797 Trial of Tom Paine's Age of Reason*, Hampton, Middx.: Bevin Books, p. 29.
21.   Bradlaugh-Bonner, op. cit., pp. 40–41.
22.   Ibid., p. 41.
23.   Clifford, op. cit., p. 43.
24.   Bradlaugh-Bonner, pp. 42–3.
25.   Ibid., p. 44.
26.   Levy, Leonard W. (1993), *Blasphemy: Verbal Offense Against the Sacred from Moses to Salman Rushdie*, New York: Knopf, p. 341.

27. Ibid., p. 344.
28. Hole, Robert (1989), *Pulpits, Politics and Public Order in England 1760–1832*, Cambridge: CUP, pp. 200–201.
29. Epstein, James (1994), *Radical Expression: Political Language, Ritual and Symbol in England, 1790–1850*, Oxford: Oxford University Press.
30. Wood, Marcus (1994), *Radical Satire and Print Culture, 1790–1822*, Oxford: Clarendon, p. 98.
31. Hole, op. cit.
32. Ibid., pp. 215–16, 218.
33. Wood, op. cit., p. 100–101.
34. Donnelly, F. K. (1988), 'Levellerism in eighteenth and early nineteenth century Britain', *Albion*, 20: 261–69, pp. 262–3; Hackwood, F. M. (1912), *William Hone: His Life and Times*, London, pp. 13–17, 24–31, 34–7 and 50–60; Smith, Olivia (1984), *The Politics of Language 1791–1819*, Oxford: OUP, pp. 171 and 190.
35. Smith, *Politics of Language*, pp. 195–6.
36. Ibid., Epstein op. cit.; Wood, op. cit.
37. Wood, op. cit., p. 125.
38. Hackwood, op. cit., p. 170.
39. Epstein, op. cit., p. 34.
40. Smith, op. cit., p. 176.
41. Hone, William (1876), *The Three Trials of William Hone, for publishing three parodies, with intr. and notes by W. Tegg. [Followed by] Trial by jury and liberty of the press*, London.
42. Colley, op. cit., Wood, op. cit., p. 107; Newman, Gerald (1975), 'Anti-French propaganda and British liberal nationalism in the early nineteenth century: suggestions toward a general interpretation', *Victorian Studies*, 18: 385–418.
43. Wood, op. cit., p. 113.
44. Hole, op. cit., p. 205.
45. Wardroper, John (1973), *Kings, Lords and Wicked Libellers: Satire and Protest, 1760–1837*, p. 200.
46. Hole, op. cit., p. 206; Berman, David (1988), *A History of Atheism in Britain: From Hobbes to Russell*, New York: Croom Helm, p. 202–3.
47. Aldred, G. A. (1941), *Richard Carlile, agitator: his life and times*, Glasgow: Strickland Press; Royle, E. (1974), *Victorian Infidels*, Manchester; Wiener, Joel H. (1983), *Radicalism and Freethought in Nineteenth-Century Britain: The Life of Richard Carlile*; Wiener, Joel H. (1988), 'Collaborators of a sort: Thomas Paine and Richard Carlile', in Ian Dyck (ed.), *Citizen of the World*, New York: St Martin's Press, pp. 104–28.
48. Aldred, op. cit., p. 54; Wiener (1983), op. cit., p. 22.
49. Wiener (1983), op. cit., p. 35.
50. Ibid., pp. 42–3.
51. Aldred, op. cit., p. 64.
52. Ibid., p. 65.
53. Bradlaugh-Bonner, p. 48.
54. Hole, op. cit., p. 105; Newman, op. cit.
55. Berman, op. cit., pp. 205–6.
56. Hole, op. cit., p. 210.
57. Wiener, op. cit., p. 49–50.
58. Aldred, op. cit., p. 85.

59. Ibid., Wiener, op. cit.; Aldred, Guy (1942) (ed.), *Jail Journal and Other Writings by Richard Carlile*, The Word Library, Glasgow: Strickland Press.

60. Royle, E. (1974), *Victorian Infidels*, Manchester: Manchester University Press, p. 34.

61. There is clearly not space to consider this agitation in detail and the reader anxious to explore this is best advised to consult the following: Aldred, G. A. (1941), *Richard Carlile, Agitator: His Life and Times*, Glasgow: Strickland Press; Hollis, P. (1970), *The Pauper Press. A Study of Working-Class Radicalism of the 1830s*, Oxford; Royle, E. (1974), *Victorian Infidels*, Manchester; Wickwar, W. H. (1928), *The Struggle for the Freedom of the Press, 1819–32*, London: George Allen & Unwin; Wiener, Joel (1969), *The War of the Unstamped*, Ithaca: Cornell University Press; Wiener, Joel H. (1983), *Radicalism and Freethought in Nineteenth-Century Britain: The Life of Richard Carlile*.

62. Carlile, R. (1825), *The Trials with the Defences at Large of Mrs. Jane Carlile, Mary Ann Carlile, William Holmes (etc.)*, London – Tunbridge Report, pp. 17–19.

63. Ibid., Campion Report, p. 20.

64. Ibid., Watson Report, p. 27–8.

65. Ibid., Wright Report, pp. 15, 17 and 56.

66. Royle, *Victorian Infidels*, pp. 36–7.

67. Levy, op. cit., p. 396; Cutner, H. (n.d.), *Robert Taylor (1784–1844). The Devils Chaplain*, London: G. W. Foote & Co.

68. McCalman, *Unrespectable Radicalism*, McCalman, *Radical Underworld*.

69. Worrall, David (1992), *Radical Culture: Discourse, Resistance and Surveillance, 1790–1820*, London: Harvester Wheatsheaf.

70. Ibid., pp. 134–146.

71. Ibid., pp. 179–180.

72. Thompson, *Witness Against the Beast*.

73. McCalman, I. (1988), *Radical Underworld: Prophets, Revolutioneries and Pornographers in London, 1795–1840*, Cambridge: Cambridge University Press, p. 203.

74. Cutner, op. cit., p. 20.

75. Levy, op. cit., p. 397.

76. Cutner, op. cit., p. 23.

77. Ibid., p. 27.

78. Hollis, P. (1970), *The Pauper Press. A study of Working Class Radicalism of the 1830s*, Oxford: Clarendon; Linton, W. J. (1880), *James Watson. A Memoir of the Days of the Fight for a Free Press in England and of the Agitation for the People's Charter*, Manchester; Thomas, Donald (1969), *A Long Time Burning; The History of Literary Censorship in England*, London: Routledge and Kegan Paul; Wickwar, W. H. (1928), *The Struggle for the Freedom of the Press, 1819–32*, London: George Allen & Unwin; Wiener, Joel (1969), *The War of the Unstamped*, Ithaca: Cornell University Press.

79. Bradlaugh-Bonner, op. cit., p. 64.

80. Barker, A. G. (1938), *Henry Hetherington, 1792–1849*, London: G. W. Foote & Co., p. 31.

81. Reports of State Trials New Series, 1839–1843 (1892), 'Reg v. Hetherington', 653–720. 26. London: Eyre and Spottiswoode, pp. 574–5.

82. Ibid., p. 572.

83. Barker, op. cit., p. 35.
84. Levy, op. cit., p. 449.
85. Royle, *Victorian Infidels*, op. cit., p. 452.
86. Holyoake, George Jacob (1864), *The Suppressed Lecture, at Cheltenham*, London, pp. 2 and 5.
87. Levy, op. cit., p. 457.
88. Berman, op. cit., p. 209–10.
89. Holyoake, *Suppressed Lecture*, p. 8.
90. Budd, Susan (1971), *Varieties of Unbelief*, London: Heinemann; Nash, David S. (1992), *Secularism, Art and Freedom*, London: Leicester University Press; Nash, David S. (1995), '"Unfettered investigation" – the Secularist Press and the creation of audience in Victorian England', *Victorian Periodicals Review*, Summer; Royle, E. (1980), *Radicals, Secularists and Republicans: Popular Freethought in Britain, 1866–1915*, Manchester: MUP; Tribe, David (1967), *One Hundred Years of Freethought*, London: Elek.
91. *Movement and Anti Persecution Gazette* No. 1, 16 December 1843, p. 5.
92. *Movement and Anti Persecution Gazette* No. 2, 23 December 1843, p. 14.
93. West Register House Edinburgh, Precognition against Henry Robinson AD 43/350.
94. West Register House Edinburgh, High Court Precognition against Thomas Paterson AD14 43/345.
95. *Movement and Anti Persecution Gazette* No. 4, 7 January 1844, p. 27.
96. Levy, op. cit., p. 460; Royle, *Victorian Infidels*, p. 85.
97. *Movement and Anti Persecution Gazette* No. 2, 23 December 1843, p. 15.
98. *Movement and Anti Persecution Gazette* No. 8, 4 February 1844, p. 61.
99. Levy, op. cit., p. 461.
100. *Movement and Anti Persecution Gazette* No. 27, 17 June 1844, p. 211.
101. Toohey, T. J. (1987), *Piety and the Professions: Sir John Taylor Coleridge and His Sons*, New York: Garland Press.
102. Ibid., Toohey, Timothy J. (1987), 'Blasphemy in Nineteenth-Century England: The Pooley Case and its Background', *Victorian Studies*, XXX (3): 315–33.
103. Holyoake Papers, Co-Operative Union Library Manchester, Pooley to Holyoake, letters 987, 1055, 1115, 1136 and others.
104. Holyoake, George Jacob (1857), *The Case of Thomas Pooley, the Cornish Well Sinker*, London: Holyoake and Company, p. 10.
105. Holyoake noted that Pooley exhibited five leading delusions, namely that the earth was a living organism, that the world was 'going wrong' and he alone could save it, Bibles should be burned to stave off potato rot, that a dead child reappears at the next birth in the family and lastly that he alone was to set the world aright. All of these, like Ginzburg's *Miller in the Cheese and the Worms*, are clearly a composite of theological musings, contemporary folk beliefs, and Pooley's own bitter experience in losing his eldest child. Holyoake, George Jacob (1857), *The Case of Thomas Pooley, the Cornish Well Sinker*, London: Holyoake and Company. It may also be noted here that whilst the Friulian Miller was accused of heresy Pooley's deviant opinions were never connected with anything other than delusion and insanity.

106. Balleine, G. R. (1956), *Past Finding Out: The Tragic Story of Joanna Southcott and her Successors*, London: SPCK; Hopkins, James K. (1982), *A Woman to Deliver her People: Joanna Southcott and Millenarianism in an era of Revolution*, Austin: University of Texas Press.
107. Holyoake, *Case of Thomas Pooley*, p. 8.
108. Toohey, *Blasphemy*, p. 280.
109. Holyoake, *Case of Thomas Pooley*, p. 14.
110. Toohey, *Piety and the Professions*.
111. Levy, op. cit., pp. 475–8.

PART TWO

CHAPTER FOUR

G. W. Foote and the *Freethinker* Prosecution: Blasphemy as Cultural Terrorism

Perhaps more than any other blasphemer in modern Britain the course which led to George William Foote's imprisonment seems to have been the most calculated action of all. Throughout Foote, and to a lesser extent his compatriots, maintained a high level of control over their own part in events as they unfolded. At first sight the motives behind Foote's actions appear to be unequivocal. He produced an explicitly atheist paper – the *Freethinker* – which, through its adoption of new journalistic styles and motifs, cultivated new audiences and spoke to these in a forthright and uncompromising manner. Foote further increased his profile with the publication of a series of illustrations which collided noisily with prevailing public tastes and moral outlooks. The use of cartoons, a medium that was new to the context of blasphemy and hence potentially powerful, can easily suggest the mistaken impression that Foote merely intended to test the contemporary scope and application of the blasphemy laws.

Many sympathetic historians have been in no doubt that Foote had simply earned his place in the roll call of the movement's heroes. Hypatia Bradlaugh-Bonner, despite quarrels between Foote and her father, portrayed his course of action and that of his fellow defendants as heroic. Moreover she took the standard secularist line of examining the case in the context of the whole history of the blasphemy laws.[1] Nicolas Walter's work and that of Jim Herrick, though echoing the same concerns as Bradlaugh-Bonner, did rather more to place the case within its cultural as much as its legal and civil liberties contexts.[2] Arthur Calder-Marshall was less convinced of Foote's libertarian *bona fides* and saw his actions as motivated by undirected malice which eventually crystallised into a quest for a decisive say in the secular movement's leadership succession.[3] The trend within the historiography which portrays Foote as the infidel crusader has, disappointingly, left the *Freethinker* case as a piece of freethought case law – more clearly part of the civil rights campaign than it obviously was but also less the clash of two conflicting cultural projects than it should be.

More subtle analyses of Foote and his motivations have tended to emphasise the part played by his literary talents and aspirations. Differences of interpretation have tended to revolve around how far his campaigns against the blasphemy laws can be distanced from his cultivation of literary society and of a literary persona. Edward Royle suggests a clear chronology from his early forays into literary criticism to a later period which followed his decision 'to sacrifice all that was dear to him' which brought him into the freethought movement and left him little or no time for his former pursuits and contacts, to his considerable regret.[4]

However, in an important article Joss Marsh argues that the links between Foote's two major preoccupations were perhaps closer than has hitherto been accepted and that such a linkage was sustained beyond the *Freethinker* case. Marsh ostensibly argues that Foote sought to 'desacrilise' the Bible through the use of the literary weapons of sarcasm, satire and profane image. This is painted as a project – part libertarian, part literary – to reduce the Bible merely to the status of a text.[5] Marsh illustrates Foote's deep distrust of the mystical and 'alluring beauty' of the King James Bible and his desire to bring to bear the new techniques of criticism alongside Paineite vocabulary upon 'the literary decomposition of the Bible'. The rewriting of biblical stories as literary conceits destabilised them and this, it was hoped, would remove their power.[6] Foote, unable to suppress the literary critic in himself, suggested that the power of the King James version came from the skill of translators lucky enough to be working in the gifted age of his idol Shakespeare and that as such the supposedly sacred book itself did not possess divine essence. Foote could therefore hardly contain his pleasure when a new translation was mooted since this would quickly desacrilise the work and the text.[7]

Marsh's work is in many senses persuasive and she argues that it is possible to identify Foote's work in the *Freethinker* with a parallel mission to desacrilise the Bible on the part of the author George Meredith. Marsh's evidence is gleaned from a number of novels but notably *Rhoda Fleming*, *Diana of the Crossways* and *The Egoist*, and presents a case for the use of coded tropes designed to satirise sentimental attachment to the Bible and to ridicule those characters that might be construed to be bibliophiles. Marsh goes as far as to suggest that:

> To look at the work of both men side by side is to witness how powerful class distinctions that informed literary stance, method, taste, and language could be overridden by the demands of the struggle against Bibliolatry and its object of worship, the Book.[8]

The parallels are undoubtedly suggestive of a wider cultural campaign against forms of Christianity.[9] The collected letters of Meredith suggest that he clearly took an interest in Foote's views and crusades. A brief flurry of letters in late 1870s suggested that Foote admired Meredith's works (one declaring him, in a *Freethinker* article, to be his favourite author) wishing them to go into cheap editions. Meredith in turn offered to promote Foote's newspaper, the *Liberal*.[10] However, Marsh suggests that the *Freethinker* was Foote's answer to the quest for the right form for a popular freethought magazine, which perhaps underestimates his previous and subsequent efforts. In some respects this conflicts with the clear intent that Foote displayed in his publication of a number of freethought newspapers and periodicals. His publication of the *Liberal* and the *Secularist* were important attempts to woo serious audiences whilst the *Freethinker* was a blasphemous artifact as much as a paper containing a regular message fortified with occasional scurrilities. All of Foote's journalistic efforts thus had a part to play in the different aspects of the lives of his secularist and Christian audiences. A new dimension to this publicly hostile reaction of some in the secular movement was almost certainly the gleeful consumption of the *Freethinker* in private. Barbed, side-splitting invective was given a legitimate place in the secularist psyche alongside sober, considered and philosophical respectability. Foote's journalism was intended to cater for both.

Foote had reverence for the world of letters but was also interested in harnessing its power for organisational objectives. Thus he entertained his own definitions of the role of literature which fit more closely with Marsh's later pronouncements on the use of satire and lampoon to at least destabilise beliefs. Meredith's literature emerges rather as a mirror for atheist or at least agnostic opinion. In the public sphere such literature was most useful as evidence for Foote's oft-touted defence that the spirit of the age was running not just against blasphemy prosecutions but that society, by neglecting to prosecute those whose opinions were as errant as Foote's own, had forfeited the right to defend Christianity. Foote clearly considered literature and journalism to have value as opinion formers in a changing age, so that the search for an heroic counterpart to Foote may equally be said to embrace pioneers of the New Journalism as much as men of letters such as Meredith. That Foote also existed in a wider spirit of criticism was also noted by Cutner who asked: 'If one was permitted to caricature a "bloated capitalist", or a "long haired envious socialist", why was it forbidden to poke fun at Jesus and his "devils" or his "cures"?'[11]

Like many of his contemporaries in the secular movement Foote's atheism had been confirmed as a result of mixing in London circles imbibing opinions which spelt the end of his nonconformist upbringing.

His entrance into the world of Victorian freethought was in many senses a typical one. Some lectures here, a pamphlet or two there and involvement in one of the bitter and protracted interpersonal arguments that so often seemed to hamstring the secular movement in its many guises. In this case Foote's particular quarrel was with Charles Bradlaugh and Annie Besant who, he argued, were using the famous Knowlton pamphlet case to enrich and inflate their own importance in the movement and for rekindling the 'old fighting days' of Richard Carlile that Foote felt should be given a decent burial. Although carping about Bradlaugh and Besant raising public subscriptions for their defence and expenses Foote was particularly critical of the concept of leadership and of the style adopted by Bradlaugh and Besant, arguing:

> It is high time that the Freethought party submitted less to its 'leading' men. Let it take its destiny into its own hands, and compel would-be 'leaders' either to work for generally recognised ends or to stand aside. Their ability and energy should not be accepted as a justification of their wrong doing: nay, the more ability and energy they possess, the farther do they lead their followers astray.[12]

Evidently at some point Foote's response to the characteristics of leadership and to Bradlaugh personally underwent a considerable seachange. His attitude to Bradlaugh's crusading instinct was dramatically altered by the visible presence of malice in those who opposed Bradlaugh's protracted attempt to gain entry to parliament. Before this occurred Foote noted that he had felt that the 'modern spirit' prevailed and also that the destruction of theology was the central achievement of the age.[13]

The progress of the Bradlaugh case was an important catalyst for the growth and development of many aspects of the Victorian secular movement and was also responsible for heightened public awareness of a series of important constitutional and moral issues.[14] The Bradlaugh case, whilst obviously providing an at least plausible motivation for Foote's activity, also represented an ingredient in the atmosphere of seige which hung over governmental activity during these years. Indeed the criminal law itself had recently failed to put its own house in order as a crucial chance to codify the criminal law and remove some of its patent problems foundered.[15] These would have simplified the law's operation and arguably have made it more coherent and accountable – aspects that were to have enduring importance in Victorian Britain. As we shall see some of these elements which appear to be external to the Foote case partially explain some of the actions of government protagonists during the affair.

To those who supported Bradlaugh's quest to enter Parliament the affair was a test of how far public opinion wished to maintain a

"COMIC BIBLE" SKETCHES.—XXXV.

A DEVIL DOCTOR.

*And Jesus rebuked him, saying, Hold thy peace and come out of him
And when the devil had thrown him in the midst, he came out of
him and hurt him not.*—LUKE IV., 35.

4.1 'A Devil Doctor', from the *Freethinker*, 13 August 1882

conservative constitutional outlook. Whilst the evolution of parliamentary procedure and tolerance during the course of the nineteenth century was an admission that Britain was to some extent becoming a pluralist culture through its acceptance of Quakers, Moravians, Catholics and Jews, there was an understanding that such evolution had its limits. Each time parliament had comforted itself that the admission of these groups was a recognition that they had earned their credentials as moral citizens and thus did not threaten the power of parliament, the sovereign or the established church. Moreover the relaxation of remaining disabilities could be seen to be examples of the enlightened benevolence of British civilisation.[16] When Bradlaugh and his compatriots extended this logic to include the rights of atheists within Victorian society they were answered by voices which steadfastly denied this.

Ostensibly this was because atheists were seen as belonging in a moral twilight. They had much of their existence confined by law to the private sphere whereby their expression of opinion was free from prosecution. Where their aspirations impinged on public perceptions of moral reality they frequently found themselves excluded from displaying and publicising their agenda or prevented from furthering their cause in ways that were tolerated when used by other minority groups. They were at this time not allowed to inherit money intended to further secularist purposes and were prevented from burying the dead with their own order of service, but only in unsatisfactory silence. Their right to affirm in court would only be granted five years after the Foote case.

Bradlaugh's campaign took the push for citizenship to the heart of political and moral power. In many respects Bradlaugh's crusade owed much to his earlier republican thinking, and arguably the strategy of Carlile and other less respectable radicals in the 1820s, which suggested that to strike at the heart of the problem – the ultimate source of the injustice – would be to bring the whole edifice crumbling down.[17] In many respects this same argument infected Foote's contribution to the cause since the *Freethinker* aimed to strike at the root and branch of Christian belief in both organised and diffusive forms and the residual moral pretensions of government through the medium of its sacred texts. In later years Foote's favourite metaphor to describe this tactic was to liken the church/state conspiracy to the boa constricter which can survive sledgehammer blows but not a needle applied to the spinal column.[18] The launch of the *Freethinker* in May 1881 was felt by Foote to provide a long-felt need both in campaigning terms but also as a journalistic antidote to the other secular papers then available. The *Secular Review*, for example, after a lively start, had fallen under the spell of William Stewart Ross (*nom de plume* 'Saladin') who distrusted any pretence at populism, preferring to keep the paper a repository of scientific and philosophically sophisticated articles intended to appeal to a middle-class and respectable working-class autodidact audience.

The *Freethinker*, on the other hand, was a mould-breaking publication in many senses of the term. It differed radically in appearance, resembling a more modern tabloid paper than more sober productions like the *Secular Review, Secular Chronicle* or the *National Reformer*. Foote was eventually to argue that his initial intention had been to include elements of scientific and literary interest but that the publication never quite attained these high ideals.[19] However the quickest of glances at the *Freethinker* indicates that Foote overstated this devotion. The first issue of the paper indicated that it would use 'any weapons of ridicule or sarcasm that may be borrowed from the armoury of Common Sense' and this proclamation was carried alongside a defence of Bradlaugh. Interestingly this defence rehearsed the secularist argument that Christianity should not be favoured within a modern political state and that anachronistic legislation to defend Christian morals had had the anomalous effect of excluding 'all the buddhist subjects of her majesty and include(ing) all the Mohammedan'.[20]

The *Freethinker* came out at 'the people's price' of one penny and was edited 'in a lively style, with a few short articles and plenty of racy paragraphs'. Moreover its popularity was extended and sustained not through advertising but through word of mouth, enabling it to out-distance every other freethought journal with its rate of progress to supply what Foote argued was a 'long-felt want' – it was selling nearly ten thousand copies a week in its early years.[21] It is here that the ambiguities in Foote's account of what happened start to emerge. It seems certain that Foote's intentions were never exact or one dimensional, indeed this lack of clarity can appear to be contrived and wilful sleight of hand. His forthright actions and the uncompromising nature of the medium through which he advocated his message demanded a response from the reader or those who construed themselves to be the victims of his blasphemies. In this respect Foote did what he could to place the responsibility for the fact he had offended upon those who were themselves offended. This had the dual purpose of making his guilt more questionable as well as adding evidence to Bradlaugh's assertion that the oppressive streak in Christianity still lay close to the central seats of parliamentary and legal power as well as other sectors which influenced public opinion. In this respect Foote's literariness and control and mastery of literary form enabled him to respond to circumstances as a reader and assimilator of literature. He emerges as being aware of the power of competing narratives which could convince a number of sides of the purity or otherwise of his intentions yet always, through the subtlety of his portrayals of himself, maintaining a control of proceedings and orchestrating a range of cultural resonances that echoed through the multifarious corridors of Victorian England.

Foote instigated a process whereby the casual encounter was a central component of the *Freethinker*'s capacity to offend since a chance and unexpected encounter with the paper was a theme which ran throughout the prosecution.[22] The importance of this element also shows that Foote clearly understood aspects of melodrama as a genre through which he could write up not only this casual encounter (as well as satirising it) but also invoke genuine public sympathy over the way that the law treated him. Melodrama itself has been described as '... the indulgence of strong emotionalism; moral polarization and schematization; extreme states of being, situations, actions; overt villainy, persecution of the good, and final reward of virtue; inflated and extravagant expression; dark plottings, suspense'.[23] Foote was to use a whole host of these elements in the *Freethinker* case. He portrayed anachronistic laws as the villain whilst extreme states of being were represented by the exhaustive writeup of his time in prison with hard labour which stretched out his martyrdom. Foote even managed to convince the *Times* and the *Daily Telegraph* that he was a simple, unlettered working man who had unfortunately fallen foul of an unjust class discriminatory law thereby portraying this as 'the persecution of the good'. Inevitably the final reward of his own virtue was his release and the apparent liberalisation of the law for which he was to claim considerable credit.

However, Foote also was able to both reverse the operation of the casual encounter and also to satirise it and both were achieved through a campaign of vilifying the Salvation Army. He argued at his trial that he and freethinkers should be protected from the vulgar street evangelism of the Salvation Army, which was, after all, a comparatively new phenomenon which, he argued, could be as frightening a casual encounter as any a Christian might have with the *Freethinker*. On this he had no better ally than Justice Stephen:

> All the more earnest and enthusiastic forms of religion are extremely offensive to those who do not believe them. Why should not people who are not Christians be protected against the rough, coarse, ignorant ferocity with which they are often told that they and theirs are on the way to hell-fire for ever and ever? Such a doctrine though necessary to be known if true, is, if false, revolting and mischievous to the last degree. If the law in no degree recognised these doctrines as true, if it were as neutral as the Indian Penal Code is between Hindoos and Mohametans, it would have to apply to the Salvation Army the same rule as it applies to the *Freethinker* and its contributors.[24]

Foote had a point which struck a chord in government circles and

AN INQUIRING BISHOP.

Scene—Shop in Manchester.

Bishop F——r: I want something suitable for a converted ballet girl, something entertaining as well as instructive.

Smart Shopwoman: Here, Sir, is just the thing—Foote's "Bible Romances;" or perhaps you would prefer Ingersoll's "Mistakes of Moses." There's a great demand for both amongst the clergy just now. The *Freethinker*, Sir, you know already.

4.2 'An Inquiring Bishop', from the *Freethinker*, 24 July 1882. A portrayal of closet clerical appreciation of Foote's work. 'An inquiring bishop' refers to the Bishop of Manchester and his criticism of the *Freethinker*.

4.3 Cover of G. W. Foote's 'Comic Bible Sketches', Part I (1885). A further depiction of clerical casual encounters with the *Freethinker* and how to satirise them.

beyond. Contemporary Home Office papers indicate just how big a public order problem the SA actually were for Sir William Harcourt. There were considerable disturbances in 1882/3 in London (January 1883), Basingstoke (June 1882) (occasioning a whole printed pamphlet on the 'Basingstoke Disturbances'), Weston Super Mare, Chatham, Bolton, Stamford, Chester and parts of Scotland.[25] Moreover 1883 was particularly noteworthy for a series of vague accusations of immorality at Salvation Army meetings which were discussed in the Canterbury Convocation by the Bishops of Oxford and Hereford.[26]

Although the full flowering of Foote's grasp of melodrama and the Socratic defence speech as useful weapons in his armoury had to wait until the courtroom the pages of the *Freethinker* provided him with considerable scope to indulge his interest in satire, lampoon and a tide of in-text biblical deliberate mis-references which Marsh describes as 'resonances of phrases which are slightly off'.[27] The *Freethinker* contained a fairly standard repertoire of gleanings from the local and national press which aimed at promoting the secular cause and undermining the religious pretensions of the established church, nonconformity and – increasingly – street-based evangelicalism. Satire and lampoon were catered for in two, sometimes waspish, sometimes simply informative, columns which carried very short, easily remembered pieces. 'Sugar Plums' was intended to be a weekly collection of stories intended to amuse and inform and might include anything from gleeful reporting of low church attendances in specific localities to epigrams from distinguished and enlightened writers on comparative religion.[28] Also on occasions it reported the continuing success and spread of Freethought.[29] 'Acid Drops' often struck a more sardonic note, containing easily retold jokes (generally at the expense of religious subjects or the clergy) and often invoking a cast of characters from generations of anti-clerical literature.[30] Occasionally the difference between the two sections of the paper could blur to the point of disappearance, or they could be supplemented or pushed aside by sections labelled 'Profane Jokes' or 'Rib Ticklers' – the latter being a title which J. W. Gott was to use to devastating effect in the years prior to the First World War.

The first issue to include an illustration was the third edition of the paper dated 3 July 1881, entitled 'Jonah on the Whale'. The succeeding editions of 1881 were similarly embellished with cartoons which re-enacted the various intellectual, linguistic and cultural attacks upon established and evangelical religions and the Bible. They mixed humour with riteous indignation to present freethinkers with representations that they could laugh at one week or be soberly moved by the next. By the end of the year the *Freethinker*'s cartoons were including representations

JONAH ON THE WHALE.

4.4 'Jonah on the Whale', from the *Freethinker*, 3 July 1881. 'Jonah on the whale' portrays Jonah playing a banjo whilst singing 'ye verie ancient song jo-nah' and uses the obvious pun with 'wail'.

of the Almighty alongside the citation of a biblical text designed to produce a discordant mock sermon. The first of these, on the cover of the 6 November 1881 edition, was comic although its portrayal of God alongside the text from Genesis ix, 13 ('I do set my bow in the cloud') was reminiscent of Blake's engraving 'The Ancient of Days'. More controversially the following week's cartoon, which took Genesis I, 16–17 as its text, depicted the supreme being using a stepladder to accomplish the fixing in the sky of the sun and moon, dressed in a conjurer's cloak-cum-smoking jacket. The following week contained the first of what became the long-running series 'Comic Bible' sketches.

It is fairly evident that the idea of cartoons as by turns instructive, offensive, comic or soberly graphic depictions of religious themes was a quick success. Their continued use in the paper confirms this as well as the decision to produce a Christmas number that would amuse freethinkers and provide a refuge from religion whilst also inflaming Christian opinion at a particularly sensitive time of year. That the cartoons were especially identified with Foote is emphasised by the fact

THE CALLING OF SAMUEL.

4.5   'The Calling of Samuel', from the *Freethinker*, 4 September 1881

THE REAL TRINITY.

4.6   '"The real trinity" of mammon, ignorance and sacred dogma', from the *Freethinker*, 11 September 1881. 'The real trinity' are opposed by an angel wielding three swords named after the progressive papers, the *Freethinker*, the *Malthusian* and the *Republican*.

"COMIC [BIBLE" SKETCH.—XLIV.

JESUS CANOEING.

" *And in the fourth watch of the night Jesus went unto them walking on the sea.*"—MATTHEW xiv., 25.

a   'Jesus Canoeing', 'Comic Bible Sketch XLIV', from the *Freethinker*, 29 October 1882

4.7   Foote's comic bible sketches traded a range of biblical images conjured from childhood, catechism and subsequent writers

"COMIC BIBLE" SKETCHES.—XXIX.

And it came to pass after these things, that God did tempt Abraham
. . . . And he said, Take now thy son, thine only son Isaac, whom
thou lovest, and get thee into the land of Moriah; and offer him
there for a burnt offering. . . . ."—Genesis xxii., 1, 2.

b   'Comic Bible Sketch XXIX', from the *Freethinker*, 4 June 1882

" COMIC BIBLE " SKETCHES.—IV.

NOAH'S ARK.

c 'Noah's Ark', 'Comic Bible Sketch IV', from the *Freethinker*, 27 November 1881

"COMIC BIBLE" SKETCHES.—XXVIII

DIVINE ILLUMINATION.

"*And God said, Let there be light; and there was light.*"—
Genesis i., 3.

d   'Divine Illumination', 'Comic Bible Sketch XXVIII', from the *Freethinker*, 28
May 1882

"I DO SET MY BOW IN THE CLOUD."—*Genesis* ix., 13.

e   'I do set my bow in the cloud', Genesis ix, 13, from the *Freethinker*, 6
November 1881

that he alone was held responsible for the *Freethinker*'s comic output by
others in the secular movement. Also when prosecution was successful he
alone prevented the publication of any further cartoons whilst he was
imprisoned, resuming them upon his release.[31] However, Foote's desire to
define his own position in relation to the other newspapers that serviced
the secularist community was also an important factor in formulating his
stance. What is clear is that both Foote's journalism and his literary
criticism were a means to an end and it is up to historians to decide the
efficacy and tactical wisdom of his attempts to achieve this end. Foote
himself did much to promote this view of his actions – in a passage

published in an early issue of the *Freethinker* and subsequently included in his own published memories of the case, Foote made plain his motives:

> ... One or two bigots, more than ordinarily foolish, have threatened to suppress us with the strong arm of the law. We defy them to do their worst, we have no wish to play the martyr, but we should not object to take a part in dragging the monster of persecution into the light of day, even at the cost of some bites and scratches. As the *Freethinker* was intended to be a fighting organ, the savage hostility of the enemy is its best praise. We mean to incur their hatred more and more. The war with superstition should be ruthless. We ask no quarter and we shall give none.
>
> Secondly we have to encounter the dislike of mealy-mouthed Freethinkers, who want omelettes without breaking of eggs and revolutions without shedding of blood. ... Truth, as Rénan says, can dispense with politeness; and while we shall never stoop to personal slander and innuendo, we shall assail error without tenderness or mercy ... .[32]

Whilst Arthur Calder-Marshall displayed Foote's journalism as an attempt to appeal to the scurrilous apprentice[33] it is clear that many in the secular movement, far distanced from the Calder-Marshall stereotype, were attracted to Foote's candour though not his style. Many local secular societies sold the *Freethinker* alongside the *Secular Review* and the *National Reformer* and it is tempting to conclude that Foote's new publishing venture filled an underestimated and important gap in the freethought market. The paper, armed with the cartoons which ranged from the ridiculous to the offensive, simultaneously provided its sympathetic reader with a weekly ration of humour as well as a degree of satisfaction at the promotion of one of freethought's most important crusades.

The *Freethinker*'s style obviously represented a break with the recently established traditions of the atheist press and also lampooned the seriousness that clustered around the centre of religious culture in the Britain of the early 1880s.[34] Not for the first time (nor, as we shall discover, the last time) Foote was invoking a piercing dichotomy between religious, humourless, stuffed shirt sensibilities alongside what he saw as sham hypocritical solemnness and the powerful side-splitting humour that its worst excesses could induce in the freethinking and sceptical public. Using his access to popular culture Foote portrayed the difference between frowning faces and broad smiling ones – what Cutner described as 'his habit of laughing at solemn nonsense'.[35] The fifth issue of the *Freethinker* contained an account of the first part of Leo Taxil's *La Bible Amusante* which took inspiration from Voltaire's treatment of religious questions. Taxil himself had a chequered career as an anti-clerical writer and Foote made conciliatory noises about appropriating a French work

1. The Tea-Meeting Curate.

2. The Calvinist.

3. Salvation Captain.

4. The Infallible One.

5. The Revivalist.

6. Broad Church.

7. Low church.

4.8 'Clerical Types', from the *Freethinker*, Summer number, 1884. As well as material from France, Foote could use widely understood English forms of anticlericalism when it suited him.

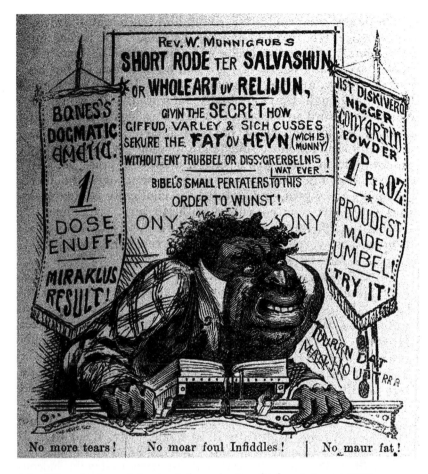

4.9 'Short Rode ter Salvashun', from the *Freethinker*, 4 August 1881

– a culture where religious archetypes portrayed as figures of fun had become a central pillar in anti-clericalism. Indeed Foote anxiously used this opportunity to lament that England itself had not developed a sufficiently virulent anti-clerical culture. This self-same culture almost made him goad the authorities and 'bigots' as well as belittle his respectable, law-abiding, secularist colleagues.

> We in England have Comic Histories, Comic Geographies, and Comic Grammars, but a Comic Bible would horrify us. At sight of such blasphemy Bumble would stand aghast, and Mrs Grundy would scream with terror. But Bumble and Mrs Grundy are less important personages in France, and so the country of Rabelais and Voltaire produces what we are unable to tolerate in thought.[36]

However the increased activity of the Salvation Army during these years raises another issue. As well as citing them in his reworking of the casual encounter Foote clearly singled them out for attack at an early stage. The cover of the edition for 4 August 1881 entitled the 'Short Rode ter Salvashun' held the movement's intentions and mode of proselitising up to ridicule.

Similarly Foote noted, in the 4 December 1881 edition of the *Freethinker*, that a sermon preached by the Bishop of Manchester against the paper displayed the two opposing tendencies of the age: 'Salvationism which turns religion into hysterics and Atheism which makes it a subject of ridicule.' However it is equally plausible to consider that Foote may have learned much from the forthright proselytising of Booth and the Salvation Army. Not only had it significantly altered the language of religious discourse but, as Judith Walkowitz points out, its female members were one of the most successful groups in the early 1880s in the hazardous task of creating new arenas of public space and colonising those previously dominated by more established and hitherto acceptable versions of religion and morality.[37] With this in mind it would not have taken Foote long to ask why God should have all the best tunes.

Despite the fact that the cartoons were instantly offensive it was rather a surprise when the *Freethinker* was eventually prosecuted for its writings. The paper had quickly attracted the attention of those seeking to use its excesses as evidence of the culture secularism sought to bring to the land. Henry Varley, the erstwhile opponent of Bradlaugh who had made several attempts to discredit his parliamentary candidature, saw in the *Freethinker* yet another avenue in his relentless fight against the President of the NSS.[38] Varley, a Notting Hill revivalist described by Foote as a 'notorious trader in scandal', produced a circular drawing the attention of members of Parliament to 'devise means to stay this hideous prostitution of the liberty of the Press, by making these shameless blasphemers amenable to the existing law'.[39]

The member for Dover, C. K. Freshfield, asked the Home Secretary Sir William Harcourt whether the government would proceed against the paper. Harcourt replied that he had seen the paper (wrongly ascribing it to being published in Northampton – this was taken as evidence by Foote that Harcourt had not seen it) but argued that more harm would come from prosecuting than by leaving it to the reprobation of all 'decent members of society'. Foote recalled in later life, with obvious pleasure, that his name had been linked in this debate to the issue of Home Rule and particularly that of moral Home Rule. The Irish Nationalist MP John Redmond, in an attempt to embarrass the Liberal government, asked Harcourt why publications which could injure public morals in England were tolerated when they would obviously be proceeded against on the Irish mainland. Harcourt retorted with the same answer he had already given. Foote's next act was to goad Harcourt into action. In an open letter he wrote:

> I tell you that you could not suppress the *Freethinker* if you tried. The martyr spirit of Freethought is not dead, and the men who suffered imprisonment for liberty of speech a generation ago have not left degenerate successors. Should the necessity arise, there are Freethinkers who will not shrink from the same sacrifice for the same cause.[40]

In response to the prosecution of Henry Seymour for blasphemous libel, which erupted early in May, Foote used it in his attempt to further provoke the authorities. Seymour had grown tired of Tunbridge Wells' NSS branch posters being defaced and had organised an evening's jocular entertainment, however the poster advertising this was prosecuted.[41] For Foote this was a further proof that the use of scurrility and cultural attack upon the rights of freethinkers seemed to be sanctioned by law or at least tacitly ignored by it and Foote openly challenged the 'bigots' to attack the leaders of the Freethought party.[42]

Though Foote was later to suffer for the outrageousness of the cartoons the initial prosecution was filed against an article by William Heaford. This article appeared over two issues of the paper (21 and 28 May 1882) and was an iconoclastic inversion of the evangelical assertion that the wavering believer must undertake a new life to be saved. Heaford suggested that 'any fool can believe' and that the heaven proposed by orthodox religionists contained an assortment of 'blood stained, crime tainted monsters' and the 'goody-goody servants of god'. Moreover the morally upright and benevolent members of mankind could skilfully spare themselves the 'affliction of salvation' by the 'trick' of sliding into sin before death. In portraying the notion of salvation as an immoral lottery and an unwished-for experience Heaford saw the atheist course of action as infinitely more noble, asking in an inversion of Bunyan 'What shall I do to be damned'. However in the midst of passages that were construed as blasphemy against the Holy Ghost the iconoclasm was tempered with declarations that the freethinker strives for a secular rather than spiritual salvation and consisted of 'the dissipation of ignorance and superstition' as well as the 'practical performance on the platform of life of principles of liberty, equality and fraternity'. In many respects this view, whilst a little distant from Foote's own political individualism, at least allowed the *Freethinker* to champion an alternative culture of morality that would later form one of the lines of defence that Foote would use at his trials.

Specifically mentioned in the indictment against Foote was a passage suggesting that the freethinker would not 'degrade himself by going through the farce of reconciling his soul to a God whom he justly regards as the embodiment of crime and ferocity'.[43] Foote had spent a pleasant day by the Thames in the company of J. M. Robertson and J. M. Wheeler and found the summons from the Lord Mayor of London to appear at the Mansion House on a charge of Blasphemy waiting for him at home.[44] Ramsey as publisher and Mr E. W. Whittle as printer were also included in the summons. Foote had been preparing himself and his readership for this for some time in melodramatic fashion. The 9 July edition quoted Dryden's Absolom and Achitaphel followed by an indulgent reference to Greek myths accusing 'priestcraft' of behaving 'like the silversmiths of Diana, they know the craft by which they have their living, although they do not affect the plain confession of worthy Demetrius'. For the man of letters devoted to literary martyrdom such language conjured up the last days of Socrates and the ministry of Jesus Christ. Indeed, these were the first names appended to Foote's evocation of those persecuted by priests which also included Hypatia, Bruno, Galileo, Voltaire and Paine – he hoped and obviously intended that his name would be added to this pantheon in the near future.

The *Freethinker* had been drawn to the attention of the Home Office as early as May 1882. Although the number for 30 April 1882, with the cover 'the first religious murder' was passed to the Home Secretary Sir William Harcourt, this was patently not the first edition that he was acquainted with. Harcourt's instinct was to seize the papers and challenge Foote to seek redress in the courts and he wrote to the Attorney General to this effect.[45] However Sir Henry James did not concur since he was concerned with the repercussions that seizure would bring, both in England but also to the delicate situation in Ireland which in mid-1882 was experiencing the worst of the land war (the *United Irishman* had already been hurriedly seized). James contended that the seizure of papers without a resultant prosecution would give the *Freethinker* credibility since the government would certainly have to pay damages into court. Importantly Sir Henry James also expressed doubts about the potential success and the character of the subsequent prosecution mounted by Sir Henry Tyler (which was aimed largely at Bradlaugh), warning Harcourt of the dangers of linking legal and governmental attitudes to 'Tyler and Co.'. For Sir Henry James the best course of action was to wait on events – an opinion which irritated Harcourt, leading him to scribble 'I do not concur in this opinion but I will wait till the pending prosecution is decided.'[46]

This case had just come to court when Foote and Ramsey did what they could to increase the stakes. The 16 July number of the *Freethinker* proudly proclaimed that the paper had been 'prosecuted for blasphemy', declaring that 'We are in for it now' with as much relief as relish. The appearance at the Mansion House was, as Calder-Marshall and Tribe suggest, probably something of an anti-climax with even Foote driven to concede that the real issue at stake was whether Charles Bradlaugh could be connected either with the publication or with the sale of the *Freethinker*.[47] The case was remanded and although subsequent counts were added it ceased to have any importance for Foote and became part of Bradlaugh's crusade.

Foote's tilt at blasphemy, however, continued and Calder-Marshall saw this as the inevitable response of a man denied his moment of glory. Once again this judgement assumes – rashly – that there was no ideology or cultural outlook lurking within the mind of G. W. Foote. Certainly his belief in access to knowledge and persuasive use of literary style, indicate an intense belief that such knowledge and skills could be used for furthering the secularist mission. Moreover he had in mind a cultural project that aimed at destabilising what he deemed to be a manifestly mistaken collectivist culture, thus liberating the individual. Although it is obviously facile to deny Foote's self-interested presentation and representation of himself, an interpretation which dwells solely on this misreads the personality of Foote and more importantly the attitudes and arguments he used in his own defence. Moreover the attitudes of those who wrote and spoke in Foote's favour, and indeed those who opposed him and saw him as something infinitely more dangerous than a mere careerist, cannot be dismissed in so cursory a fashion.

The 30 July edition of the *Freethinker* was a hurried single sheet concoction, largely because the printer, Whittle, had lost his nerve. The issue enabled Foote to acknowledge the flourishing state of his own defence fund, the imminent dissociation of Bradlaugh from the *Freethinker*'s mission and that English Law had been neglected enough to become a 'veritable Augean Stable to be cleansed'. This same article also began the process of invoking distinguished legal opinion in favour of Foote and his compatriots. In this case the recent attempted codification of the Criminal Law and its author Sir James Fitzjames Stephen's opinion that judge-made law was too capricious was increasingly cited as evidence that the law of blasphemy was neither established nor settled.[48] Stephen was a valuable source for suggesting that a whole range of statutes existed as anachronisms, lending further weight to the claim of Foote and the secularists that they were also the promoters of progress in seeking their deletion.[49] Indeed Stephen's leading biographer James Colaiaco characterised his declared mission as legal philosopher and journalist to be to 'reconcile democracy with culture' using the tolerant administration of the latter to counteract the perceived disadvantages of the former.[50]

Throughout this period Foote and Ramsey's use of cartoons continued to have the desired effect. The 13 August edition contained a cartoon depiction of Christ casting out demons entitled 'A Devil Doctor'. This and subsequent issues of the paper continued to arrive on Harcourt's desk, sent by concerned members of the public. One letter, from a Walter Grover to Harcourt, enclosing the 13 August 1882 'Devil Doctor' copy of the *Freethinker* (see Fig. 4.1) complained:

> That such an infamous periodical so calculated to bring religion into ridicule & disrepute, can be disseminated in our public thoroughfares without restraint – whilst in other respects the supervision of our national morality is ostensibly the subject of such rigorous supervision, appears somewhat strange....
>
> The retaillers of these periodicals are undoubtedly of the lowest and probably of the poorest class – but the opportunities afforded in the streets of a widespread distribution of this pernicious matter & of the inculcation of a proportionate amount are perhaps incalculable.[51]

This letter itself is revealing since it posited the unfortunate results of the casual encounter with the *Freethinker* and followed this with an established narrative concerning its pernicious influence upon public morals.[52] Moreover a number of enduring social myths – the obscenity of the publication, the 'obviously' poor and lower class origin of the paper's vendors – were paraded not for the first or last time. The importance of these two elements and Foote's desire to combat them both appears in his vehement and almost obsessive refutation of the former and his realisation of his power to use the latter.

Foote's decision to defend himself suited his own wider purposes. As such the lone voice which could, when appropriate, cry in the wilderness had an intense journalistic appeal and placed Foote squarely in the company of Socrates, Bruno, Paine and the others. However the decision also had repercussions for Foote's sense of narrative creation and his control over the progress of this martyrdom. As matters unfolded Foote could control the presentation of the case from courtroom speech to the outraged feeding of public opinion through his journalism. This was a significant aspect of the portrayal of the episode since the *Freethinker* could continue the crusade and set new boundaries of taste and distaste – whilst *Progress* kept Foote, and his readership, in touch with the more intellectual arguments espoused by his supporters. Despite this the *Freethinker* could still make strategic appeals to higher principles as well as define its readership for the eyes of officialdom and the wider public. The 20 August edition reminded its audience of the Pooley case through an appeal to the 'working men' to defend freedom of thought 'not only on the selfish ground that an attack upon one form of thought is a menace to all, but because education, being witheld by the rich and powerful from the nation as a whole, is at work'.

By September the paper had turned the whole of its front page over to

GOING TO GLORY.

4.10 'Going to Glory', from the *Freethinker*, 3 September 1882. Infinitely more impressive than some of the earlier cartoons, this tableau depicts the injustice of the Christian doctrine of forgiveness around the protagonists in a case of murder. The murderer enters heaven (diagonally upwards), encouraged by the doctrine of repentence whereby the clergyman wipes his sins from a blackboard. The victim, however, falls (diagonally downwards) to hell, mourned by a grieving widow and orphan. Note the Salvation Army caps worn by the angels.

4.11   'The Salvation Dodge', from the *Freethinker*, 1 October 1882

a cartoon representation of the theme 'Going to Glory'. This portrayed the unforeseen metaphysical consequences of the Christian doctrine of forgiveness. Altogether this cartoon is considerably more impressive in design and execution than those pirated from Taxil – displaying a rather more stern view of Christian theological shortcomings. The original must have raised eyebrows with its full page treatment and more sophisticated artwork and graphical impact. Once again the Salvation Army are lampooned in this cartoon since two of the angels welcoming the 'murderer' to heaven wear caps bearing the legend 'SA'. In October Foote followed this up with a more forthright full page cartoon entitled 'The Salvation Dodge'.[53]

Although the older, smaller format cartoons returned in November Foote and Ramsey were steeling themselves for a particularly incisive attack upon the citadel of Christian belief. For the 1882 Christmas number Foote revisited the notion of providing holiday reading for freethinkers, as he had in the 1881 number which had blended serious political expression with biblical parody in its portrayal of Bradlaugh in the Lion's den. This time the Christmas number dispensed with the newsworthy material that had previously filled the 'Acid Drops' and 'Sugar Plums' columns, substituting a number of sustained parodies and lampoons variously in prose, verse and cartoon form. Most notable was the cartoon life of Christ depicting Jesus worshipped by the animals in the stable (captioned 'The Wise Ones') as well as parodies of the Wedding at Canaan and the discussion with the elders portrayed as a disrespectful youth casting spells to bewitch 'the Jerusalem Bigwigs' and rather pertinently being 'run in for blasphemy'. Most notorious of all was the cartoon based on Exodus xxxiii, 23 depicting the deity clothed in old, worn out trousers. This image was completed by the sight of (depending upon how mischievous the reader was) either a rogue shirt tail or rank flatulence emanating from a hole in the almighty's trousers. In truth this was another subtle piece of the extension of disbelief and humourous ridicule since Foote had already printed an orthodox representation of this text culled from a Dutch Bible of 1669. The use of this cartoon was a clever piece of inversion since the use of the earlier, arguably as ridiculous, cartoon had been forced on him by the reservations his printer had entertained regarding the use of comic Bible sketches.[54] However Foote's instinct was to shun the safety of caution – a course of events in which he saw 'neither glory, honor, nor profit'.[55]

The publication of the Christmas number set matters in motion once again at the Home Office. The Under Secretary of State, Lushington, informed Harcourt that Sir Thomas Nelson acting for the City of London again intended seizure of the papers – this time enraged by the conspicuously heightened attempt at blasphemy contained within the

9. He turneth water into wine.

a   'He turneth water into wine', from the *Freethinker* 'Comic Life of Christ', Christmas 1882

10. He preacheth from the Mount.

b   'He preacheth from the Mount', from the *Freethinker* 'Comic Life of Christ', Christmas 1882

4.12   Excerpts from the Christmas number's 'Comic Life of Christ'. Note Figure 4.12f, 'He is run in for Blasphemy'.

16. He visiteth Hell and preacheth to the Devils.

c   'He visiteth Hell and preacheth to the Devils', from the *Freethinker* 'Comic Life of Christ', Christmas 1882

1. He is annunciated.

d   'He is annunciated', from the *Freethinker* 'Comic Life of Christ', Christmas 1882

2. He getteth born in a manger, and is worshipped by wise ones.

e   'He getteth born in a manger, and is worshipped by wise ones', from the *Freethinker* 'Comic Life of Christ', Christmas 1882

15. He is run in for Blasphemy.

f   'He is run in for Blasphemy', from the *Freethinker* 'Comic Life of Christ', Christmas 1882

Christmas number. Nelson argued that the earlier caution on the part of the Home Office had been shown to less outrageous editions of the *Freethinker* and believed that the Christmas number was obscene within the meaning of the letter Lord Campbell's act of 20 & 21 Vic. cap. 83. Lushington himself noted that the local imperative for action against the *Freethinker* could, if not checked, easily overtake the Home Office desire for vigilance tempered with caution. Displaying a measure of weariness Lushington argued that the edition was profane rather than obscene and noted that such distinctions were liable to get 'mixed up especially in the mind of the Lord Mayor'.[56] Harcourt's reply was more admiring of Nelson's desire for action and expressed regret at having his owns hands tied in the matter by a higher authority.

The overall attitude of Harcourt appears surprising. Finding the *Freethinker* distasteful was not a strange attitude in itself but the blatant desire to bring the full force of the law to bear against Foote and his compatriots lacked wisdom, judgement and tact. Indeed the dedication of Harcourt to securing a conviction and the full measure of punishment before the law recurs as an enduring, and perplexing, theme throughout the Foote case.

Thus a second prosecution was brought respectively against Foote as editor, Ramsey as publisher and Kemp as printer and it was this which was heard first. Once again traditional accounts of the case have focused upon the explosive effect of the cartoons but it should be remembered that this was not a unanimous impression. When Foote, Ramsey and Kemp attended committal proceedings at the Mansion House the solicitor instructed by Sir Thomas Nelson mentioned the Exodus and Life of Christ cartoons only at the end of a long list of alleged blasphemies that took in material from page 3, page 5 and the penultimate verse of the poem 'A Ballad of the Gods'. After some evidence intended to establish the responsibility for the *Freethinker* the depositions were signed the following day and committal made for trial on 26 February.[57] However, after an intervention by the Prosecuting Counsel, Sir Hardinge Gifford, the defendants first faced the case against them at the Old Bailey on 1 March before Justice Ford North where they faced an indictment for publishing 'certain blasphemous and impious libels'. In his account of the case Foote made much of the fact that the indictment also described the defendants as 'wicked and profane persons, instigated by the devil'.[58]

In his opening address to the jury Sir Hardinge Gifford drew attention to the fact that Foote, Ramsey and Kemp were accused of 'contumellous and disrespectful reproaches against the Christian religion and the Holy Scripture' and laid great emphasis upon the fact that disrespect was clearly involved in cartoons, poetry and prose throughout the Christmas

SERIOUS BIBLE SKETCHES.—I.

A BACK VIEW.

FROM A DUTCH BIBLE OF 1669.

And the Lord said, ... I will put thee in a cleft of the rock, ... and thou shalt see my back parts: but my face shall not be seen.—EXODUS xxxiii., 21—3.

a   'Serious Bible Sketch I', Exodus xxxiii, 21–3, from the *Freethinker*, 6 August 1882

4.13   Two portrayals of Exodus xxxiii, 21–3, 'And I will take away mine hand, and thou shalt see my back parts; but my face shall not be seen'. Foote's own cartoon was offensive, but his inclusion of the seventeenth-century Dutch equivalent is none the less intended to suggest that the situation is inviting both smut and ridicule.

MOSES GETTING A BACK VIEW.

b 'Exodus xxxiii, 21–3', from the *Freethinker*, Christmas number, 1882

number. The conclusion of his address effectively challenged the judge and jury to decide that the line of propriety had been crossed:

> If the publication in question did not speak for itself, and in a way that no language of his could express, of hideous and outrageous blasphemy no such offence could be known to the law.[59]

Once again evidence was considered which sought to clearly link Foote with the publication of the *Freethinker*. It was discovered that the *Freethinker* was registered at Somerset House with Ramsey entered as the proprietor of the paper, whilst Kemp signed himself as printer and publisher of the paper.[60]

All this was necessary since Foote's defence rested partly upon there being no evidence that he was responsible for the paper – a fact that was not accepted by Justice North. Although the gallery applauded Foote's efforts the plain truth was that the effect of at least some of the evidence he offered was nullified by the attitude and frequent interventions of Justice North. He was opposed to Foote quoting from works outside those mentioned in the indictment and using them to establish that 'opinions like those expressed here extensively prevail'. Justice North argued 'That is not the question at all. If they extensively prevail, so much the worse, what somebody else has said, whoever that person may be, cannot affect the question in this case.' Justice North was determined that such evidence should not be admitted that in any way constituted what Foote claimed was a 'justification' of the libel – the matter was solely a question of whether the defendants themselves were guilty of the libel.[61] This was perhaps the start of an increasingly dim view that judges were to take of the whole nature and use of expert evidence. Although Foote was still able to read extracts from the works of John Stuart Mill, Viscount Amberley, T. H. Huxley, Matthew Arnold, Shelley, Swinburne and others, Justice North prevented him from handing a copy of Fox's libel act to the jury, preferring that he should inform them as to the necessary points of law to be considered. Characteristically Foote himself took this to be an affront to his own prowess as his own makeshift defending counsel. Justice North's final intervention was to shorten Foote's exposition of the *War Cry*, obviously tested by the length of his defence, dismissing it as evidence.[62]

Justice North's summing up took place in the absence of Sir Hardinge Gifford – a circumstance which Foote was to declare indicated the partiality of the judge. The essence of this speech was to suggest that Foote's numerous citations and examples were irrelevant and observing that the law defined the meaning of blasphemy, and it was for the jury to say whether the publication was a blasphemous libel within the definition of the law:

If by writing or otherwise anyone denied the existence of the deity, throwing abuse, contumely, and outrage upon sacred subjects, scoffing at God, the Trinity, or the Holy scriptures, that by the law was blasphemy. The question, therefore, was whether the publication before them was a blasphemous libel within that definition.[63]

When the jury retired to consider their verdict Justice North took the opportunity to hear another related case against Henry Cattell, a newsagent of 84, Fleet Street, who was indicted for publishing the libels cited in the Foote, Ramsey and Kemp case by exposing them for sale in his shop. The Jury convicted Cattell, but recommended him to mercy on the ground that he might not have known the contents of the paper and Justice North postponed sentence while awaiting the outcome of the main case against Foote et al. After two hours the jury considering the Foote case returned to court, declaring that they could not return a verdict. Despite further promptings from Justice North to reach a conclusion the matter remained unresolved and he discharged the jury intending to try the case the following week.

Justice North then refused Foote and the other defendants' application for a renewal of their bail which Foote later described as 'simply vindictive' and Calder-Marshall as 'unjustifiable'.[64] In some respects these decisions only made sense if during his conduct of this and the subsequent trial Justice North genuinely considered the defendants to be a serious threat to public morals. Certainly Foote was at every stage unrepentant and had very publicly left instructions for the continuation of the *Freethinker*. Such contingencies would have been temporarily unnecessary with an extension to bail and Justice North may well have suspected that fresh assaults upon the Christian religion would be inevitable. With this began Foote's rich vein of prisoner rhetoric which was to prove essential to his creation of martrydom.

Foote had also hoped that the inability of the jury to reach a verdict would lead to the entrance of a *nolle prosequi* and rapid release but, as Calder-Marshall points out, the conviction of Cattell on a charge of selling libels meant that further proceedings against the publisher of those libels was inevitable.[65] Foote declared that he was certain his case was hopeless when he resumed his place in the dock the following Monday. The proceedings followed the course they had run the previous Thursday as the prosecution concentrated on the 'loathsomeness' of the *Freethinker*, as well as its likely effect upon those who chanced upon a shop retailing the publication or those who inadvertently read its placards in the street. The prosecution then argued that the liberty of opinion was in this case being abused and, in a departure from the line taken in the first trial, suggested that the crime of blasphemy was no more obsolete than theft or murder and its apparent decay was due to the inherent morality of the British public that had hitherto made its use unnecessary.[66] This was followed by the restatement of evidence intended to prove responsibility for the alleged libels.

When Foote spoke he drew the jury's attention to the disabilities he had laboured under in preparing his defence from a prison cell and further expressed contempt for Justice North's refusal of bail.[67] Once again Foote's protestations of being hampered in the preparation of his defence must have appeared spurious to a jury that was, like its predecessor, treated to a considerably long and pedantic performance.[68]

Again Foote's defence was followed by a statement by Ramsey and on this occasion Kemp's counsel submitted that his client did not contest that he had sold the papers. After the judge's summing up the jury deliberated for a few minutes without leaving the court and promptly returned a verdict of guilty against all three defendants. In pronouncing sentence Justice North referred to Foote as a man whose intelligence had been led astray in choosing to 'prostitute his talents to the service of the devil'. More importantly Justice North conveyed to Foote that his many quotes from what were mistakenly deemed acceptable publications were fruitless since the judge maintained that the *Freethinker* was 'totally different from any of the works you have brought before me, in every way whatever'.[69] However Justice North had been saving his bombshell until last when he sentenced Foote to twelve months imprisonment with hard labour. Ramsey received a sentence of nine months on the grounds that he had merely acted under the instruction of others whilst Kemp's sentence was three months. Cattell was ordered to enter into his own recognisances for £200 and find one surety in £100 and to come up for judgment when called upon. It was at this point that Foote faced the bench and uttered his famous words 'My lord, I thank you; it is worthy of your creed.' The court itself was in uproar upon hearing the sentence and, after attempts to restore order, the judge was obliged to have the police clear the gallery.[70]

There is absolutely no doubt that the severity of the sentence shocked many present, from Foote's supporters through to neutral observers. The *Daily Telegraph* refused to take these disturbances at face value, claiming that it was:

> easy enough to pack a gallery with sympathisers with a particular defendant; nor is it difficult to create a certain feeling of pity towards prisoners when there is seen to be an array of legal talent on the side of the prosecution, and the defendants are left to fight their own battle as best they may.[71]

William Stewart Ross, a fellow freethinker who opposed Foote's strategy, was nonetheless shocked and appalled by the proceedings and the verdict that had been given. In his editorial in the successive edition of the *Secular Review* Ross admitted openly that he had 'more or less opposed the editorial conduct of the *Freethinker*' but eulogising Foote's court appearance he spared no rhetorical flourish:

> Our Freethought martyr had stood in that dock the live-long day, facing the flashing scabbard of the sword of justice, the purple and ermine of the judge, and the heavy gold chain of the sherrif [*sic*] ... confronting these antique paraphernalia like the genius of the living present facing the rude symbols of the dying past. We felt proud of our young colleague in the forlorn hope of Humanity, and never prouder of him than when the verdict of 'Guilty' had been brought in, and, pale as marble, but firm as steel, he faced the Christian judge.[72]

In some respects the attitude of Ross displays a hard and unrelenting earnestness that is somehow absent from Foote. In calling almost for a secular crusade Ross gave the blasphemy laws, and the response he wanted to them from freethinkers, the uncompromising shiver of earnest medievalism:

> Let us put out the blood-blurred glimmer of this baleful and falling star, and then men may join hand in hand, and form round the earth one vast encircling ring of universal brotherhood. ... Let our kindness for Christians intensify our hatred against Christianity. ... Our motto is 'prison ruin; but no surrender'. I should regret, knowingly and wantonly, to outrage the feelings of any man or woman; but my colours are nailed to the mast and come fine, come prison, come life, come death, I shall not lower the old flag by one inch to escape the dungeon or the gallows.[73]

Despite this strong language which ran contrary to some of Foote's rational requests for a more liberal legal outlook within society, Stewart Ross's profession of martyrdom must have rung a little hollow in the ears of the three defendants as they contemplated their coming months in prison.

*   *   *

The conviction and severity of the sentences sparked Foote and Ramsey to petition Harcourt at the Home Office complaining of the obsolescent antiquity of the offences, the inability of the first jury to agree a verdict, the severity of the sentences, their previously good character, and the consequences for their reputations as citizens and businessmen. Individually Ramsey protested that he 'had reasonable grounds for believing that the proprietorship of the newspaper would not be held to be an offence at law'. Foote, meanwhile, concentrated upon the various

TRIAL FOR BLASPHEMY.

4.14   Foote's enemies indicted for blasphemy, from the *Freethinker*, Christmas number, 1883

instances of Justice North's partiality in hearing the case and thence began a long campaign of complaint about his treatment in prison. Characteristically Foote rounded off this petition with a statement that his petition was not 'based on personal grounds but on the peculiarity of my offence and the severity of my sentence alone'.[74] The attitude of the Home Office was considerably less than sympathetic since those in Harcourt's department once again considered that the rarity of the offence was largely attributable to Foote's forcing of the realm of the profane far beyond the pale. The absence of prosecution for 50 years was 'probably due to the circumstance that during that period no equally blasphemous production has been published and hawked about in such an intolerably offensive manner'.[75]

However the reaction in the public domain to the trial, verdict and sentence was less easy to explain or answer. Letters were received from all sections of the country and, rather embarrassingly for Harcourt, all sections of opinion. Petitions arrived from Gateshead, London, Leicester and Dewsbury enacted only hours after the verdict had been declared. Several were addressed to Gladstone and must have given Harcourt cause to consider that significant sections of liberal opinion had been stirred against his actions. The letter of W. Wilmer of Manchester was typical, combining the concern of the liberal in politics with that of the liberal Christian. He wrote and asked if Gladstone could mitigate the sentence:

> I cannot find words to express my indignation and shame that such an incident should be possible in the 19th century, and as a Christian blush for the creed which answers its opponents with 12 months hard labour ... as an English Liberal I earnestly entreat you to take some prompt action in the matter which a great number of earnest Christians will undoubtedly consider a national scandal to religion.[76]

Other letters began to identify the sentences as alien to the spirit of the age, a refrain that rapidly became a central component of the numerous petitions that were to arrive at the Home Office with increasing regularity. Whilst some attacked the nature of the sentences others were stirred by their severity and it is here that a view more sympathetic to Harcourt's actions emerges. Sir Robert Leake, enclosing a letter from an irate constituent, ventured to suggest that a lighter sentence would have served the goverment's purposes better.[77] Harcourt must have been angered by such advice since the decision of those in his department to acknowledge the letter of MPs privately was robustly questioned by Harcourt himself who scrawled 'why privately' over the file.

By the end of March Charles Bradlaugh's activities in London and the provinces on behalf of the three prisoners had borne fruit. Petitions, substantially commissioned by Bradlaugh himself, were received from

various London suburbs, the West Riding of Yorkshire, and Blackburn –
all of them contained the by now standard assertion that the blasphemy
laws were contrary to 'the spirit of the age'. Whilst sections of opinion
coming out in favour of a reduction in sentence were one thing, a
petition with widespread support from those who could be described as
opinion formers was quite another. A petition from James Sully which
finally reached Harcourt at the end of May had a whole host of
influential signatures, some from unexpected sources. Amongst the
clerical signatures were those of the Presidents of the Congregational and
Baptist Union respectively and also the principal of New College Oxford.
Whilst a small number of MPs signed, the large number of newspaper
editors prepared to sign the petition was significant in what it said about
those who were in the business of opinion forming. R. H. Hulton of the
Spectator was also joined by P. H. Hill of the *Daily News* as well as the
editors of the *Manchester Guardian* and *Liverpool Daily Post*. The
literary world was represented by Herbert Spencer, G. J. Romaines and
Leslie Stephen amongst others, whilst a host of the academics who
signed included T. H. Huxley and Henry Sidgewick.

The professional judgments of Harcourt and Justice North were also
questioned through the numerous signatures of legal professionals also
appended to the petition. This particular petition concentrated upon the
scale of sentence and was in some respects unwelcome support for Foote
since he would have preferred a line of attack which saw the whole
proceedings as anachronistic and absurd. In the event the petition towed
a moderate line and merely sought remission of the sentence. Its argument
was to deny 'sympathy with all insulting attacks on religious belief, and
while not questioning the right of society to prevent by suitable means the
publication of such insults, respectfully submit that the punishments
inflicted in the present instance were excessive'. This interpretation of the
Sully petition is given further credence by the appearance of John
Tyndall's signature alongside a coda which while considering 'the
punishment to be "excessive"', nonetheless believed that '... the ribaldry
in which some of our professed Freethinkers do not scruple to indulge,
renders them in my opinion, enemies of true freedom'.[78]

By early June more powerful and exalted opinions were being
expressed as to the wisdom and justice of the government's stance in the
matter. The recently enthroned Archbishop of Canterbury Edward White
Benson hurriedly sought Harcourt's attention on the affair. Benson
himself had been founding president of the Church of England Purity
Society in early 1883 and barely a month had passed since his
enthronement at which his sermon had called for a new moral crusade in
this area.[79] Despite this the imprisonment of Foote and Ramsey evidently
gave him significant disquiet since it reflected badly upon the Christian

religion. This was not simply the religion that was in the various common vocabularies that thronged the whole affair but focused particularly on the much-discussed link between Church and State. Since this critique was an established part of the secularist intellectual legacy the Archbishop could have been forgiven for his concern – particularly since he had not been in office for many weeks. Benson argued that punishment could not be justified by either particular events or the lessons of history:

> Greek states found 2000 years ago that when even death was made the penalty for every marked offence against the ancient church and state, the offences steadily increased.[80]

Moreover the Archbishop was further concerned that Freethought or at least blasphemy and godlessness would conceivably be granted their own martyrs to rank alongside Bunyan and Foxe. This, however, was not the crux of the matter. The Archbishop was deeply concerned that religion and its presumed authority were to be the victims of the *Freethinker* trial and that Foote and Ramsey's offence was much better viewed as blows against 'the upward instincts of humanity'.[81] Despite this it seemed clear to the Archbishop that the intellectual misdemeanour of doubt was punished with the same severity that was used against the felony of scurrility. He made an illuminating comment when he noted that a course of action embracing the Indian solution of a crime of 'wounding with deliberate intention the feelings of any person' would do much to soothe the problem. This so-called Indian code solution eventually became a rallying cry for moderates who called for reform of the blasphemy statutes until well into this century.[82]

The Archbishop clearly saw that the destruction of potential religious sentiment '… the whole hope of seriousness in the thoughtless and ignorant' was the greater crime than 'questioning the scriptures'. It was abundantly clear to the Archbishop that the punishment of Foote and Ramsey was inappropriate if it was conducted merely in the name of Christianity and was positively damaging if the relationship between Church and State was to be carelessly rattled in the face of secularists, nonconformists and liberal anglicans.

Although Harcourt wanted to offer reassurances about the public and private motives behind the Liberal Government's stance on the matter Archbishop Benson was still less than content. While he thanked Harcourt for a copy of the indictment and for the assurances that Christianity would not be dragged through the mud he was anxious to disentangle an unfavourable interpretation of religious orthodoxy and ideology from what should be seen as political and moral matters:

> It should be stated fairly that the Christian is at least as anxious as the non-Christian that punishments should not be excessive, and

that these offences should be viewed in their real sight as violations
of human decency and dealt with accordingly.

It is not just that it is popularly received that Christianity as a
faith makes offences into crimes which would not be crimes
otherwise. ...[83]

Although Harcourt felt the matter would become clearer after it was
discussed in Parliament the Archbishop was, by the following month,
growing impatient. By 5 July he wrote to Harcourt telling him that he had
arrranged to consult with Lord Selborne and that the appeal 'over your
head' should not be viewed with too much embarrassment.[84] The
conversation between Selborne and the Archbishop allowed the former to
reiterate Harcourt's line on the prosecution and the conviction during
which he proffered a copy of W. Blake Odger's pamphlet of legal
precedents (Digest of Libel and Slander) which he advised the Archbishop
to consult. However the Archbishop was not wholly convinced and in the
reply, which Selborne also enclosed to Harcourt, he indicated that he was
clearly convinced that the opinion of authorities like Odger and Stephen
were that the law still paid great attention to the matter contained in cases
of blasphemy rather than the manner in which it was expressed.[85] This
obviously left contemporary public opinion 'to suppose that the
punishment of these men is for attacking the Christian *faith*, and not only
for the abominable modes they employ'. However the Archbishop
stopped short of attending a meeting of Foote's sympathisers at St James's
Hall which, in his eyes, would have been 'condoning ribaldry on
religion'.[86]

The archbishop was further convinced that the view of the
government, and his own position, could be explained by a 'luminous
question in the House of Lords' which should be asked by a Christian
layman with the intention of arguing that 'it is outraged decency and not
impugned doctrine which is being avenged'.[87] Selborne's advice in his
covering letter was to refuse to be involved in the plan and his reasons
for this refusal appeared legally and politically quite sound. He had no
wish to put the Law Lords on the spot by asking them to pass opinion
on laws that they themselves had considerable power in framing.
Furthermore the intention behind the question was clearly that Justice
North had entertained motives other than legal duty in his sentencing of
Foote, Ramsey and Kemp, leaving Selborne to wonder precisely which
side the Archbishop thought he was supporting:

I think it highly inexpedient at the present time, to keep alive and
ferment discussions (in quarters no means friendly to those
intentions which his grace has at heart) as to the manner in which
the duties of the judges, or of your own office, in the cases which
have been recently before the courts, have been discharged: it is
certain (whether here Justice North's words were discreet or not or

his sentence too severe or not), that he is an honourable and concientious judge, where the object was to do his duty... .[88]

Eventually Harcourt and Selborne were persuaded to have the relevant question asked. This act was received with scarcely concealed glee by the Archbishop who thanked Harcourt for the 'skillfulness' [sic] with which he had answered the question which had, in his eyes, exonerated established Christianity from the guilt pertaining to Foote and Ramsey's imprisonment.[89]

The matters which lie at the bottom of this exchange are in many respects puzzling. Why was Harcourt prepared, even willing, to upset the Archbishop of Canterbury? Why was Archbishop Benson himself so interested in the case, enough to potentially embarrass the Home Secretary by appealing 'over his head' to Lord Selborne? Certainly the attitude of the liberal administration to the Anglican establishment in the first years of the 1880s was not the most cordial. After ten years of wrangling the Burial Amendment Act had reached the statute book only in 1880. Although the Archbishop's predecessor had given ground on the issue the eventual measure kept most of the existing privileges of the Anglican church regarding burial fees and so on relatively intact. Moreover the evidence of the Harcourt papers suggests that the attempt to amend them again (which became the Burial Amendment Act of 1884) had begun in early 1883. Whilst it might be an overstatement to venture that Harcourt saw the Foote case and its eventual judgment as a means of embarrassing the Anglican hierarchy by association he must certainly have considered that this apparent association, at least in the short term, did the Liberal party no harm amongst its nonconformist supporters. The role of the Archbishop may appear to have, at least partly, encompassed a desire to consolidate his own recent appointment and to resist any fresh challenge to the privileges and rights his office was designed to protect.

Whatever the attitude of Harcourt and the ecclesiastical establishment to the conviction and imprisonment of Foote, Ramsey and Kemp there was little that any of them could do to prevent the situation becoming a picaresque melodrama. This spawned its own heroes, heroines and villains as well as providing regular and significant copy for national as well as freethought papers. Foote himself took the lead in this with a series entitled 'Prisoner for Blasphemy' which ran for many weeks in the *Freethinker*'s compatriot paper *Progress* outlining the whole story from the outset to what Foote inevitably saw as a successful conclusion. This was later collected together as a pamphlet.[90] Any thoughts on the part of the authorities that Foote, Ramsey and Kemp would prove to be model prisoners during their confinement were rapidly undermined. Foote readily adopted the mechanism of prison and confinement as a further demonstration of Christian oppression and his conduct during his confinement reflected both this understandable sense of outrage and the need to produce regular and riveting copy through this adoption of a new public persona.

As early as May 1883 Foote petitioned the prison governor with a tirade of complaints, some repeated from the trial (refusal of bail and the severity of the sentence) and others emerging as consequences of his confinement. The most important of these latter complaints was the fact that Foote, Ramsey and Kemp entered Holloway prison sentenced as second-class misdemeanants which led Foote to rebuke the authorities for treating him 'like a common felon'. Foote noted that Lord Coleridge had been surprised at such treatment and was prepared to pass a concurrent sentence with first-class status had the jury found the defendents guilty at this subsequent trial. Foote then outlined the physical privations that assailed him in prison. He complained – stridently – of the alteration that prison life had had on his habits, occasioning 'enforced disuse of my faculties' and making his imprisonment 'far more severe than that of ordinary criminals'. He also suffered stomach problems, nausea and loss of appetite alongside debility of his vocal powers and literary skills – the last two of these, if true, the authorities had considerable cause to be thankful for. Certainly the medical officer was prepared to concede that both Foote and Ramsey had suffered considerable deterioration in their respective conditions as a result of the prison regime – a matter in which the governor concurred. Foote's petition ended with a request for remission of sentence or restoration to first class misdemeanant status which he had briefly enjoyed while on remand and a request for Ramsey to be treated in a similar fashion.[91]

Harcourt pushed for the letter of the law to be observed, noting on these files that Foote and Ramsey could expect no alteration of their status since the judge should have had due regard to this when sentencing. Whilst the complaints from Holloway may appear to be an attempt to make the captivities of Foote, Ramsey and Kemp simply more comfortable there was a little more to the vehemence of Foote's special pleading since he cited it as a further example of Christian injustice. This injustice now took on a tripartite form embracing injustice of indictment, injustice of trial proceedings and injustice of sentence. This denial of first-class status emphasised still further that blasphemy was regarded as criminal, not simply in the mechanical operation of the law but also, more significantly, that the discretionary element that senior law officers and government ministers were supposed to regulate would similarly be used harshly against the blasphemer. In this respect the flat denial of such status was a mistake by Harcourt which Foote could use to the full as it became an indispensable part of his martyr narrative – with a resultantly corrosive effect on public opinion.

Foote's own access to the public stage whilst in captivity was aided by a regular round of family visitors and others from the freethought fold and these visits themselves caused an edgy prison governor to express concern to the Home Office. The visits of, amongst others, Edward Aveling, Annie Besant and Joseph Symes and the prospect of Kemp and Ramsey themselves becoming visitors to an incarcerated Foote seemed too much to bear. This concern was also heightened by the fact that Foote had also been detected in a clandestine correspondence. Foote's later reports of his time in prison which emerged as the two versions of 'Prisoner for Blasphemy' dwelled incessantly upon the conditions of his confinement. The inadequacy of diet, the poor ventilation caused by the misuse of blackleading within his cell became cause for retrospective complaint that readers were encouraged to shudder along with. This shudder could be intensified by Foote's accounts of his fellow inmates – the 'repulsive specimens of humanity, survivals in our civilised age of the lower types of barbarous or savage'.

More important still Foote's confinement entailed an opportunity to undergo the nearest equivalent to a secularist trial of faith. Confined to gaol with reading restricted to the Bible, the Book of Common Prayer and a hymn book Foote underwent the secularist approximation of John Bunyan's confinement. In some respects this 'trial by seclusion' should not be underestimated. Deprived of like-minded company or alternative reading materials or means of writing the terms of incarceration must have represented a stern test for those whose atheism was as firmly in the public domain as was Foote, Ramsey and Kemp's. The prison regime effectively represented a distilled form of Christianity which, Foote's crusade continually argued, society had long since left behind. His verdict on systematically reading the Bible (twice) was that its contents confirmed still further his atheist opinions and he furthermore resented the totalitarian methods that had persuaded him to endure this.

Whilst Foote was convinced his insufferable behaviour was instrumental in speeding his release Sir William Harcourt had left instructions to be notified when Ramsey had completed three-quarters of his sentence, perhaps indicating that he saw no advantage in prolonging the punishment unnecessarily. This view was also forced upon him by the collapse of the third trial and the liberal treatment of Foote and the defendants by Coleridge. This encouraged those sympathetic to the plight of the prisoners to transfer their attention from protesting against the severity of sentence to campaigning for their release.

Foote himself singled out the support of Admiral Maxse's work in organising petitions and letter writing for special praise, declaring that he 'valued his sympathy even more than his assistance'.[92] By July 1883 the mass meeting in St James' Hall, which Archbishop Benson had fought so shy of, amounted to an impressive display of public support for the prisoners' release. Alongside the usual freethought representatives were some clerical and semi-clerical fellow travellers like Stewart Headlam, Moncure Conway and the Unitarian W. Sharman, who had renounced his living to campaign for the repeal of the blasphemy laws and to whom Harcourt had earlier refused permission to visit Foote.[93]

Eventually the matter was raised in Parliament through the member for Leicester, Peter Taylor, who questioned Harcourt as to his intended course of action particularly in relation to ordering remission of the remaining sentences. In his reply Harcourt managed to tie himself rather injudiciously in knots whilst he chided the opposition benches for suggesting that they would countenance a minister 'interfering with the making and the adminstration of the law, and transfering it from Parliament to the Executive and to a Minister of the Crown'. Harcourt, initially stating his detachment, went on to betray his opinions in the matter of the sentences. Whilst admitting that he did have power to alter these he argued that the special circumstances of any case should be considered. This opened the way for him to express that he considered the publication which had caused the affair was 'a scandalous outrage upon public decency' and that it was 'in the most strict sense of the word an obscene libel'. This was a miscalculation which suggests that it was not only Lord Mayors who, in an unguarded moment, could confuse the issues of blasphemy and obscenity. This potential accusation was to provide important ammunition for Foote and Ramsey's ideological fight against the forces ranged against them. Ramsey in particular responded swiftly with a petition to Harcourt on this and an offer to supply new copies of the Christmas number for another trial, this time for obscenity – an offer which was not surprisingly never taken up.[94]

The matter was eventually resolved when the prisoners were finally released. Kemp left prison in May 1883, according to Foote 'in a state of exhaustion', whilst Ramsey was released in November to be met by a crowd of sympathisers who thence conveyed him to the Hall of Science. This of course was built to the crescendo of Foote's own release which duly came on 25 February 1884. The attempts of the authorities to bundle their awkward charge onto the street in the early hours were thwarted by Foote's own insistence upon taking his time over breakfast in a final theatrical display of stubbornness. After twelve months Foote had no intention of missing his other breakfast at the Hall of Science and the chance to address his friends and admirers.

Although this last act marked the end of Foote and the *Freethinker*'s involvement with the law the matter did not rest here. Whilst Foote himself returned to his journalism and continued the crusade – the comic Bible sketches reappeared and the originals were republished in a single pamphlet – he was never called to account again.[95] In many respects this was no disappointment since activating the laws and their punishments was clearly enough for all who were connected with the case. Foote then set rather noisily to work retelling and nuancing the narrative of his trial and incarceration. Although it is possible to detect considerable egoism in Foote's account of events, a factor which clearly did not endear him to some contemporaries and to historians like Calder-Marshall it is easy to forget that the Foote case was *the* blasphemy case of this generation. In contrast to the hapless Pooley the authorities were distinctly unlucky to be pitted against an articulate and shrewd opponent who had a reading public at his disposal that were warming to the variety and numerous cadences that the new journalism was capable of conjuring and manipulating. If Foote was insufferable for Calder-Marshall one wonders whom he would rather have seen in the dock – the more subtle although disreputably rakish rogue Aveling or the sombre serious and dour Stewart Ross.

The third, and most significant, trial which Foote underwent in this series was before Justice Coleridge who had prosecuted in the Pooley case of 1857. Foote's defence was treated more sympathetically as he was able, this time, to offer his expert evidence that the spirit of the age allowed the *Freethinker* to stand alongside Mill, Huxley and the others. After another divided jury had been unable to agree the prosecution dropped the case. This last trial was particularly notable for Coleridge's pronouncement in which he confirmed much received opinion but instituted a significantly new departure. Whilst Coleridge entertained the suggestion that the law might be a bad one he nevertheless argued that it should be obeyed. None the less he went considerably further in arguing that as a result of England's cultural diversity Christianity could no longer be considered to be a part of the law of the land. Moreover he compounded this with a plea for the development of toleration as civic virtue and duty:

> It is also true, that persecution is a very easy form of virtue. A difficult form of virtue is to try in your own life to obey what you believe to be God's will. It is not easy to do, and if you do it, you make but little noise in the world. But it is easy to turn on some one who differs from you in opinion, and in the guise of zeal for God's honour, to attack a man whose life perhaps may be much more pleasing to God than is your own. When it is done by men full of profession and pretension, who choose that particular form of zeal for God which consists in putting the criminal law in force against some one else, many quiet people come to sympathise, not with the prosecutor but with the defendant.[96]

However, the liberal interpretation, which distinguished between 'matter' and 'manner', did not alter the practice of law or its day-to-day operation.

Those who were moderate or respectful in their denial would remain immune whilst the purveyors of ridicule would be easy targets. Effectively, a legally-established class bias was enshrined in this judgment.

The *Freethinker* prosecution was undoubtedly a landmark prosecution in the history of blasphemy prosecutions. Without doubt the machinations of Harcourt and the Home Office, the attitude of Justices North and Coleridge and the skill of George William Foote ensured that a very public stage was prepared for the discussion of the precise religiosity of late Victorian society. However, Foote's defence stretched beyond blasphemy to questions of equal treatment in the realm of free speech and towards a free trade in knowledge. Moreover the resolution of Justice Coleridge in the third trial contained important signposts for what a modern blasphemy law could look like.

Foote's arguments in his own defence did not simply seek to refute the charge of blasphemy against him. They were in effect a culmination of processes of social, political and religious change that society had undergone since it had last been pressed to consider the offences of blasphemy and blasphemous libel. Certain motifs which appealed to the increased modernisation and civilisation of society were portrayed time after time in Foote's defence, as was the argument that knowledge, free speech and access to both of these were the essential rights of free citizens. In linking the question of access to knowledge and freedom of opinion Foote could argue that he was appealing to the spirit of an age which had witnessed a vast expansion in the scope of the political nation as well as changes in the scope and nature of literate communities.[97] As such Foote's stance and defence during the case rested on appealing to those who had benefited from these changes and were prepared to see their full implications adopted and promoted.

On many occasions Foote discussed the necessity of his actions and the necessity of prosecution. This was frequently to be his answer to freethinkers who disliked the candour and tone of his attacks upon Christianity – to demonstrate that a practice was anachronistic it had to be shown to be so even if it convicted a whole culture and the spirit of the age. Thus throughout his trial Foote took the opportunity to scare his colleagues in the secular movement and wider informed opinion with the spectre of a resurrected literal Christianity which would be prepared to desecrate the tombs of Darwin and Mill. The keynote of his trial was to emphasise that the law and culture of Britain had surely moved beyond the medieval relic that he portrayed blasphemy to be. So anachronistic was this law, that Foote repeatedly pointed out that it simply appeared to protect the state religion since the link between Church and State was implicit in it. Thus logically the laws offered no protection to Catholics or Nonconformists and indeed the alarming assertion that the denial of the doctrine of the Trinity by Unitarians was contrary to statute sent many scurrying for legal advice.

Although Foote's defence indicted the law of the land he also spent considerable time referring to the individuals involved in the case. Varley, Tyler, Harcourt and Justice North, all were seen as motivated by malice and prejudice. Foote was even able to suggest that the recently created office of Public Prosecutor was capable of considerable partiality in the exercise of its actions. As befitted an individualist Foote argued that this situation had much wider implications for Victorian society since, with the blasphemy laws in place, the apparatus of the law and by implication the State could be used to further individual grievances. By using this critique Foote also made sure that the whole episode was given the stench of 'Old Corruption' which echoed the republican critique of Bradlaugh, Thomas Paine and Richard Carlile.

Despite this display of fortitude and initiative one of Foote's greatest triumphs was to persuade the public at large that he was representative of the unlettered working man whose welfare and opinions had vexed the governing classes since 1867. There were in fact two major points of argument that were being alluded to here. Foote's citation of Mill, Swinburne et al. was a classic demonstration that polite 'doubt', the studious use of literary conventions and a sanction of an expensive cover price was almost certain to guarantee the writer freedom from prosecution.

While some papers such as the *Daily Telegraph* were outraged by the actions of Foote and his compatriots a significant number were opposed to the prosecution. *The Times*, the *Standard*, the *Daily News* and the *Morning Advertiser* all expressed the view that blasphemy prosecutions were an anachronism. The *Spectator* was one paper among many that spotted inconsistencies in the legal interpretation of blasphemy which oscillated between defining it as the 'thing said' and 'the manner of saying it'. Most importantly it emphasised that the issue was the lack of understanding between the class that frames laws and the class that usually breaks them. Whilst this was a victory of sorts it was a fact that this supposedly more liberal application of the law rested upon the opinion of one judge just as Foote's earlier conviction could be said to have done. Foote argued that there was not a clear definition of blasphemy in any statute and that this had considerable implications for civil liberties, since without such a definition prejudice and taste became the main arbiters in the matter. Once this situation was allowed to flourish then injustice, partiality and tyranny would follow.

Although Foote and others in the secular movement were wont to ascribe the actions of government and individuals to either personal or collective prejudice they were in a sense ignoring the genuine fear that gripped Victorian society about how morality was to be maintained and promoted.

A MERRY CHRISTMAS.
Inside and Outside.

a 'A Merry Christmas', from the *Freethinker*, Christmas 1882: Foote's 1882 Christmas message on Christian hypocrisy

4.15 Foote could also use illustration for very serious effect

b   'The God of Battles', from the *Freethinker*, 5 November 1882: in the wake of Tel-el Kebir, Foote pronounces on Christianity and militarism

Many saw Christianity as the mainspring of the country's laws as well as the leading influence upon behaviour within society. It should be remembered that alongside the Foote case Harcourt had to worry about a whole series of challenges to strict and moral government during these years, ranging from the scandals of female white slave traffic to Brussels which brought about a Criminal Law Amendment Act ushering in new police powers and raising the age of consent, through the persistent menace of crime supposedly linked to the consumption of Penny Dreadfuls, to the continued activities of Irish terrorists operating out of New York which itself resulted in legislation to control the access to explosives.[98] Indeed these concerns motivated Harcourt's desire to retain centralised control of the police in the metropolis which held up the introduction of a bill to reform the governance of London until 1884. That the latter was viewed as confiscation may also have been a consideration in the Corporation's procedure against Foote et al. By demonstrating their willingness to act against immorality they showed their powers to be active and relevant.[99] Foote and Ramsey and other potential blasphemers as a result were cast as the sworn enemy of morality and for this reason their offence was often confused with obscenity, as indeed it was at the three trials. Significantly this last charge was hotly denied by the defendants who stressed that society had surely moved beyond the false and often morally ambiguous messages of Christian scripture.

The trials and subsequent imprisonment cemented the reputation of Foote and it was an easy accession for him to the presidency of the National Secular Society. Though he refused to compromise on the material he published and, indeed, invited subsequent prosecution the *Freethinker* was never to be troubled again. This did not, however, prevent the Home Office from watching the paper closely and as late as the 1920s the authorities contemplated prosecution. The blasphemy laws themselves remained intact despite attempts to repeal them in the aftermath of the *Freethinker* trial. Indeed Sir James Stephen became a leading critic of the Coleridge judgment suggesting, very publicly, that it confused matters by spuriously introducing a decency test with no substantial precedent for it.[100] Stephen argued that the law was unaltered from Hale's time and examined closely the authorities which Coleridge had used. He also took a contrary opinion to the judgment's interpretation of these and argued that, though draconian and out of step, they were the clearest possible case for the law's removal rather than 'prolong its existence and give it an air of plausibility and humanity'.[101] Moreover Coleridge's judgment, so Stephen argued, introduced a worrying complacency over religious debates since it was nowhere established in law that reasonable criticism of such matters was possible. Indeed, Stephen also had an important point to make when he suggested that calmness and decency were probably the last emotions

4.16   G. W. Foote as portrayed on the cover of the *Freethinker*, 1 July 1883

present in such discussions. His conclusion was that the law was not based upon a 'desire to prevent pain' but on a principle that Christianity was to be protected on the assumption that it was true – a situation which he defined clearly as persecution.[102] Henceforth Justice Stephen became the guiding hand behind the formulation of a repeal measure which was to have considerable longevity into this century.[103]

Meanwhile, judicial opinion was able to take comfort in the assumption that the law's regulation could be left to the onward advance of public taste and the wisdom of individual judges. This confidence was to prevail undisturbed until the next generation dusted these laws off for use in the Edwardian period, this time primarily against public speakers. What the Foote prosecution proved to the discomfiture of liberal England was that the Common Law was not simply used to defend the common man against the pretensions of centralised autocratic power. It refused to accept responsibility for some of the legal system's power, instead preferring to let the sensibilities of individuals or even Foote's much-publicised 'spirit of the age' regulate its use. However this left several hostages to fortune. The law could be misinterpreted, reinterpreted in the light of theological developments or could be used by the determined to forward personal grudges and to trawl medieval and early modern case-law to do so. Moreover Coleridge's judgment seemed to make the law less anachronistic and actually workable and this fuelled a considerably long-running argument with J. F. Stephen's interpretation of the law which was ostensibly still raging beyond the Edwardian period.

The Foote case was in a sense the Victorian attempt to settle the law of blasphemy and modernise it. Whilst Foote went to prison for 12 months the effect of the last case to be heard was to change the law significantly. The new emphasis from Justice Coleridge was on the fact that the 'manner' made the casual encounter increasingly central to the offence. It was not what was said but the context was all important – how the words or images struck an individual in the immediacy of first being confronted with them. This seemed to go hand-in-hand with other Victorian fears of suddenly being confronted with the moral abyss where free love, moral anarchy, family limitation and the dissolution of sacred institutions became complete. In short, a fear of what modernity might mean. All of these were aspects which were to be further explored in the Edwardian period.

Notes

1.   Bradlaugh-Bonner, Hypatia (1934), *Penalties Upon Opinion*, London: Watts & Co., pp. 95–108.
2.   Herrick, J. (1982), *Vision and Realism: A Hundred Years of the Freethinker*, London: G. W. Foote & Co., pp. 18–32; Walter, Nicolas (1990), *Blasphemy Ancient and Modern*, London: Rationalist Press Association, pp. 49–55.
3.   Calder-Marshall, Arthur (1972), *Lewd, Blasphemous and Obscene*, London: Hutchinson, pp. 169–92.

4. Royle, E. (1980), *Radicals, Secularists and Republicans: Popular Freethought in Britain, 1866–1915*, Manchester: MUP, p. 100.

5. Marsh, Joss Lutz (1991), '"Bibliolatry" and "Bible Smashing": G. W. Foote, George Meredith, and the heretic trope of the book', *Victorian Studies*, 34 (3): pp. 315–36.

6. Ibid., p. 318.

7. Ibid., p. 320.

8. Ibid., p. 325.

9. Joss Marsh has significantly enhanced her examination of Foote and his links to wider literary genres in *Word Crimes: Blasphemy, Culture and Literature in Nineteenth-Century England* (University of Chicago Press, 1998). This unfortunately arrived as this book was going to press. My engagement with this interesting and informative work must thus wait until another occasion.

10. Meredith, W. M. (1912) (ed.), *Collected Letters of George Meredith*, London, Letters 19 August 1878, 31 December 1878 and 30 May 1879. In the first of these Foote declared, 'I admire the fight you are making, and class you among the true soldiers.'

11. Foote, G. W. (1932), *Defence of Free Speech, being a three hours' address to the jury in the court of Queen's Bench before Lord Coleridge, on April 24, 1883. New edition with an introduction by H. Cutner*, London p. 3.

12. Foote, G. W. (1878?), *Mr. Bradlaugh's Trial and The Freethought Party*, p. 15.

13. Foote, G. W. (1886), *Prisoner for Blasphemy*, London, p. 18.

14. Arnstein, W. L. (1957), 'The Bradlaugh Case: a reappraisal', *Journal of the History of Ideas*, XVIII (2): pp. 254–69; Arnstein, W. L. (1962), 'Gladstone and the Bradlaugh Case', *Victorian Studies*, V (4): pp. 303–30; Arnstein, W. L. (1962), 'Parnell and the Bradlaugh Case', *Irish Historical Studies*, XIII (51): pp. 212–35; Arnstein, W. L. (1965), *The Bradlaugh Case: A Study in Late Victorian Opinion and Politics*, Oxford: Clarendon Press; Bradlaugh-Bonner, Hypatia and J. M. Robertson (1894), *Charles Bradlaugh, a record of his life and work*, London; Royle, E. (1980), *Radicals, Secularists and Republicans: Popular Freethought in Britain, 1866–1915*, Manchester: Manchester University Press; Tribe, David (1967), *One Hundred Years of Freethought*; Tribe, David (1971), *President Charles Bradlaugh, M.P.*, London: Elek.

15. Brown, Desmond H. (1992), 'Abortive Attempts to Codify English Criminal Law', *Parliamentary History*, II (1): pp. 1–40.

16. Colley, Linda (1992), *Britons: Forging the Nation*. While Linda Colley argues that the provinces emphatically opposed the repeal of the Catholic Emancipation act she concludes with an assertion that the eventual passage of the act renewed confidence in the British imperial civilising mission.

17. McCalman, I. D. (1984), 'Unrespectable Radicalism: Infidels and Pornography in Early Nineteenth Century London Movement', *Past and Present* (104): pp. 74–110; McCalman, I. D. (1993), *Radical Underworld: Prophets, Revolutionaries, and Pornographers in London, 1795–1840*, Cambridge: Cambridge University Press.

18. Foote, *Prisoner for Blasphemy*, op. cit., p. 18.

19. Ibid.

20. *Freethinker*, vol. 1, no. 1, May 1881.

21. Foote, *Prisoner for Blasphemy*, op. cit., p. 17.

22. Mrs Mary Ward (1888), *Robert Elsemere*, Rosemary Ashton (ed.), Oxford: Oxford University Press, 1987. See Marsh, Joss Lutz (1991), 'Bibliolatry' and 'Bible Smashing', op. cit.

23. Brooks, Peter (1976), *The Melodramatic Imagination: Balzac, Henry James, Melodrama and the Mode of Excess*, New Haven: Yale University Press, p. 11.

24. Stephen, James Fitzjames (1884), 'The Law on Blasphemy and Blasphemous Libel', *Fortnightly Review*, March 1884, 289–318; Foote, *Prisoner for Blasphemy*, op. cit., p. 12.

25. PRO HO45 9613 A9275. See also Begbie, Harold (1920), *Life of William Booth: The Founder of the Salvation Army*, London: Macmillan, and Mews, Stuart (1988), 'The General and the Bishops: Alternative Responses to De-Christianisation', in T. R. Gourvish and Alan O'Day (eds), *Later Victorian Britain, 1867–1900*, Basingstoke: Macmillan, pp. 209–28.

26. Begbie, op. cit., pp. 17–23; Mews, op cit., p. 223.

27. Marsh, op. cit., p. 321.

28. See for example *Freethinker*, 20 November 1881, p. 125 for a 'Sugar Plums' column which contains a piece reporting low church attendance in Ipswich and a piece from Ernest Renan who argues that enforceable religious conformity belongs to the age of pre-medieval city states and has largely been superceded by the modern taste for tolerance and enlightenment.

29. See for example the note in 18 June 1882, p. 197 referring to the success of the *Freethinker* in Scotland which as far north as Inverness was reported as selling over six copies per week.

30. The issue for 9 July 1882 for example contained a story which playfully pulled a host of otherwise revered religious terms and descriptions down to a level of abuse. The paper reports a wedding at which the Revd H. M. Simms turned a woman out of the church by 'practising a little muscular Christianity on the grounds that she, and some of her compatriots, were in the habit of attending a rival gospel shop'.

31. Foote, *Prisoner for Blasphemy*, op. cit., p. 19.

32. Ibid., p. 21.

33. Calder-Marshall, op. cit.

34. Nash, D. S. (1995), '"Unfettered Investigation" – the Secularist Press and the Creation of Audience in Victorian England', *Victorian Periodicals Review*, Summer, 28: pp. 123–35.

35. Foote, *Defence of Free Speech*, op. cit., p. 2.

36. Foote, *Prisoner for Blasphemy*, op. cit., p. 20.

37. Walkowitz, Judith (1992), *City of Dreadful Delight: Narratives of Sexual Danger in Nineteenth-Century London*, op. cit., London: Virago.

38. Calder-Marshall, op. cit., p. 180; Royle, op. cit., p. 272.

39. Foote, *Prisoner for Blasphemy*, op. cit, p. 22.

40. *Prisoner for Blasphemy*, p. 24.

41. See Calder-Marshall, op. cit., pp. 181–2 for the suggestion that the timing of the Seymour trial did not follow the chronology outlined by Foote in *Prisoner for Blasphemy*.

42. Ibid., pp. 24–5.

43. *Freethinker*, 16 July 1882.

44. Foote, *Prisoner for Blasphemy*, op. cit., p. 26.

45. HO 45 9536/49902, Liddell to James, 23 August 1882.

46. Ibid. Memo of Sir William Harcourt 2 September 1882.

47. Calder-Marshall, op. cit., pp. 183–4; Tribe, *One Hundred Years of Freethought*, op. cit., p. 156.

48. Colaiaco, J. (1983), *James Fitzjames Stephen and the Crisis of Victorian Thought*, pp. 92–3, 202–3.

49. *Freethinker*, 25 July 1882.
50. Colaiaco, op. cit., p. 2.
51. HO 45 9536/49902, Grover to Harcourt 13 August 1882.
52. Interestingly this letter is accompanied in its PRO file by a similar one regarding the publication *Town Talk* which contained sensationalist articles exposing the evils of prostitution. The correspondent was also similarly concerned with the consequences of encountering '... these most terrible bills' carrying headlines 'in the largest of letters' with the legends '"*How the women hide their shame*", "*Prostitutes at the Westminster Aquarium*" and "*Fallen Women*"'. The correspondent was concerned that this would 'make it altogether unfit for any lady or respectable woman to walk through the city'. The coda to this used the language of moral outrage and the plea for moral re-armament to frame a widespread objection to this onslaught that could have referred as equally to the *Freethinker* as to *Town Talk*:

> I cannot conceive that it can be possible that there would be no means of suppressing these fearful publications in this the most civilised and Christian country in the world, – & it is a national disgrace that the moral characters of the young men of our city should be lowered & ruined as they must be by the constant issue of such degrading Bills. (HO 45 – 9536/49902)

53. The Salvation Army were considered to be the direct enemy of secularists by none other than Edward White Benson himself. See Mews, Stuart (1988), 'The General and the Bishops: Alternative Responses to De-Christianisation', in T. R. Gourvish and Alan O'Day (eds), *Later Victorian Britain, 1867–1900*, Basingstoke: Macmillan, pp. 209–28, esp. pp. 215–16.
54. Foote, *Prisoner for Blasphemy*, op. cit., p. 38.
55. Ibid., p. 49.
56. HO 45 9536/49902 Lushington to Harcourt, 31 January 1883.
57. *Freethinker*, 11 February 1883.
58. Foote, *Prisoner for Blasphemy*, op. cit., p. 41.
59. *Daily Telegraph*, 2 March 1883.
60. Ibid.
61. Foote, *Prisoner for Blasphemy*, op. cit., pp. 72–3.
62. Ibid., pp. 74 and 78.
63. *Daily Telegraph*, 2 March 1883.
64. Foote, *Prisoner for Blasphemy*, op. cit., p. 82; Calder-Marshall, op. cit., p. 188.
65. Calder-Marshall, p. 188.
66. *Daily Telegraph*, 6 March 1883.
67. There is an interesting exchange in HO 144 114/A25454 which suggests that Foote and Ramsey were almost prevented from conferring over the weekend due to the neglect of the prison governor. Even when Harcourt was appraised of this oversight those in his department were anxious that the prisoners should be 'entitled to the privileges of unconvicted prisoners but no more'.
68. *Daily Telegraph*, 6 March 1883.
69. Ibid.
70. Ibid.
71. Ibid.
72. *Secular Review*, 10 March 1883.
73. Ibid.

74. HO 144 114/A25454/26 & 27 petitions of Foote and Ramsey 7/3/83.
75. Ibid., notes appended.
76. Ibid., Wilmer to Gladstone 7 March 1883.
77. Ibid., Leake to Harcourt 9/3/83.
78. Sully to Harcourt 9 May 1883.
79. Bristow, Edward J. (1977), *Vice and Vigilance: Purity Movements in Britain Since 1700*, Dublin: Gill and Macmillan, pp. 100–101.
80. Papers of Sir William Harcourt 1880–85 (M.S. Harcourt Dep.) Miscellaneous correspondence files Box 212, Archbishop Benson to Harcourt, 5 June 1883.
81. Ibid.
82. Macdonell, John (1883), 'Blasphemy and the Common Law', *Fortnightly Review, new series*, June 1883, pp. 776–89, p. 789.
83. MS. Harcourt Dep. Archbishop Benson to Harcourt, 8 June 1883.
84. Ibid. Archbishop Benson to Harcourt 2 July 1883, 5 July 1883.
85. Stephen, James Fitzjames (1884), 'The Law on Blasphemy and Blasphemous Libel', *Fortnightly Review*, March 1884, pp. 289–318.
86. MS. Harcourt Dep., Archbishop Benson to Selborne, 16 July 1883.
87. Ibid.
88. Ibid., Lord Selborne to Harcourt, 19 July 1883.
89. Archbishop Benson to Harcourt, 26 July 1883.
90. Foote, *Prisoner for Blasphemy*, op. cit.
91. HO 144 114/A25454. Petition of G. W. Foote to Harcourt, 24 May 1883; Report of Prison M.O. of Holloway Gaol, 23 May.
92. Foote, *Prisoner for Blasphemy*, op. cit., p. 165.
93. HO 144 114/A25454. Holloway prison governor to Harcourt, 7 July 1883.
94. Foote, *Prisoner for Blasphemy*, op. cit, p. 168.
95. Ibid., Foote, G. W. (1889), *Defence of Free Speech, being a three hours' address to the jury in the court of Queen's Bench before Lord Coleridge, on April 24, 1883*, London.
96. Coleridge, Ernest Hartley (1904), *Life and correspondence of John Duke, Lord Coleridge*, London, p. 291.
97. Anderson, Patricia (1991), *The Printed Image and the Transformation of Popular Culture 1790-1860*, Oxford: OUP; Walkowitz, Judith (1992), *City of Dreadful Delight: Narratives of Sexual Danger in Nineteenth-Century London*, London: Virago.
98. Bristow, Edward J. (1977), *Vice and Vigilance: Purity Movements in Britain since 1700*, Dublin: Gill and Macmillan, pp. 92 and 107; Dunae, P. (1979), '"Penny dreadfuls": later nineteenth-century boys' literature and crime', *Victorian Studies*, XXII: pp. 135–50. Harcourt could also be unremitting in other contexts. He refused to offer clemency to Tom Dudley and Edwin Stephens, the defendants in the infamous 'cabin boy' cannibalism case. See Simpson, A. W. B. (1984), *Cannibalism and the Common Law*, Chicago.
99. Doolittle, Ian (1983), 'Obsolete Appendage? The City of London's Struggle for Survival', *History Today*, 33 (May): pp. 10–14.
100. Stephen, James Fitzjames (1884), 'The Law on Blasphemy and Blasphemous Libel', *Fortnightly Review*, March 1884, pp. 289–318. Stephen White has thoughtfully drawn my attention to the fact that Stephen's criticism of a fellow serving judge was almost unprecedented.
101. Ibid., p. 315.
102. Ibid., p. 318.
103. *Freethinker*, 24 May 1885.

CHAPTER FIVE

Boulter, Stewart, Pack and Gott: Blasphemy, Conflict and Public Order

The apparent liberality of the Coleridge judgment prevented Foote from ever appearing in court again although this did not prevent successive Home Secretaries from showing interest in the *Freethinker*. The later *Jerusalem Star*, a publication by James Ramsey which blended lampoon skit and scurrility, was similarly observed from a watchful distance but this paper fell victim to the repetitive nature of its content and ultimately the collapse of its circulation.[1]

The clearly invoked connection between blasphemy and obscenity appeared to be vindicated in the context of the Havelock Ellis/Watford University Press Affair. Opponents of freethought culture had long been able to invoke a series of episodes that cemented this connection within the popular mind. Richard Carlile's Malthusian publications, such as *Every Woman's Book* and his relaxed attitude to marriage was a favourite subject for reproach as was the excessive libertinage of earlier blasphemers such as Sir Charles Sedley. Later in the nineteenth century there were still closer and more serious ideological connections to be made, if only sometimes by association. The Secular Society at Leeds, for example, let its hall to a disreputable group which resulted in a police raid and the incident gained the infamous sobriquet of the 'Leeds Orgies'.[2] Similarly the relationship of Bradlaugh and Besant came under close scrutiny in the context of the Knowlton pamphlet trial and in many circles Annie Besant's reputation was damaged irreparably. Towards the end of the century organisations like Oswald Dawson's Legitimation League, which argued for the legal recognition of children born outside the marriage contract, always lay on the fringe of the secular movement and were also believed to be a refuge for quasi-anarchist opinion.[3] This connection was reinforced in the public mind by the actions of those involved in the Watford University Press affair, in which a disreputable publishing venture which combined aspirations for serious social education with elements of ribaldry became the centre of intense police activity. Following a melodramatic and farcical police raid thousands of books were seized, many of which were works by Havelock Ellis.[4] The serious side of the incident was that the company's publishing programme contained a large quantity of birth control literature and other malthusian works as well as having tantalising links to anarchism. The development of Neo-Malthusianism in England has been discussed by a number of protagonists within the movement and also by historians.[5] Certainly the Neo-Malthusian answer to social problems and deprivation became widely discussed in politically radical and socialist circles. The argument ostensibly suggested that family limitation was a pivotal and generally underrated solution to a variety of social and political problems. The pressing question of distribution and redistribution of resources within society was paramount within this discussion, although radicals also saw family limitation as a putative answer to the 'Woman Question'. Meanwhile Secularists considered Neo-Malthusianism as a valuable weapon which could be used to de-mystify what they saw as religious pretensions to moral jurisdiction over man's nature.

The Edwardian period proved itself once again to be another era in which society reinvented the offence of blasphemy, as it was to do with each successive generation. Whilst it could be said that this reinvention took place as a natural consequence of the Foote case sliding from memory it was also true that the protagonists in the Edwardian cases brought new facets, related to style, content, intention and ultimate goal to the crime. Most striking to the observer is that where Foote exhibited wit and the willingness to indulge in the accepted, if in his case rather barbed, conventions of rhetorical discussion there was a manifest refusal of the Edwardians to indulge in this. Gott, Pack and Stewart in their journalism and in their public discussions emphatically pulled no punches. There was little of the literary pretensions of Foote or Hone and much of the wilful portrayal of themselves as dangerous enemies of society.

A further difference from Foote was the association of Pack, Stewart and Gott with forms of socialism. All three of them were prime movers in the establishment of the Freethought Socialist League which had its headquarters in Bradford. There has often been an assumption that secularism and freethought were intimately connected with the health and prosperity of liberalism.[6] But there is also scope for more detailed research into the enduring nature of theistic and atheistic critiques of society in socialism. There is clearly a case for considering that socialism in the Edwardian period was engaged in an evaluation of what may be called 'the Religion Question'. Much of this turned upon the investigation of the association of religion with capitalism and the former's arguably appalling record of fostering and condoning its progress. Likewise the fact that religion appeared in league with the capitalist state in suppressing the spread of birth control knowledge was a further cause for campaigning. Such religious and state-fostered objections to birth control always claimed ostensibly to be directed at the protection of morality. In this respect this was one conspicuous area in which the labour movement sought to campaign against religion and capitalism combined. Attempts to criticise existing moral conceptions and to construct new ones rapidly became a major area of debate and discussion from the Edwardian period onwards.[7] Gott and Pack were emphatically convinced that what they saw as the recent influx of Christians into the socialist movement was a concerted attempt to 'nobble' it. The Freethought Socialist League's manifesto contained the legend 'Christism can never be anything but a religion for slaves' and declared further that 'Socialism is a political and industrial movement based upon Secular Philosophy.' The purpose of this secular philosophy was '... to dispel superstition; to spread education; to disestablish religion; to rationalise morality; to promote peace; to extend material well-being; and to realise the self-government of the people'.[8]

The extensive publishing programme of the Freethought Socialist League also contained a number of titles which aimed explicitly at undermining Christianity and its moral record. Capitalism was likewise indicted as enjoying not only biblical sanction but the material and moral support of the various forms of ecclesiastical establishment. What may have worried the authorities still more was the sort of company that this movement was keeping. Bradford was also the powerbase of J. Greevz Fisher who stood as a Liberty candidate in 1892, arguing for voluntary taxation, female emancipation and an end to compulsory education.[9] However members of the American anarchist milieu such as Moses Harman and Melfew Seklew were frequent contributors to *The Truthseeker* newspaper. The latter, arguing for a moral anarchism which he linked to promotion of the ego, specialised in material that was similar to that which Gott was to produce and he courted arrest in the same fashion.[10] American anarchism had in particular gained a bad name from the 'Haymarket Massacre' in 1886 in which seven police were killed and over 60 demonstrators injured by a bomb, for which a number of anarchists were imprisoned and others hanged.[11] Moreover, as the new century began anarchists were responsible for the assassination of President McKinley and a number of European royal figures.[12] Whilst Seklew and Harman may have been portrayed as peaceful social radicals harrassed unnecessarily by the police their English associates can not really have been surprised at the attention these individuals elicited from local and government agencies.[13] Even indigenous associates of the movement like Guy Aldred were to have extensive careers in the anarchist organisations of Great Britain. Aldred indeed had links with the syndicalist influences that were at work in the later Edwardian period and actually stood trial in 1909 for alienating the 'Indian native liege subjects of the King'.[14]

a   *The Truthseeker* cover, March 1904

5.1   Anticlericalism *Truthseeker* style

PROSECUTED FOR BLASPHEMY !

THE PARSON

TROUSERS AT ABOUT THE PRICE OF STOCKINGS See page 12.

b   *The Truthseeker* cover, February 1904

Thus the furore which greeted the various cases against John William Gott, Ernest Pack, Thomas William Stewart and Harry Boulter all deserve to be viewed in these contexts. All these men did much consciously to bring prosecution (though scarcely punishment) upon themselves but in doing so they nonetheless argued that a wider ideological battle was to be fought as a matter of necessity. Whilst at least one of the prosecutions against Gott was concerned with the written word, all of the others were responses to immediate public order problems. While the offence of publishing blasphemy must clearly appear calculated – particularly when the Foote case is considered – the blasphemous conduct of a public meeting attended by the forces of order has perhaps more calculation still. In the context of a public meeting the reaction of audience and police could be gauged while the speech or illustration was in progress. As such, the performance, content and Coleridge's famous 'manner' could be finely judged, in the first instance by the speaker, to produce a desired effect. But it should be remembered that a judgement of the propriety of the remarks or rhetoric used was also demanded of the forces of authority present. Indeed, the advert for Pack, Tom Jackson (another associate) and Stewart contained in *The Parsons' Doom* described them as 'The Unholy Trinity' and implored the public to ask for the 'the Lecturers who command large crowds' and the lecturers who 'create a sensation when they speak'.

In activating the local forces of order and morality all of these cases opened up once again a distinction between provincial and metropolitan attitudes and, it should not be underestimated, ways of perceiving and protecting morality. Stewart and Gott, in particular, through their actions were able to demonstrate a heightened need for awareness of the issues inherent in an offence like blasphemy. Likewise others felt they needed to protect morality in the environs of Edwardian Leeds – as we shall see with mixed results. This demonstrated that the application of the law, if not partially applied, at the very least exhibited the personal stamps of those who policed it at the highest level.

In some previous accounts the importance of this context has been overshadowed in the discussion of legal precedents set during this period most particularly in the Bowman case. Bradlaugh-Bonner, somewhat optimistically, saw the decision in this to refute objections to a secularist bequest as accepting that criticism of religion was valid, ending once and for all the 'part and parcel' argument.[15] Whilst this was clearly important we should not forget the other side of this equation – the lingering potential for an explosive and immediate moral panic. For the authorities, confronted by Gott, Pack, Stewart and Boulter, such men represented a serious and real moral danger. They combined attacks upon the scriptures with the supposedly profligate and indiscriminate spread of birth control ideas, literature and appliances. To understand

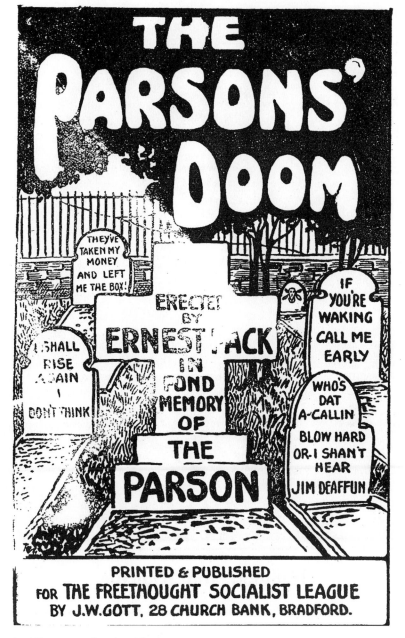

5.2   The cover of Pack's 'The Parsons' Doom'

Religion and Ridicule.

5.3   Portrait of Ernest Pack, from the cover of 'A Blasphemer on Blasphemy'

PETER DISCOVERS A LACK OF FAITH.

But when he saw the wind boisterous, he was afraid: and beginning to sink, he cried, saying, Lord, save me. —Matt. xiv., 29, 30.

5.4 Matthew xiv, 29, 30, from *The Truthseeker* (various editions)

this panic is to go part of the way to understanding the importance of the cases covered in this chapter.

John Gott has proved an elusive man for historians. His appearances in the Labour and Socialist papers of the period are tantalisingly enigmatic and his own journalistic enterprises were themselves idiosyncratic and lacking the formal systematic approach of even the most outrageous satirical work of the previous generation. His newspaper *The Truthseeker* was published sporadically from 1894 onwards and often alternated between an existence as a text-orientated journal to periods as a repository for collections of cartoons and pictorial depictions which rendered it more or less an occasional adult pamphlet. Despite the *ad hoc* nature of the periodical many of the cartoon's design and execution were infinitely more sophisticated and impressive than the rather amateurish examples that Foote had borrowed from Taxil and elaborated upon. Once again traditional accounts of the Gott episode have concentrated upon the scurrility of the work which brought him to court and have neglected the more serious critiques of Christianity and depiction of freethought ideology that was also part of his journalistic canon. Whilst he could have a customary tilt at various clerical stereotypes – an idea he clearly borrowed from Foote (long after Foote himself had borrowed it) – he was also capable of cartoons that celebrated the philosophy of Thomas Paine or the genuinely moving 'The Cry of Mankind' which depicted humankind cast adrift in a malevolent universe shackled to superstition.

Gott's business arrangements were scarcely more orthodox. *The Truthseeker* contained regular adverts for Gott's clothing business which started life as a tailoring shop and gradually evolved into a full scale clothing club. These adverts in some respects provide a partial insight into Gott's idiosyncratic world. Gott advertised the sale of birth control and Malthusian pamphlets such as J. R. Holmes's *Theory and Practice of Neo-Malthusianism*, Allan Laidlaw's *Sexual Love* and Seklew's *Liberty Luminants* (the last of these selling supposedly 600 copies at one meeting alone) alongside more established freethought staples by Haeckel, Laing and Tyndall. These adverts appeared with those promoting Gott's clothing business which sold 'Special Parcels' of cheap clothes combined with textile remnants. This business eventually specialised in employing freethinkers who had been turned out of other employment. He had agents throughout the West Riding, the North East, the North West and London as well as having outposts in Scotland. Occasionally the two areas of Gott's business would meet when his special parcels would be completed by the inclusion of his cheap tea and a 'parcel of advanced literature'. The precise nature of the literature involved is hard to discern and it may be that this route constituted a

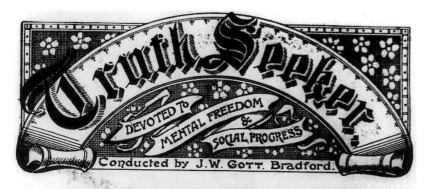

THOMAS PAINE.

Reprinted from The Truthseeker published at 28, Lafayette Place, New York, U.S.A.

The Truthseeker is published on the 1st of each month, and can be had from all Newsagents, TO ORDER; or post free, 12 months, for 1/6, from The Truthseeker Company, 36, Villiers Street, Bradford, Yorks.
Wholesale London Agents: Freethought Publishing Co., and A. & H. Bradlaugh Bonner.

5.5 Gott commemorates Tom Paine, from *The Truthseeker* (various editions)

THE CRY OF MANKIND.

a   'The Cry of Mankind', from *The Truthseeker* (various editions)

HOW MANKIND IS CRUCIFIED BETWEEN TWO THIEVES.

b   'How mankind is crucified between two thieves', from *The Truthseeker* (various editions)

5.6   *The Truthseeker* was prepared, however, to use cartoons for the graphic display of serious sentiment and argument

c   'Faith', from *The Truthseeker* (various editions)

method of distributing material that would have attracted even greater
police attention.

   Nonetheless it was also certainly true that Gott, Pack and Stewart
hardly did their best to avoid the attention of the authorities. An
example of this quest for public attention and interest is furnished by an
incident which Ernest Pack turned into a *Truthseeker* pamphlet. By 1903
the 'triumvirate' were already well known to the police and authorities
when a case was brought to court in Leeds under the Town's 1842
Improvement Act.[16] The prosecution, however, made a distinct mess of
presenting the evidence against Pack. The dates of the alleged offence
mentioned on the different summonses laid against Gott, Pack and
another associate George Weir were at odds with one another. Likewise
the procedure regarding the marking of the purchased copies of the
pamphlet broke down in court as witnesses could not identify precisely
the copies they had purchased. The prosecution withdrew its case and
left hanging in the air the suggestion that the proceedings and at least
part admonishment of the defendants had served their purpose. Pack's
response was to goad the authorities further by seeking to prolong their
pursuit of him. With obvious annoyance at being cheated of his 'fun' he
avowed to carry on selling the prosecuted pamphlet and went out of his
way to identify his opinions with those contained in the offending
edition of *The Truthseeker*. Most potently of all he questioned in court

a   'Tools for Making Christians', from *The Truthseeker* (various editions)

b   'Why the Devil can't I be saved?', from *The Truthseeker* (various editions)

5.7   Gott's version of the casual encounter

whether the police were sufficiently qualified to regulate opinions and attitudes or if they were simply the tool of other malevolent interests. His subsequent pamphlet reporting the case contained a letter from George Jacob Holyoake who reiterated this sentiment:

> Policemen are very excellent persons in their place, but as theological judges they are detestable.... Policemen are examined in muscle – not in theology.... The fact is that they are put forward by persons who are ashamed to appear themselves.[17]

Holyoake's letter also reiterated the prevailing objection entertained by secularists that 'there is more coarseness in the Bible and more blasphemy in some branches of Christianity than was ever spoken on Woodhouse Moor or printed in Bradford'.[18] Likewise Pack responded by quoting Ingersoll's litany upon the evils of blasphemy which justified attacks upon Christian culture and its shaky presumption in defending the supposed beliefs of a potentially uncommited majority against a committed and vocal minority:

> To persecute the intelligent few at the command of the ignorant many; that is blasphemy
> To forge chains; to build dungeons for your honest fellow man; that is blasphemy
> To pollute the souls of children with the dogma of eternal pain; that is blasphemy.[19]

From this unfortunate prosecution the authorities learned a hard lesson which they were to digest locally for a number of years, however their scrutiny of the activities of Pack, Gott and Stewart did not end here. The Pack prosecution was followed in February 1908 by the arrest of a London lecturer named Harry Boulter for speeches delivered in Islington which denied the existence of Christ and an at least semi-intentional threat to kill anyone Boulter found to be a Christian. This case was presided over by Justice Philimore and it was clear from the first that Boulter's primary offence had been the dissemination of his views, although clearly a public order dimension was also present in the apparent threat to the safety of Christians.[20] Philimore's reconfirmation of the Coleridge decency test was to be reiterated in Home Office memos which surveyed the blasphemy laws when they were discussed in the 15 years which followed. When Boulter reneged on the terms of his discharge by repeating his blasphemy he was imprisoned for a month, once again drawing press and parliamentary attention.

Boulter built upon Foote's rhetoric of confinement and was able to demonstrate just how obstructive and mischievous the blasphemer could be during the course of his imprisonment – even entitling a later report of the experience 'How I fell among thieves'.[21] Boulter's 'plight' reached J. M. Robertson who also received notice that he had been refused books of secular instruction, given inadequate opportunities for exercise and had been insulted by the prison chaplain. Robertson noted rather caustically that 'Insulting the freethinker I suppose, the chaplain might regard as part of his duties but here again he should be either silent or treat all his prisoners alike'.[22] Whilst in itself this mischief amounted to very little it did occur around the time when other correspondents chose to write to the Home Office on the matter of blasphemy. Alf Carrick, later to campaign vigorously on the matter, noted that the maintenance of the laws which within two months were to trap Boulter, were related to the enduring conception that religion and morality were linked.

> You might reply that a belief in religion is necessary to morality. I do not say you believe this, but I meet the objection should it be raised. Religion and morality are quite distinct from each other, both in their origin and in their contents. Religion has often been opposed to morality, and the opposition of morality to religion has been a vital element in every progressive movement of mankind. Ruskin in his 'Lectures on Art' pointed out the importance of distinguishing the idea of religion from the idea of morality; the former signifying 'the feelings of love, reverence or dread with which the human mind is affected by its conception of spiritual being' while the latter is the 'law of rightness in human conduct'. It is possible for people who sincerely reject Christianity to live upright and honourable lives.[23]

The polarisation of opinion in this area is, however, also demonstrated by the reply to this petition which emphasised that blasphemy outbursts bear some comparison with slander, obscenity, libel and indecency. Seeking to refute the accusation that only opinions were being attacked the Home Office emphasised that it was playing a game of expediency with morality and public order. Since the number of potential beneficiaries of blasphemous publication could not be matched in number with those outraged by the offending material thus, like its libellous and obscene counterparts, it should be prevented from public forums. Once again parallels with the Foote case and its wider public order and morality concerns are instructive. The same Edwardian period Home Office files contain urgent letters from police authorities in Birmingham who were concerned about the implications of inflamatory public speeches – two of which had recently occurred. One resulting in an unemployed mob storming the Council House in an attempt to force entry whilst another was made a few nights later by a contingent of unemployed who had arrived from Manchester. Similarly an inflammatory speech which linked the recent assassination of the King of Portugal to the possibility of a similar act in Britain was also reported at length and conceivably once more drew the link with anarchist activity made earlier in the decade.[24] Likewise Thomas William Stewart's activities in Birmingham were caught in the spotlight of this attention.

The Chief Constable C. H. Rafter had ensured notes were taken of speeches which might be 'of a blasphemous or treasonable nature' but was sensible enough to place the offence in perspective by staying his hand in case too much unwelcome attention was drawn to the matter.

Stewart's scrutiny by the authorities was to bear fruit for both of them in his arrest again in 1911 when the authorities at Leeds proceeded against him. Stewart, who by now went under the lecturing *nom de plume* of 'Dr Nikola', had combined his freethought lectures with advertising consultations on methods of birth control and the treatment of sexually transmitted diseases. This time Stewart and Gott were indicted for separate offences. Stewart's was for addressing the crowd on '... impious, blasphemous and profane matters' whilst Gott had been summonsed for selling at the same meeting a self-published comic pamphlet *Rib Ticklers or Questions for Parsons*. This particular pamphlet is hard to assess in terms of its intentions although most historians dismiss it as a piece of juvenilia.[25]

Once again the direction of the case, at both committal and assizes, turned around the authenticity of the evidence – in particular the originality of notes taken of Stewart's speech. But three interesting and ultimately related emphases emerged from this case. Firstly, in their writings in support of their action both Gott and Stewart in *The Truthseeker* demonstrated that they entertained a rather different interpretation of the Coleridge dictum than that which prevailed in legal circles. A particularly verbose article written under the pseudonym S—B publicised what it considered to be the widely-held opinion amongst secularists that the views of Coleridge had 'given the coup-de-grace to the perfidious and musty old statutes of the third William'. There was a clear confusion as to which laws the atheist's lectures were being prosecuted under since, when Stewart refused to desist from lecturing, a second information laid against him was framed as though it were a part of statute law. Whilst there was considerable misunderstanding in both camps on this matter the overriding impression given is that men like Gott and Stewart believed that the Coleridge dictum provided them with unequivocal protection rather than offering a sophisticated and refined decency test. At his trial Stewart reiterated the opinion that the case-law established by Coleridge's acceptance of Starkie, reconfirmed by Philimore in the Boulter case and Justice Darling in 1909, led him to believe that his utterance of the relevant opinions expressed at this meeting was legal.[26]

The precise nature of these opinions was the subject of a second area of intense dispute which the case highlighted. Stewart had addressed the crowd on the apparent injustice of the doctrine of salvation and faith – a popular freethought argument which Foote had illustrated graphically with his cartoon 'Going to Glory'. He postulated that his honest denial of the scriptures (despite a, to his mind, moral life) would lead the Almighty to throw him over the battlements of heaven. His supplication was followed in his speech by a representation of that offered by Dr Crippen. Crippen's acceptance of scripture, his acceptance of the Catholic Church's offer of resurrection and exhibition of shameless wit on the subject of murdering his wife in the knowledge that the Almighty would look after her would prove acceptable and he would be, in Stewart's words, 'given a harp'. From this exposition of the injustice of salvation Stewart concluded that 'God is not fit company for a respectable man like me ... I would rather be in hell with honest men!'[27]

Thirdly, Stewart's defence turned interestingly upon the fact that public opinion and the opinion of numerous local authorities had not intervened against these self-same opinions which had openly been expressed for many years. He produced a number of witnesses including Ernest Pack and George Weir who testified both that Stewart had used the same words on numerous previous occasions and that their substance had been published in a work, *Mistakes of Moses*, by Robert Ingersoll. In some respects Stewart had a legitimate point to make here. If the material had been exposed to the gaze of the public in both written and oral form on many separate occasions then questions had simply to be asked about the occasion which had led to prosecution. Justice Horridge, however, appeared to wave aside Stewart's assertion that the previous airings of his views which had not resulted in breaches of the peace were 'not in any way conclusive'. What the defendants may have been justified in asking was whether there was something particularly different about the Leeds of 1911? An answer in the affirmative would be an admission of two things of which secularists would have required to take considerable heed. If Leeds *was* different then the court and public opinion should take account of whether specific interests were motivated against Stewart and were able to shelter behind the notion of public opinion. The second and perhaps more serious point was to emphasise that if public opinion had hardened against Stewart in Leeds then this was a clear indication that the spirit which underlay the Common Law of Blasphemy was significantly misplaced. The Leeds prosecution appeared to demonstrate that the law and its interpretation could become conservative as much as follow the path of progressive liberality which lay behind the essence of the Coleridge judgment and its subsequent reconfirmations.

In his summing up Justice Horridge began reasonably enough with a reiteration of the Coleridge decency test and suggested that:

> ... the law of England has advanced very much – people are allowed unlimited freedom of thought and expression as long as that expression is given vent to in language which I will call for the moment, decent... .[28]

However the summing up then took a distinctly different turn which outflanked Stewart's optimistic assertion about how far the liberal assumptions of the Coleridge dictum could be pushed in practice. Horridge introduced to his summing up a consideration of the context in which the expression of opinion actually occurred. He suggested Stewart was

> ... free to speak what he likes as to religious matters, even if it is offensive, but when we come to consider whether he has exceeded the limits, we must not forget the place where he speaks, and the persons to whom he speaks. A man is not free in a public place to use common ridicule on subjects which are sacred to most people in this country; he is free to use argument.[29]

Horridge continued by asking the jury to decide whether the words of Stewart constituted 'a fair discussion on a religious subject', drawing particular attention to his use of the word 'respectable' in the phrase 'God is not fit company for a respectable man like me.' Horridge then emphasised that the jury should remind themselves that such sentiments were expressed in a public place and that they must decide whether they were 'maliciously said for the purpose of hurting the feelings of any religious people who might be near'. Whilst the Rationalist Press Association's *Literary Guide* argued that this made blasphemy '... neither more nor less than the crime of vulgarity'[30] the Home Office itself was particularly comforted by a passage which was underlined in the notes of the case. This once again represented what could legitimately be judged to be the most succinct expression of informed legal opinion.

> Therefore you see as long as you express yourself in argument, as long as you express yourself calmly, you may attack anything you like. The question is whether you have used language for the purpose of annoying religious people – language which is likely to irritate, and lead possibly to even a breach of the peace by religious minded feelings being hurt to such an extent by the language used. So long as it is kept within fair limits, there is no annoyance.[31]

From the defendants' point of view, and arguably that of all secularists, Horridge's summing up also contained the extraordinary statement that he was

> ... always glad that a jury has to decide these questions, because they have not got to give reasons for their decisions. They have not got to justify them in argument.[32]

In some respects this represented a significant move towards what was to become the supremacy of public opinion in the matter of blasphemy. Horridge's pronouncement went further in downgrading the notion of the 'spirit of the age' which had motivated defences since Foote's, as well as further marginalising any expert evidence presented from literary texts. This principle was replaced by the notion of jurymen deciding the level of offence on the basis of what Horridge described as 'common sense'. However, what was undisclosed here was that juries were also able to reflect wider societal changes in both secular and religious directions. Just as jury members were absolved from sharing their legal opinions they were equally absolved from having to justify or defend any religious opinions and feeling that they held.

In the event the jury decided – without leaving the stand – that Stewart and Gott were both guilty. Stewart was sentenced to three months imprisonment without hard labour whilst Gott was imprisoned for four months. Stewart reiterated Foote's famous thank you and its attack upon Christianity, adding an interesting gloss in the words '... and great may be your reward in Heaven'. Whilst this was obviously a premeditated squib there was nonetheless a serious side to this phrase which emanated through the press reports to the rest of England. Perhaps blasphemers really considered that judges believed they were doing the Lord's work and would certainly have heightened the concern of secularists who felt threatened by Christian culture. Moreover for them it visibly pulled the rug from under any notion that the law was theologically tolerant and presided over by those who were impartial.

Meanwhile blasphemy was increasingly being considered a public order problem and this was perhaps related to the growing levels of civil disobedience and unrest which characterised the years immediately preceding the First World War. Boulter was again arrested and imprisoned whilst the Bradford and Leeds agitation was carried further by Tom Jackson who made the connection with the government's wider concerns, seeing the blasphemy prosecutions as '... a malignant resolve to repress a rising tide of proletarian militancy'.[33] Jackson also claimed that the pursuit of the attention of the authorities was '... simply to force them to prosecute and imprison, prosecute and imprison, until they got sick and tired of doing it'.[34] Although Tom Jackson eventually got his wish the authorities in Leeds and elsewhere continued their policy of rooting out blasphemy in its guise of public order threat. Jackson's appearance before the Leeds' Stipendiary Magistrate – the first ever under the Town Police Clauses Act of 1847 – ended in a brief imprisonment whilst Jackson's own stubbornness also led to further prosecution.[35] The Nottingham branch of the NSS had to endure the imprisonment of two of its members, D. C. Muirhead and Frederick Chasty, after an address at an open air meeting. Likewise another lecturer, Stephen Edward Bullock, who had learned his trade as a public orator with the Church Army, was arrested after a lecture at Rotherham which resulted in three months imprisonment, again meted out by the Leeds assizes.[36]

Both Gott and Stewart attracted the attention of the authorities once again as publisher and orator respectively; Gott for the new pamphlet *The*

Parsons' Doom which also included the earlier *Rib Ticklers* pamphlet. This time the Home Secretary advised against prosecution of the publication on the grounds that it would do more harm than good but emphasised the growing concern of blasphemy as a public order problem.[37] Further perusal of the pamphlets led the Home Office in some interesting directions. Leading civil servants who prepared the briefing documents on the pamphlet argued that the 'vulgarity of their production' was so intense that they could only be produced with financial gain in mind. This was a startling admission which further emphasises the extent to which the Home Office was starting to panic. It demonstrated the long-discussed gulf between the mores of polite society and the street corner in exceptionally sharp relief. Moreover it postulated for the official mind the existence of a sub-culture devoted to the ridicule and vilification of established moral values and assumptions – one that was prepared to put ideas like neo-malthusian family limitation into practice. If Gott, Pack and Stewart were motivated by financial gain then there was clearly an avid and worrying market for their wares of all kinds. The connection between the actions of Gott and moral concerns were emphasised by Home Office scrutiny of Gott's bookstock mentioned in the pamphlet. The numerous works of Neo-Malthusianism which Gott had advertised rather transparently as 'Red Hot Stuff' led the Home Office to take action since they were 'contrary to all good morals'.[38] So worried was the Home Office that the briefing papers asserted that allowing private prosecution by members of the public to regulate the matter was not enough. The view taken suggested that

> The matter seems to be one of which the Home Office should take official cognisance and in which it should assume some responsibility. If Gott has contumaciously repeated the offence for which he was successfully prosecuted by the Leeds Police the necessity of enforcing respect for the law seems to require that the matter should be referred to the Director of Public Prosecutions for his observations on the advisability of a further prosecution.[39]

From this point onwards the Chief Constables of Bradford and Leeds were asked to keep a closer watch on Gott, Pack and Stewart lest it be required that they move against them. Perhaps ironically, when a local authority next moved against Stewart it was at Wolverhampton in 1913. A number of police officers took verbatim notes of Stewart's speech and their survival in the Home Office papers gives the historian a clear sense of their content. They appeared to mix spontaneity with an established set of anecdotes that once again possibly owed much to music hall comedy. What is also evident from these notes is that they contained material which both the police and Home Office considered blasphemous, evident from extensive underlining:

> You who are Christians believe in the Nicene or Apostles Creed – 'I believe in God the father almighty maker of heaven and earth, and in Jesus Christ his only son our Lord who was conceived by the holy Ghost born *of the Virgin Mary, suffered under Pontius Pilate, was crucified dead and buried. He descended into hell – and stopped there for the weekend (laughter) – Do you Christians believe that was so?' On the third day he rose from the dead went up to Heaven and sat on the right hand of himself* (laughter).[40]

Potential threats to public order were present in the form of hecklers whose remarks were reported in these same notes. However what really served to link blasphemy in this instance to obscenity was that Stewart's wife was selling birth control literature, by application, at the meeting. This was compounded by Stewart referring to his activities as a medical advisor in potentially offensive terms: '... Every child is an accident... *God doesn't send them. If he does I have beaten him something like 200,000 times.*'[41]

Moreover Stewart's wife also distributed information about a subsequent meeting to be held behind closed doors at which family limitation and the prevention and cure of sexually transmitted diseases would be discussed. All told Stewart was indicted on four counts – three of these were ostensibly obscenity charges linked to the offer for sale of the neo-malthusian pamphlets whilst the last was a charge of blasphemy. In the event it was only on the last of these that Stewart was convicted, receiving a sentence of four months.

The feeling amongst much informed public opinion was that whilst Stewart had been publically acquitted of the obscenity charges some element of them was effectively present in the blasphemy conviction, a view which a glance at Home Office opinion on the verdict seems to vindicate:

> There is nothing illegal in the sale of such goods nor do I think the pamphlet could properly be held to be indecent but the fact that 'blasphemy' is used to push such a trade is a very material point in estimating the bona fides or otherwise of the blasphemer.[42]

The Home Secretary Reginald Mckenna himself even used the connection with obscenity as a means of refusing a remission of Stewart's sentence. The resulting adjournment debate allowed Arthur Lynch to observe that Labour members and their supporters 'may infringe some of the obsolete Acts of which the British Constitution is full... obsolete Acts which are brought out of the darkness after 500 years to punish political opponents'.[43]

A campaign to release Stewart sent numerous petitions to the Home Office. The Metropolitan Secular Society staged an open air meeting to protest against the sentence which was attended by over 5000 people.

The fruit of this meeting was an extensive petition calling for Stewart's release and the repeal of the laws. A copy of this same petition was received from the RPA signed by Sidney Webb, Arnold Bennet, Flinders Petrie, Edward Carpenter, Walter Crane, Gilbert Murray, Graham Wallas, Bertrand Russell and a number of Oxford and Cambridge academics.

The appearance of Gilbert Murray on this petition was interesting since the Home Office files contain a letter of Murray's to the *Nation* newspaper which vindicated the view that the conviction for blasphemy was unconnected to any stigma of obscenity. Anxious to placate public opinion this letter was clearly kept in reserve by the government to be produced when needed. Whilst it must have comforted the government, with the passage of time it appears to demonstrate that the cleave between polite and popular street culture was widening. Of particular disquiet to freethinkers would have been Murray's lack of surprise or indeed lack of concern for this state of affairs:

> one must certainly admit that they [the lectures]were not uttered in a purely scientific spirit; they are rough, popular and controversial, intended to raise laughter, intended to irritate or confound. They do not show much critical spirit or good taste. *But there is nothing obscene; nothing, in the ordinary sense of the word, immoral; certainly, no language which I can conceive as deserving the serious notice of the law.*[44]

*　　*　　*

Gott continued to offend throughout the war, serving sentences in 1916, 1917 and 1918. His last, and most serious, offence which brought him dramatically to public attention was in 1922 when *Rib Ticklers* surfaced again in a case of obstruction which later became one of blasphemy. The material which landed Gott in trouble on this occasion was his comparison of Christ to a circus clown entering Jerusalem on two donkeys. The case was distinctive because of Justice Avory's pronouncement that the pamphlet did not need to cause a breach of the peace but had only to contain the possibility of doing so, even upon reflection. Avory indicated that if those of strong religious beliefs and the community in general were protentially moved to act then the matter was blasphemous. Avory's summing up also extended the influence of both the casual encounter and inflated sense of melodrama which the Coleridge judgment had encapsulated through its heightened sense of the 'manner' in which offence occurred.

> You must put it to yourself, supposing you received by post some abominable libel upon yourself ... what is your first instinct? Is not the instinct of every man who is worthy of the name of a man – the

instinct is to thrash the man or the woman who has written a libel on him? and that is why the law says that it is calculated to provoke a breach of the peace... . You must ask yourself if a person of strong religious feelings had stopped to read this pamphlet whether his instinct might not have been to go up to the man who was selling it and give him a thrashing, or at all events to use such language to him that a breach of the peace might be likely to be occasioned, because that would be quite sufficient to satisfy this definition.[45]

As a result Gott was sentenced to nine months in prison with hard labour and remains to this day the last individual to be imprisoned for blasphemy. At appeal Avory's opinion and the sentence were confirmed and it should be noted that the Criminal Justice Administration Act of 1914 had made the application of hard labour as a component of sentencing discretionary.[46] In particular the Chief Justice's opinion rested on how far Gott's sentiments would inflame even a mild sympathiser with Christianity – as such his opinions were judged to be a threat to the community and a threat to public order. Leonard Levy points out that this was significant since the Coleridge decency test had left the matter of public order and breach of the peace as an open question. Likewise he observed that this state of affairs invoked the spectre of police and public order protection for Anglicanism whilst breaches of the peace occasioned by attacks on Catholics or Jews would have to be covered more clumsily under other legislation.[47] As Levy suggests, the notion of likelihood to provoke breaches of the peace as a cornerstone of the offence made prosecution and conviction considerably easier – indeed, it potentially opened the way for individuals to be so offended by all manner of atheist propaganda as to undertake violence. This case moved Courtney Kenny to produce his famous examination of the law pertaining to blasphemy which begins by noting precisely this change.[48]

The campaigns of Gott, Pack and Stewart were relentless and single-minded and cost them considerably in time, money and energy. Gott suffered most, with the death of his wife during one imprisonment and the cruel shortening of his own life during the 1921–22 imprisonment. Tom Jackson's hope that their campaign would make blasphemy prosecutions seem ridiculous was, to say the least, counterproductive. All three defendants were regarded as dangerous threats to public order and were linked in the official and increasingly the popular mind to all sorts of other moral and political conspiracies. Whilst Gott may have been the only one left engaged in this activity by 1921 he was still proving the laws were workable and in regular use. Worse still, the action taken against him left the law arguably more draconian in its potential operation than it had been at the start of the Edwardian period. A clear irony was that before the Avory judgment the campaign of these

J. W. Gott, as A4.32, Armley Gaol.

5.8   Gott in prison uniform surrounded by his publications, from *The Truthseeker* (various editions)

individuals had gone some way towards highlighting the iniquity of the law. As a result lawyers and members of government circles were persuaded that the law was more of an embarrassment than a worthwhile form of legal protection for religion. Whilst the wishes of government and its advisors to extricate themselves from a clearly harsh situation were admirable their ability to produce a satisfactory solution was to be tested beyond endurance. These attempts to find a legislative solution to the problem, against the backdrop of the campaigns of Boulter, Pack, Stewart and Gott, forms the substance of the next chapter.

Notes

1. Nash, D. S. (1995), 'Unfettered Investigation' – the Secularist Press and the Creation of Audience in Victorian England', *Victorian Periodicals Review*, Summer.
2. Royle, E. (1980), *Radicals, Secularists and Republicans: Popular Freethought in Britain, 1866–1915*, Manchester: Manchester University Press, p. 63.
3. Dawson, O. (1895), *The Bar Sinister and Licit Love. The first biennial proceedings of the Legitimation League*, London; Dawson, O. (1897), *Personal Rights and Sexual Wrongs*, London; Oliver, H. (1983), *The International Anarchist Movement in Late Victorian London*, Beckenham: Croom Helm, pp. 144–5.
4. Calder-Marshall, Arthur (1972), *Lewd, Blasphemous and Obscene*, London: Hutchinson, pp. 193–229.
5. Micklewright, F. H. Amphlett (1961), 'The Rise and Decline of English Neo-Malthusianism', *Population Studies*, XV: pp. 32–51; Standring, G. (1914), 'Reminiscent Notes on the Neo-Malthusian Movement', *The Malthusian*, XXXVIII (3, 15 March): pp. 19–20; Standring, G. (1919), 'Memories and Musings of an Old Malthusian', *The Malthusian*, XLIII (9, 15 September): p. 69; Standring, G. (1919), 'Memories and Musings of an Old Malthusian', *The Malthusian*, XLIII (6, 15 June): pp. 43–4.
6. Royle, op. cit.; Budd, Susan (1971), *Varieties of Unbelief*, London: Heinemann.
7. Nash, David S. (1991), 'F. J. Gould and the Leicester Secular Society: a Positivist Commonwealth in Edwardian Politics', *Midland History*, 16: pp. 126–40.
8. Pack, E. (n.d.), *The Parsons' Doom*, Bradford: Freethought Socialist League, p. 13.
9. Royle, op. cit., p. 225.
10. *The Truthseeker*, July 1904.
11. Avrich, Paul (1984), *The Haymarket Tragedy*, Princeton: Princeton University Press.
12. DeLeon, D. (1978), *The American as Anarchist: Reflections on Indigenous Radicalism*, London: Johns Hopkins University Press, pp. 81–2.
13. Moses Harman himself had in fact gone through a phase immediately prior to the Haymarket bomb incident in which he saw dynamite as a social panacea. See Sears, Hal D. (1977), *The Sex Radicals: Free Love in High Victorian America*, Kansas: The Regents Press.

14. Aldred, G. A. (1948), *Rex v. Aldred*, Glasgow: Strickland Press; Aldred, G. A. (1955), *No Traitor's Gait! The Autobiography of Guy A. Aldred*, Glasgow: Strickland Press.
15. Bradlaugh-Bonner, Hypatia (1934), *Penalties Upon Opinion*, Watts & Co., p. 127. This case effectively ended the prohibition on bequeathing legacies for secularist purposes.
16. *The Truthseeker*, September 1903.
17. Pack, E. (1904), *A 'Blasphemer' on 'Blasphemy'. The latest Leeds Police Fiasco*, Bradford: Freethought Socialist League, p. 4.
18. Ibid., p. 5.
19. Ibid.
20. Bradlaugh-Bonner, op. cit., p. 118.
21. *The Truthseeker* 1911.
22. HO 144 871/160552 Robertson to Home Office, 17 July 1909.
23. HO 144 871/160552 Carrick to Home Office, 9 January 1908.
24. HO144 871/160552/20.
25. Royle, op. cit., pp. 279–80; Levy, Leonard W. (1993), *Blasphemy: Verbal Offense Against the Sacred from Moses to Salman Rushdie*, New York: Knopf, p. 502.
26. HO45 10665/216120/18.
27. Ibid., Pack, E. (n.d.), *The Trial and Imprisonment of J. W. Gott for Blasphemy*, Bradford: Freethought Socialist League, p. 31.
28. HO45 10665/216120/18.
29. Ibid.
30. *Watt's Literary Guide*, 1 January 1912.
31. HO45 10665/216120/18.
32. Ibid.
33. Morton, Vivienne and Stuart Macintyre (1979), *T. A. Jackson, A Centenary Appreciation*, London: History group of the Communist Party, p. 9.
34. Ibid.
35. Bradlaugh-Bonner, op. cit., p. 124.
36. Ibid., Royle, op. cit., p. 280.
37. HO45 10665/216120/49.
38. Ibid.
39. Ibid.
40. Ibid., testament of Bernard William Molton, 29 September 1913. (Italicised words underlined in the original.)
41. Ibid. (Italicised words underlined in the original.)
42. HO 45 10665/216120/59.
43. Hansard, 23 February 1914.
44. HO45 10665/216120/59. (Italicised words underlined in the Home Office original.)
45. R v. Gott 16 Criminal Appeal Reports 87, 1922.
46. Bradlaugh-Bonner, op. cit., p. 125.
47. Levy op. cit., p. 502.
48. Kenny, Courtney (1922), 'The Evolution of the Law of Blasphemy', *Cambridge Law Journal*, 1: pp. 127–42.

CHAPTER SIX

Attempts at Repeal and Extension: 1913–38

The question of what to do with the blasphemy laws entered the agenda of secularists and government alike, with increased urgency as the Edwardian period drew to a close. Whilst the former asked for the final destruction of the dubious legal status of the offence the latter was increasingly persuaded to listen to these pleas. Indeed the Gott case of 1920/21 eventually provided further evidence that the law was neither impartial, clear, nor demonstrably acting within the interests of society at large.

That the precise letter of the law was not at all clear to many even informed Edwardians was emphasised in an illuminating exchange between George Greenwood, the Labour MP and the Home Secretary Reginald Mckenna in 1911. Greenwood, through a parliamentary question, drew Mckenna's attention to the two contrary interpretations of the blasphemy laws extant in different editions of J. F. Stephen's *Digest of Criminal Law*. This of course was the preamble for Greenwood to enquire whether an alteration of this state of affairs was pending or even contemplated. Whilst Mckenna fended off the enquiry and its implications various civil servants were canvassed for their opinions. These tended to dismiss the differences out of hand and to marginalise the notion of Stephen as a legitimate legal authority:

> J Stephen's view, if it was correct at any time, must now be regarded as an irrelevant archaism – there have been enough cases of blasphemy during the last 50 years to establish Coleridge's view (which Sir J. Stephen considered nonsense) beyond question.[1]

Greenwood, however, persisted and a written question noted that Stephen had inserted a rubric calling for parliamentary action to remedy the parlous state of the blasphemy laws expressly as a response to the Coleridge judgment against Foote. This statement also declared that Stephen believed the only real solution would be total abolition. Such a comment only appeared in the 1894 and subsequent editions, a fact which Mckenna put down to the eccentric editorial taste of Stephen's own son. Moreoever the effect of Mckenna undermining the Stephen criticism was to pronounce that the 'law may be regarded as settled'.[2]

The popular and substantially believed official notion that the law was 'settled', and perhaps more importantly irrelevant, was further emphasised in 1913 when a Bill to amend the blasphemy laws was discussed in Parliament. The Bill itself aimed at ensuring that '... no criminal proceedings shall be instituted in any court against any person for schism, heresy, blasphemy, blasphemous libel, or atheism'. In truth the Bill was aiming to equalise the legal status of atheist belief alongside both Anglicanism and other religious faiths. To this end it sought the repeal of elements contained within 1 Edw. 6 c. 1 (An Act against such persons as shall irreverently speak against the Sacrament of the Altar) as well as parts of the Elizabethan Acts of Supremacy and Uniformity – the second of these proposals would have abolished the penalties for acknowledging the Pope. Acts for uniformity of public prayer dating from Charles II's reign as well as 9 & 10 William were also targets as was the 1819 Criminal Libel Act (60 Geo 3. & 1 Geo 4. c. 8), from which the word blasphemous was to be removed. More controversial, in the light of the recent problems in Leeds and those connected with the Boulter case, was the proposal to remove the word 'profane' from the Metropolitan Police Act of 1839 (2 & 3 Vict. c. 47) and the Town Police Clauses Act of 1847 (51 & 52 Vict. c. 64).

Home Office commentaries on this putative legislation offered a curious mixture of complacency and alarm. It was noted that the bill would only be worth bothering with if members of the House could be convinced that the law was still likely to be used and that the question of blasphemy as opposed to blasphemous libel was of 'purely historical interest'. However the recent threats to public order in the guise of Gott, Pack et al. were recognised by the rejection of the proposal to repeal the Town Police Clauses Act. This was, however, seeking to prevent the construction of a serious, probably 'indefensible' legal anomaly:

> To the majority of persons who use the public streets profane language is quite as likely to be offensive as indecent or obscene language – and it would be unreasonable to say that persons who annoy inhabitants or passengers by the one should be punished, while persons who produce the same affect by the other shall have immunity![3]

Another commentator summed up the tenor of Home Office opinion of the Bill's intention when he asserted that 'no one would be the better for its repeal except those who want to make themselves offensive to their neighbours'. One other opinion from someone at the Home Office signing themselves H. B. suggested that repeal was totally unnecessary; that the law of blasphemy was far from obsolete since it was '... on the contrary a striking instance of the Common Law adapting itself to the times and changing in accordance with a general change of view in regard to religious matters'. Moreover H. B. considered that blasphemy was analogous to crimes such as sedition and treason whereby public expression of such opinions, with its obvious public order dimension, was intrinsic to the offence. This view was extended in his written memo which drew analogy with the law relating to defamatory libel to emphasise that the essence of the offence was the threat to public order.

> It is much the same with blasphemy, and blasphemous language of the kind that is prosecuted probably outrages the feelings of a much larger number of people than merely obscene language would; while a defamatory libel may be perfectly true, and offensive to the feelings of one individual only, but yet be criminal. If the religious views of the majority of the nation changed so much that blasphemy ceased to be offensive to them, juries which represent the average man would cease to convict. This is the safeguard against a harsh application of the law.[4]

This argument went further, in both confidence and complacency, to suggest that whilst it was, as a matter of principle, desirable for the law to protect all religious feeling the burden of experience suggested that it was only Christianity which was regularly attacked – 'if it were shown that aspersions on the Jewish religion were regular occurrences [then] a case could be made for extending the blasphemy laws'. He further asserted that the principle of the Common Law was itself embodied in the two extant public order statutes, the Metropolitan Police Act and the Town Police Clauses Act, and that this might usefully provide a platform for future treatment of the offence. If the blasphemy laws were to be abolished he admitted that the use of these two acts would effectively contain the potential public order problem. Moreover it was 'by no means a bad thing that juries should occasionally have an opportunity of showing by their verdicts the view they take of blasphemy, and that judges should lay down the law about it, *Procedure by indictment is an effective safeguard against an abuse of the law*'. This was followed by another reiteration of the Indian Code solution which would empower the courts to decide the legal status of individual religious sentiments.[5] This view is particularly intriguing. The latent support for the traditional notion of the English Common Law as responsively organic is here counterbalanced by an enduring belief in the power and desire of public opinion to uphold, sometimes retrospectively, Christian versions of morality. In this paradigm such public opinion did the law's thinking for it. Moreover the effectiveness of public order legislation was a convincing argument for excluding blasphemy from the public sphere and that this apparently offered protection to the blasphemers themselves.

Whilst this Bill failed during 1913 it was reintroduced in the next session of Parliament. This time Asquith himself took an interest and indicated that he was broadly in favour of repeal, since the existing Statute Law should be swept away since it served no useful purpose. Whilst Asquith considered the Common Law to be adequately constrained by the Coleridge judgment the Statute Laws, he concluded, should be clearly and quickly abolished. Their application appeared to him to be a lottery regarding prosecution and interpretation with the one obvious trend being the increasing likelihood of their enforcement against the 'comparatively ill-educated'. However he was also concerned that laws pertaining to breach of the peace and offensive/violent language should remain and that as long as this caveat was observed the Bill could expect government support, albeit with appropriate amendments in committee.[6]

This attempt to repeal the blasphemy law, like its predecessor, foundered due to lack of support and was overwhelmed by other government business. With the onset of war, questions of the defence of morality and public perceptions of it became paramount. Many of the attitudes of Edwardian England towards religious dissent were summed up by various provisions contained in the Defence of the Realm Act. Once again Gott found himself in the dock as a result of the rapidly changed atmosphere.

*   *   *

The post-war period witnessed further attempts to repeal the laws relating to blasphemy. The 1922 bill foundered whilst the 1923 bill introduced by Harry Snell at least received a second reading, despite instructions from the whips office to block it. Both these bills were identical to the 1913 bill but this time both had substantial support from the Labour members of the House. One conceivable motivation for this support, more important than Gott's quasi-socialist connections, was the resurrection of Foote's claim that the law worked partially against the uneducated and constituted an attack of freedom of speech and an enduring form of tyranny. The *Daily Herald* received a number of letters to this effect which it gleefully printed.[7] Once again the gulf of understanding emphasised by the Home Office's renewed assertion that the blasphemy laws were modern and acceptable was demonstrated in the context of the Gott case. Essentially this was a recognition that Gott had turned the matter from one of tolerance into one concerning the maintenance of public order. The Home Office expressed surprise at the introduction of a repeal bill in 1923, ostensibly on the same grounds that had influenced them in the pre-war period. As far as they were concerned the law was settled and the Gott case was so manifestly beyond the pale that they asserted with confidence:

that a man is not free in a public place where passers by, who might not willingly care to listen to him knowing what he was going to say, might accidentally hear his words, or where young people might be present – a man is not free in such places to use coarse ridicule on such subjects which are sacred to most people in this country such conduct might well lead to a breach of the peace from hot-headed believers.[8]

Once again the issue of the dichotomy between articulate commentary as opposed to mere lower-class contumely was central in the minds of civil servants. Uppermost was the urge to reiterate the summing up in the case against Gott which was invested with comfort for critics and despair for adherents. Justice Avory's summing up emphasised that Gott's publications could be dismissed as

> ... vilification, ridicule or irreverance of the Christian religion and of the scriptures. Is it in any sense argument? Is it in any sense within the bounds of decent controversy on religious subjects? Is it anything more than vilification of sacred subjects and contemptuous – contemptuous and insulting? ... Speakers who attack the Christian religion, or distribute pamphlets of that character, are not intellectual reasoners upon religious controversies. They select public places where decent orderly subjects resort, and indulge in, as the two last-mentioned cases indicate, language of a character likely to provoke a breach of the peace.[9]

This placing of Gott and his dialogue firmly beyond the pale had the effect of persuading the Home Office that repeal of the blasphemy law was in many respects irrelevant. Sir Charles Schuster was convinced that the Bill was a waste of Parliament's time, suggesting that the antique ecclesiastical authority cited in the Bill had effectively been dead for some time although he concluded that

> This being the law, it would be most unfortunate now to remove the prohibitions against, and the penalties for, blasphemy and blasphemous libel, whether at Common Law or by statute. 'If violent, offensive or indecent words' (per Lord Buckmaster at p. 470) are used, there is no reason why the offender should not be prosecuted. If they are not used, there is no offence.[10]

Despite the manifest refusal of Parliament to act the issue of blasphemy law repeal drifted on into the 1920s without resolution. By 1924 the Society for the Abolition of the Blasphemy Laws was already well versed in the arguments with which it was to confront the government of the day with frequent petitions on this occasion and hereafter. Chapman Cohen reiterated the established arguments that the laws were effectively an anachronism, that Coleridge's definition was at considerable variance with that accepted by statute law and that Christianity itself was discredited by the retention of such laws. These arguments were augmented by others which highlighted what the Society considered to be the unscrupulous use of its provisions. Drawing upon the distant rather than recent past Cohen pronounced that

> ... at times the Blasphemy Laws have been used, as towards the end of the eighteenth century and the beginning of the nineteenth, as a cover for preventing political agitation and obstructing the political education of the masses. ... It has also been used to prevent fulfilment of contracts made between christians and freethinkers. It has been used to prevent copyright in books. It has been used to prevent a parent having the custody of a child. It has also been used very frequently to prevent the paying over of legacies, when it was assumed that the legacies might be used for anti-christian propaganda.

Another strand of argument emphasised the uniqueness of blasphemy as an offence which appeared increasingly isolated within the general canon of the law. Cohen noted that blasphemy was the only area in English law policed by the notion of decency in the conduct of argument and that this, in itself, was a very one-sided debate with what he viewed as a predetermined outcome:

> The only person who can say whether his feelings have been wounded by a criticism is clearly a Christian. He is the prosecutor, he decides, he judges, he sentences. It is the only case where a thing like that occurs, and consequently it is, as Mr Asquith admitted some years ago, quite a partial law, one that can never demand the respect that all law should demand of citizens.[11]

The law was also demonstrated to be increasingly incompatible with notions of a free and pluralistic society when Cohen declared the protection of the Anglican church alone as a travesty which Catholics, Jews and Mohammedans should not accept. This suggestion that society was diversifying and that the law needed to accommodate this further was emphasised when Cohen suggested that blasphemy prosecutions came in waves. More importantly the Common Law did not actually prevent, despite what some who saw it as a defence of morality might argue, potentially blasphemous opinions from being held – privately or otherwise. Cohen argued that the Common Law actually acted as an incitement to transgress and provide psychological succour for diverse opinions. 'When a law is regarded as unjust it is never a great difficulty to find men who are ready and even eager to break it. It invites attack, and, as a matter of fact, I think it often gets it for that reason.'[12]

The influence of the Gott case was also present here although in truth it did not represent all of the arguments faithfully. Gott may have been straining at the leash of what was acceptable but this did not necessarily make him the vanguard of a new society. Moreover he could all too easily be dismissed by the hostile as a reason for the retention of the blasphemy laws personified. The deputation and its instigators the NSS were anxious to distance themselves from the manner of Gott's protest, declaring that their interest in his case 'was a matter of opinion which we had to defend'. Having made this disclaimer Cohen pressed the attack further, using the Gott case as an example of the inadvisability of applying the full rigour of the law.

Cohen then reminded the Home Secretary Arthur Henderson that this matter had been long overdue for action. Mckenna had promised an end to government-inspired prosecutions and had left a memo of his actions though neither had been acted upon. The Society's deputation to Henderson also included representatives of the liberal Christian viewpoint who echoed Cohen's assertion that the blasphemy laws discredited Christianity itself. The Revd Dr Walter Walsh went so far as to argue that the dictates of conscience and personal morality should be allowed free rein:

> If the opinions seem to the speaker to be pernicious, to be detrimental to human morals, and contrary to reason, he is even entitled, in my judgement, and I think I carry the whole deputation with me, to denounce anything that appears to him to be of the nature of superstition and to be likely to cloud the clear thinking and even to contaminate the ethical nature of persons who believe it.[13]

Walsh went on to suggest that religious iconoclasm was necessary for religious progress and that such liberty that existed had been produced by this very process. He called for an end to the state's ability to interfere in matters of tone since this had always been used by the law as an attempt to control scurrility rather than what he saw as debate.

> For example, a university don who is an expert in language, skilled in classical synonyms, and who understands the use of language, will very deftly and skilfully with a stiletto stab in the back some ecclesiastical dogma to which he may be pledged; do it so skilfully that few people will notice it, and the law certainly will take no account of it. But if a Hyde Park orator, carried away with enthusiasm, uses a bludgeon to assail the same superstition as his more cultured colleague, very likely he will be hauled up and panelled for blasphemy.[14]

Whilst this sought to point to the inequity of the law it failed to note that judges and chief constables really were interested in the use of the bludgeon, the whipping up of enthusiasm and the more explosive effect that these could have, and had previously had, on real audiences in real situations. Henderson's reponse to this deputation was, to say the least, disappointing. He, like Mackenna before him, expressed sympathy but was unable to offer parliamentary time for the matter. Thus blasphemy once more dropped out of parliamentary focus and was not to be seriously considered again until the end of the decade. George Lansbury introduced the same bill as had done the rounds in the early 1920s to parliament in each of the following four sessions. Whilst it reached a second reading on each occasion instructions from the Home Office strove to ensure that the bill would be overcome by other business. However there was also a significant groundswell of opinion which felt that repeal would create a potential hostage to fortune. In 1927, contemporaneous with yet another attempt to push Lansbury's bill beyond a first reading, was the Second Reading and debate of a bill which sought to prevent seditious and blasphemous teaching to children. This bill linked blasphemy with communist agitation in the guise of socialist forms of education which it considered to be a danger to the State. However, the need to unlock this connection was spotted and an amendment strove to remove the word blasphemous from the bill which itself foundered.[15]

When another repeal bill was introduced in 1929 the Home Secretary J. R. Clynes was confronted by another deputation which, in addition to Cohen and Walsh, included Graham Wallas, Harold Laski and the veteran reformers Canon Donaldson and Frederick Verinder. The deputation, which was introduced by Revd Reginald Sorensen, Free Church minister and Labour MP for Leyton, noted that nothing had changed since the previous deputation. Contained in this assertion was the presumption that the blasphemy laws and in particular the Common Law offence of blasphemous libel had been retained because its use was at least hypothetically contemplated. Sorensen carefully rehearsed the standard history of the offence, taking in a paraphrase of the Hale judgment and noting not only that the blasphemy as 'part and parcel' cornerstone argument was iniquitous, but also that it could be fatally destroyed by the disestablishment of the Anglican Church. The frailty of the Coleridge dictum was also discussed with, unsurprisingly, clear support for Stephen's view that the Coleridge interpretation was contrary to law and covered the denial of doctrines rather than the form of the denial. The, by now familiar, notion that the blasphemy laws were contrary to a perceived spirit of the age was given a new twist by the suggestion that the imprisonment of Carlile and his shopmen for publishing Paine's 'Age of Reason' would be 'quite temperate Higher Criticism, as it would now be called, of the Old Testament'. Whilst this at first sight appears a deft point to make such a view would have cut no ice with the Home Office's belief that the law itself had safely evolved since these incidents.

In arguing its case the deputation chose also to focus on what it perceived to be anomalies of interpretation concerned with the conduct and outcome of the Boulter case. Attention focused upon Justice

Philimore's embrace of the Coleridge dictum which appeared to sit rather uneasily with what the deputation described as the impression 'that the real offence was for him the offence of spreading opinions which he considered to be wicked'. Graham Wallas took the logic of this argument further when he suggested that Philimore had been disposed to treat Boulter lightly on the basis that his opinions had been spoken rather than written and that the publication of these opinions would have compounded the offence – a clear indication that the nature of the opinions constituted a significant part of the offence.[16]

Thus the application of the law was shown to be muddled, inconsistent and capable of almost arbitrary interpretation. Wallas suggested that the way forward would be for parliament to frame and enact laws relating to public peace which could be used to protect all religions. Although the Home Office would almost certainly have argued that other laws effectively operated in this manner anyway, Wallas's arguments had certainly shown that chinks in legal administrative practice and jurisprudence certainly existed. Moreover Wallas's parting shot was to reiterate Philimore's own comment that judges are entrusted with the administration of the law whether they like them or not and that such a situation was a further argument as to why the Common Law offence of blasphemy should not be left to judges to interpret.

Canon Donaldson, a former member of Stewart Headlam's Guild of Saint Matthew, reiterated the established spirit of the age motif and noted that the potential blasphemer could be exposed to corporal punishment. Such relics, he argued, when enacted, had a disproportionately damaging effect upon Christianity as well as lowering the overal sanctity of the law:

> ... we have learnt ... that there is a boomerang effect from any attempt to exercise this law; that is to say, it discredits religion infinitely in the minds of just and fair-minded people, and it does real harm to the cause of good in every direction, whether you name it by the name of God or not ... do not let us have a law which presumes that the Christian Faith is part of the English Statute book. ... I believe that I represent a very large body of clergy and laity in the Church of England in what I have said.[17]

This particular critique carried with it considerable power since clergymen could, in some senses, justly claim to speak for Christianity and to know better than the government about how to engage in defending it from its foes. However as we shall see the presumption by the clergy to speak with authority for their own laity and for nominally diffusive Christians could itself appear to be, on occasions, an anachronism.

Whilst Chapman Cohen substantially repeated his objections which he had voiced earlier in the decade, on this occasion he offered the charge that the law itself was a danger to moral values and was capable of being applied carelessly. Cohen further charged that the forces responsible for social progress in moral matters could simply find themselves swamped by a new tide of blasphemy prosecutions. In other words whilst the law remained a moveable feast then no opinion former, holder or disseminator could consider themselves to be beyond the reach of the law.[18] In reply the Home Secretary J. R. Clynes admitted that he was sympathetic to the cause of reform but closed the door to any government involvement in the issue. Instead he hoped that a private members' bill would be the answer since the composition of the Commons may have allowed the proposal to stand a decent chance. Although Clynes had pleaded that lack of time prevented the government from taking any action he was nonetheless strongly warned off by officials in the Home Office. In a document intended to brief Clynes for the meeting he was advised that repealing the statutes against blasphemy was an irrelevance whilst the operation of the Common Law offence could safely be left to the sound judgement and practice embodied in the Coleridge judgment and the case-law that it subsequently influenced. The decision to proceed with prosecutions was once again seen as regulated by the steady and trusted hand of public opinion. Whilst the old statutory provisions, it was admitted, would remove grievances concerning the one-sidedness of the law this course should only be followed '… *provided the law against speech or action tending to breach of the peace is safeguarded*'.[19]

This extremely important proviso was the axis around which Home Office objections to blasphemy repeal turned on this occasion. Alarm was expressed at the possible disappearance of the Common Law offence which, it was held, would prevent prosecutions against breaches of the peace which would henceforth only be punished by a magistrate's binding over order. The briefing paper also baulked at the description of the current law as 'this last obstacle to freedom of thought and speech' and suggested that the Society for the Abolition of the Blasphemy Laws be challenged to show that the current law was enforced unjustly. The only way the government should agree to take action was if the bill could be altered to keep alive the Common Law as explained by Justice Avory in the Gott case.

With a Labour victory the previous year, 1930 saw the bill considered in Cabinet as well as receive a second reading during which the labour member for Bermondsey Alfred Salter spoke movingly of the penalties meted out to his Quaker ancestors.[20] However, elements of the casual encounter appeared in misgivings offered by Sir Charles Oman and James Lovat-Fraser who both spoke of the intolerably blasphemous caricatures that could be found on the continent. Lovat-Fraser even described how he restrained his younger brother from 'wrecking' premises, offering them for sale. Henry Scrymgeour-Wedderburn even detected the hand of communist agitation behind the proposal.[21]

By this stage Clynes was echoing the advice of his department in recommending that the bill be amended in committee so as to ensure that breaches of the peace could still be encompassed by the law, and said as much in Parliament.[22] Subsequent advice from the Home Office also saw alteration of the law as inevitably linked to dangers inherent in the 'spirit of the age' argument so frequently expounded by Cohen, Snell and the others. If this were acknowledged then the law should protect all forms of religious belief – a rhetorical suggestion in Home Office memos which was clearly intended to appear unreasonable.[23] Of more immediate importance was the growing belief that testing what constituted a breach of the peace in this context could prove to be both difficult and capable of introducing worse iniquities and inequalities than the original repeal was intended to remove:

> The more devout and pious are less likely to cause a breach of the peace but *they* are the people who, if any, need protection from having blasphemous insult thrust upon them. The factious on the other hand are specially likely to feel constrained to breaches of the peace, and they will be protected or will have a remedy.[24]

In addressing this problem the Home Office advised that the bill be amended. Various suggestions were offered, any of which would have considerably reduced the bill's attempt to deal with grievances. The route of amendment involved either safeguarding the power to prosecute in cases where a breach of the peace occurred or creating a new offence of penalising attacks upon all religious feeling, backed up by the power to imprison rather than merely fine offenders. To lend weight to these suggestions passages from the Indian Penal Code (section 295a & section 298) the Metropolitan Police Act of 1839 (section 54, 12 & 13) and elements within the Good Rule and Government Byelaws which covered indecent and threatening language were offered as potential models and useful areas of guidance. From this discussion two amendments emerged; one appending a proviso regarding actual breach of the peace and another intended to protect religious feelings by prohibiting the use of language, drawing, gesture or representation intended to insult or wound and 'calculated to cause a breach of the peace'.[25]

Advice from the Director of Public Prosecutions was firmly against the second course of action and the dangers inherent in the creation of a new offence which would have had considerable civil liberties repercussions. Interestingly the DPP was more concerned with the fact that the 'cleansing of the stables' that the bill appeared to represent was going too far in both moral and legislative terms. The bill would have abolished all offences against religious belief and the DPP focused particularly on the fact that this would remove any disciplinary control of Anglican clergy as embodied in the Church Discipline Act of 1840. Similarly the all-encompassing nature of the bill would also circumvent the provisions of the Burial Laws Amendment Act which prevented addresses which contained contempt for the Christian religion.[26] Moreover the DPP anticipated trouble in the provisions which sought to protect religion of any kind, although it was not made clear whether this objection was to the law being extended beyond the Anglican denomination or beyond Christianity itself.[27] Mindful of the public order concerns of the Home Office and local chief constables the DPP suggested that the offence be liable to arrest without warrant. This contained the interesting twist that this would protect the person who has uttered provocative language noting the charged context of street politics since 'the risk of rough handling by outraged listeners is a wholesome check upon blasphemers'.[28] Once the potential blasphemer had been arrested the DPP suggested that such cases might come before quarter sessions where such offences had previously gone to assize courts – all of which could be accomplished while preserving the spirit of the Coleridge judgment.

This last stipulation concerning the trial of the offence would have had a quite ambiguous effect. On the one hand the suggestion that the crime could become a misdemeanor tried in a lower court might appear to suggest that the DPP was prepared to see the crime downgraded in importance. However the involvement of quarter sessions would have represented the application of more localised forms of justice located in individual cities and boroughs. In some respects this was precisely the sort of localised arena for justice that opponents of the blasphemy laws had long argued against. Part of Foote's early defence had been that partisan interests had used his predicament as a means of promoting the City of London's civic profile in the face of the imminent parliamentary reform of local government. Similarly aspects of the Gott case and the Stewart case of 1912 had striven to emphasise the intolerant attitude of the Leeds Constabulary and Bench to behaviour which had been long tolerated in other localities. In their push for national legislative solutions, those who opposed the blasphemy laws urgently sought to establish national standards and national interpretations of the law. Although Foote's early paranoia about the partisan political nature of the office of DPP may have seemed plausible in the early 1880s as a long-term development it must have been welcomed by libertarians and opponents of the blasphemy laws. Despite this 1929 witnessed a Director of Public Prosecutions whose advice to the Home Office appeared calculated to unravel many years campaigning for the appreciation of blasphemy as an issue which should be regulated by national standards of definition and implementation.

After some consideration the DPP, J. A. Stainton, offered the Home Office three versions of the amendment that might be considered. Whilst one sought to define the expression of blasphemy to include words, writing and publishing content which would outrage and provoke breaches of the peace the more liberal versions sought to distinguish between attacking and impugning religious convictions and merely impugning them in the course of potential breaches of the peace.[29] These three clauses appeared to have embraced different aspects of the Indian Code solution without following through its logic of universal protection for all religions. The first identified explicitly, in the manner of the Indian Code, the methods by which offensive matter could enter the public domain yet required a proof of calculated intention on the part of the blasphemer to 'outrage the religious convictions of any persons and thus to provoke a breach of the peace'. The two others ignored the catalogue of means in favour of a more generalised statement which aimed at protecting the religious convictions from any assault upon them regardless of the intention of the offender and, arguably, of the offended against. These in truth were ill-fitting attempts to adapt the Indian Code to English conditions. In their way they perhaps represent a recognition that religion needed protection as an aspect of personal conviction rather than as a widely accepted social ideology. However they were also designed to close the door to total abolition of the laws related to religious opinion which the bill represented and constituted an attempt to liberalise the law without conceding the case for a pluralisation of its application.[30]

The Home Office itself was by now convinced that the solution was to, as far as possible, 'allow the bill to die' – particularly since some opposition saw the potentially successful enactment of the bill as introducing 'the Russian tyranny'.[31] This clearly meant that government could see a political cost in administering the *coup de grace* itself. Thus it hoped that amendments would perform this unenviable task while the Home Office continued in its round of canvassing opinion and gathering evidence so that it could influence any course the bill and its proceedings might take. Eventually the government was forced to act furtively through the refusal of Ernest Thurtle, the Labour MP for Shoreditch and a frequent sponsor of repeal measures, to co-operate in what he saw as the clear emascalation of the bill he had introduced. The amendments that were eventually suggested curbed the open-ended freedom that the bill as it stood unamended appeared to offer. Legal opinion offered by the Parliamentary counsel suggested that the bill as it currently stood would

... be to allow any person to say whatever he liked about the Christian religion, however gross or scurrilous his language might be and even though his language might tend to provoke a breach of the peace.[32]

The Parliamentary counsel also noted with some alarm that the proceedings in parliament indicated that many members were convinced (erroneously) that conduct to provoke a breach of the peace was an offence under general law rather than being covered by local acts which some areas were not subject to. Government amendments would draw the proposed legislation back from a dangerous brink only by sweeping away the existing ecclesiastical and statute law, saving the ability of the ecclesiastical courts of the Church of England to discipline their own clergy. In addition to this one amendment created a new statutory offence making it criminal to attack religion 'in words which no decent person would tolerate'. The amendment went further to outline what this phrase meant by suggesting that they should be scurrilous, 'calculated to outrage' and intended to provoke a breach of the peace. The proposal to take the blasphemy laws beyond Christianity was also excluded by this series of amendments, largely on the grounds that it represented an extension of the laws. However, advice from the Committee stage of the bill was less than helpful. It recommended amending the bill to prevent the actions of an individual 'outraging the religious convictions of any other person'. This was modelled on the revised Indian Code of 1927 which had substituted the public order influenced notion of 'outrage' for the previously introspective notion of 'wounding'. The logic of recourse to the Indian Code was also stated as a recommended amendment – that the protection of all religions should be strongly linked to the question of breach of the peace. The report argued that this, however, could not be done without sweeping away all existing laws – ecclesiastical, common or statute – related to blasphemy.

This restatement, or redefinition, of the offence itself opened a whole new can of worms which the Parliamentary Committee had considered at length. The phrases 'religion' or 'religious convictions' were clearly an essential part of the offence and the Committee admitted that this '... has no very precise meaning. Is it for instance to be an offence to attack Mormonism or the Agapemonites?'[33]

The Committee, aware of the Gordian knot it had tied, offered a way out of the problem. Clearly any attempt to define the word religious was farcical – as the Committee itself pithily stated 'The draftsman by a stroke of the pen would have to solve a question which has been the subject of theological controversy for centuries.' Citing religions by name was a dangerous strategy which would cause endless debate about which religions to include or exclude. The impossibility of reaching such decisions was manifest and indeed the suggestion that such decisions might be rescinded in the light of scholarship was clearly hinted at in the example cited of a recent work which argued that Hinduism was 'hardly worthy of the name of religion'. Moreover this whole state of affairs would make the law a perpetual moveable feast and would do nothing to settle the matter once and for all, an element that was clearly uppermost in the minds of those at the Home Office. If the blasphemy laws were to be altered at all this should only be done if a satisfactory long-term resolution could be had. The solution that the Parliamentary Committee suggested would be to leave the definition of 'religion' out of the measure. This was an outcome which must have greatly pleased some at the Home Office since it served to keep the sovereignty of public opinion, in the shape of juries, untouched. The Parliamentary Committee, however, pointed out that such juries would be pronouncing on the vexed question that theologians had previously baulked at. Moreover there was also an inherent problem of identifying words which appropriately drew the line between 'fair criticism' and 'outrageous attack'. Put simply, this objection uttered concerns that legislation would prevent temperate criticism which would have no universal measure of outrageousness other than the sensibilities of the religious adherent so attacked and the predilections of the jury. The Indian Code emphasis on intention was no help here either since

> The ordinary law is that a man is held to intend the natural consequences of his acts. Any clause requiring a jury to look beyond the natural consequences of the acts proved in evidence, and to look into the mind of the prisoner would be a considerable departure from the present law and would lead to great difficulty in its application.[34]

The analogy of the law of libel was similarly considered and rejected. In this instance a successful defence that the words complained of were true and publication was in the public interest was unworkable when brought to the example of blasphemy. Visions of courtroom attempts to prove the truth or otherwise of words spoken against various deities had an air of farce and the committee wisely suggested that such protracted proceedings would clearly offend believers far more than any potentially blasphemous publication or utterance was likely to. The committee saw the only way out in a proposal which asserted that the matter published 'must not only be calculated to provoke a breach of the Peace but must also be in its nature grossly offensive'. Once again the Committee admitted that there were problems even here, not least in the definition of the central words used in the new offence. The definition of 'scurrilous', garnered from the OED, was taken to mean, somewhat unhelpfully, 'using such language as only the license of a buffoon can warrant; characterised by coarsensess or indecency of language, in jesting or invective; grossly opprobrious or jocular'. Such a definition of the law would clearly have inflamed any cases conducted under its auspices – only a small leap of imagination is necessary to envisage what (albeit in very different ways) Holyoake, Foote or Gott would have said in court and the press about such a law. The Committee was rather happier with its formulation of the notion of outrage which again, courtesy of the OED, was taken to mean 'to do violence to; to subject to outrage; to wrong grossly, treat with gross violence or indignity'.

The use of the word 'publication' was also given consideration. Despite the apparent wish of some to extend the law to cover actions and conduct, the Committee swiftly agreed that this would represent an inadvisable extension of the laws. Clearly the Parliamentary Committee realised the express need to minimise potential grievances and to limit the potential use of the law as far as possible. The Committee also recognised that the government were intending to exclude Northern Ireland from such legislation since the Government of Ireland Act gave Stourmont powers to legislate for such matters and any interference from Westminster would amount to 'constitutional impropriety' on the part of the Imperial Parliament. The situation in Scotland was slightly different since its exclusion from such an Act was on the grounds that the Lord Advocate's powers represented sufficient discretion to regulate the law.

When these amendments were put to Ernest Thurtle he argued for a total omission of the word 'religion' from the Act. However it was pointed out to him that this would leave the law capable of being used against political convictions – a situation which J. A. Stainton suggested would leave the Criminal Courts occupied for months after each general election. Whilst accepting this Ernest Thurtle was not prepared to become the instrument of the government's preferences in the matter and resolved to think about this and the lengthy memo on the historical nature of the offence which Stainton gave him.[35]

When the Bill did appear in Parliament the government amendments were swiftly followed by a number of others from various members. These had the effect of abolishing the legal proceedings for schism, heresy or atheism whilst allowing the maintenance of laws against blasphemy and blasphemous libel (although some sought to install a regulatory authority in the form of the Attorney General). Significantly the amendments veered away from the Indian Code solution by denying protection to non-Christian religions and – most disquieting for the government – the effect of some amendments destroyed the legal jurisdiction over the Anglican clergy.

Certainly the language used in some of these amendments indicates that attempts to circumscribe anti-Christian opinion and its modes of expression were fraught with potential difficulties and would have posed severe difficulties for judges and juries alike had they ever made it onto the statute book. The amendment suggested by Lovat-Fraser and Commander Southby, for example:

> Provided that if any person, by words, writings, or pictures, scoffingly or irreverently ridicules or impugns the doctrines of the Christian faith, or utters or publishes contumelious reproaches of Jesus Christ, or profanely scoffs at the Holy Scriptures or exposes any part therof to contempt or ridicule, he shall be guilty of a misdemeanour punishable by fine and imprisonment without hard labour.[36]

In this instance the notion of irreverence or scoffing could conceivably have been applied to a wide range of literary, religious and journalistic works. Once again, this time unwittingly, such an amendment would also have retrod the arguments concerning anti-trinitarian views which had surfaced in the nineteenth century. The fact that the reckless use of such words was creating hostages to fortune was more than evident to Ernest Thurtle who complained that some of these amendments would make matters worse than they currently were. Any chances of the law being amended through this bill collapsed rapidly and the rest of this debate degenerated into attempts to appoint blame for the collapse of the measure and the patient work of Ernest Thurtle and the others.[37]

The attempt to sweep away prosecutions for blasphemy and blasphemous libel surfaced again in 1936 and 1937 this time with an amended title – The Religious Prosecutions (abolition) Bill – and was a clear attempt to close the loophole which would have undermined the discipline of Anglican clergy. Interestingly the Bill also proposed to extend its provisions to take in Scotland. This time the Home Office arranged with the whips office to have the measure blocked throughout each session and clearly learned their lesson since it was deemed expedient to prevent it gaining even a second reading.[38]

*   *   *

An overview of these attempts to end the capacity within the British legal apparatus to punish blasphemous utterings appears to be an unco-ordinated series of lost opportunities and misunderstandings. Many of the arguments of repealers seemed reasonable to all but the most blinkered of parliamentary opponents. The laws were manifestly contrary to the 'spirit of the age' – in this context a surprisingly consensual concept – and their continued existence obviously still enshrined various forms of inequality related to religious faith and class. This inequality did not simply undermine the citizenship of atheists and agnostics but also the followers of non-Christian forms of religion. Even here the exclusion was not complete since Muslims would receive protection for some of their beliefs where they overlapped with Christianity. This was just starting to have an important imperial dimension. Acknowledging some of these inconsistencies in private the Home Office, on occasions, even admitted that the law itself could be seen to have been badly expressed, to have evolved haphazardly and to have no clear purpose or guidelines related to its application. This situation was becoming increasingly untenable since it seemingly imposed a universal British religio-moral culture over what had become a vastly different society.

With these elements in mind the intransigence (or more accurately inertia) of successive governments appears mystifying. Traditionally moves for repeal had provoked at least mild interest and support from the libertarian and secularist wing of liberalism and, as the century progressed, was gaining support amongst labour members of parliament and outside who responded to the class discriminatory rhetoric which could be invoked around the law. Despite this, admittedly modest, level of support the measure clearly had no long-term political advantage for any party which would care to adopt the measure as its own. Significantly the successive Bills introduced to the House were always private members' bills which then involved their promoter in considerable work to gain any sign or semblance of support from the government.

Some of the arguments advanced by repealers and those opposed to the laws as they currently stood were themselves on occasions not calculated to make the decision for government easier. The introduction of the Indian Code solution into the argument frankly did not help matters and merely dragged the debate into dangerous waters. Once the whole question of extending the laws beyond Christianity came on the agenda it was no surprise to find civil servants and senior government figures baulking at problems associated with finding a working definition of religion. Similarly the attempt to repeal a supposedly 'British' blasphemy law without considering the manifestly different legal history and religious culture of Scotland and, to a lesser extent, Northern Ireland showed a considerable lack of foresight.

Significantly there was a groundswell of opinion voiced during these debates which, far from dragging its feet over the enactment of obviously overdue legislation, argued quite vociferously and articulately against any alteration of the Blasphemy laws as they currently stood. The murmur of opinions which spoke darkly of repeal encouraging wholesale challenges to morality was not entirely extinct. This opinion was generally expressed in its mildest form as a presumption that an alteration in the laws would only affect a very small, generally undeserving, minority whose actions and sentiments could be painted as beyond public sympathy. As we have seen there was also a more sophisticated school of thought which argued that the legal sanctions against blasphemous libel, since they were a part of the Common Law, actually functioned quite adequately. The premise that the Common Law was capable of evolution to engage with the 'spirit of the age' still had currency and was enhanced by the belief and evidence that juries were capable of deciding the question in response to this. This argument had a circular integrity whereby any attempt to change this state of affairs could be regarded as an intrusion upon the sanctity of the Common Law and simultaneously to be acting contrary to the 'spirit of the age' as expressed by the decisions of juries. The atmosphere of weariness which appears to hang over the continuous attempts to alter the law was a reflection and crystallisation of the central issue which was the irreconcilable differences between two unmistakably opposed interpretations of the justness or otherwise of the laws pertaining to blasphemy and blasphemous libel. Increasingly, during these years, the battle appeared to be a protracted extension of the Coleridge versus Stephen debate.

The Coleridge Judgment itself was the basis behind the opinions which emanated from the Home Office. The Coleridge distinction between matter spoken and the manner in which it was spoken was in this context a very important one. The judgment had opened the door for the assertion that Christianity was no longer part and parcel of the law of the land and this could cheerfully be seen by the Home Office as an advance which now tolerated shades of the agnostic and atheist opinion that had so often caused an embarrassment to the Liberal and Tory administrations of the 1870s and 1880s. The Coleridge assertion that so long as the decencies of debate were observed all doctrines could be criticised seemed at times to turn the affair into one related solely to matters of public order – an area that the Home Office felt much more comfortable with. Moreover, as we have discovered, this particular episode in its evolution was confirmation that the law could still adapt and evolve. The concentration upon the manner of the expression meant that individual instances of alleged blasphemy could pass through several filters to determine whether a specific line had been crossed. From police constable, or 'man and woman on the Clapham Omnibus', through Chief Constable to Attorney General and Judge the law could almost be seen to carry its fair share of checks and balances as each individual weighed the evidence of offence against a psychological scale of propriety and decency. This process had its apotheosis in the jury system which gave very public and strategically important pronouncements upon the nature of public taste and the boundaries of propriety. The whole system, seen in these terms, had an impeccable logic which relied upon the march (or, as its opponents would have said, slow crawl) of toleration and as such its servants in the Home Office hotly defended its record as being entirely in keeping with the 'spirit of the age'.

The system was not monolithic nor indeed necessarily inflexible, yet it did contain its contradictions and assumptions that could be identified in some quarters as anachronistic. Firstly, while the argument that such a system contained checks and balances had some logic it was also true that the individual stages of this had nonetheless the devolved responsibility of policing and applying the law in their hands. One obviously potentially perilous aspect of this was the action of local policemen, ranging from the police constables who had arrested Stewart to the actions and opinions of chief constables who had insisted on action against Gott. Occasionally, as at Leeds, this could appear dangerously like a more arbitrary summary justice administered by individuals with vastly varying ideas and competence. A second problem which highlighted this conception of the law as a potential anachronism was the accusation that the existing law and the system which regulated it defended only Christianity and visibly the Anglican branch of it. The second half of this accusation is more easily dealt with. The attacks upon religious sensibilities made by Gott were considered beyond most measure of the proprieties of debate, making the case against him clear cut. The fact that such cases were now considered primarily on the manner of the statement involved further served to distance consideration of the precise doctrine or religious text attacked. When we also consider the more ecumenical attitude that began to prevail within, for example, the English Catholic hierarchy from the turn of the century onwards a tacitly agreed version of Christian fundamentals served to iron out the doctrinal inconsistencies that had served defendants so well in the years before the Coleridge dictum. At this period this blending of sacred doctrines into a language and rhetoric of religious feelings was, on the face of it, an advance in religious tolerance. As we shall see, however, this was to have a significant and unforeseen impact at the end of the twentieth century. The accusation that the regulation of opinion had not kept pace with the increasing plurality of society was rather more difficult to refute. Public opinion and the opinion of local officials was mobilised solely in the defence of the Christian religion. Although the Indian Code solution was frequently mentioned, and this clamour heightened from the Edwardian period onwards, enthusiasm for its adoption in administrative circles was minimal.

The attitude of repealers rejected many of the assumptions outlined above. Again this stemmed from the conflict between the Coleridge and

Stephen interpretations of the blasphemy laws. In following the attitude of Stephen those who sought repeal were convinced that this was always less likely once the law appeared to become more reasonable as a result of reform. Suppression of opinion had appeared to die under Coleridge, to be replaced by emphasis upon the manner and context of expression. The Stephen argument that the law was objectively a bad law and needed to be shown to be thus was still influential and, it could be argued, remained at the back of the minds of those like Stewart , Pack and Gott who deliberately set out to attack the law through transgression. Another fundamental objection to the law and its practice was that it made the interpretation of the law itself less exact and considerably more open to debate. Whilst the supporters of the Coleridge interpretation heralded this as a positive virtue those who perceived themselves to be, at least potentially, most likely to be subject to the law and its application were less impressed. There was an overwhelming dislike of the notion that the law would be interpreted by those who were not strictly speaking fully qualified to pronounce on such matters. Policemen, however professional as law enforcement agents, obviously had no formal theological training. Whilst this was a problem in the context of blasphemous publication the situation could be interpreted as considerably worse than this in the case of public meetings. The police, as those constrained by the need to keep public order, would exercise their prerogative to take action purely and simply upon this imperative. Still worse the abdication of responsibility for the law to the untrained was perpetuated and made more iniquitous in the presumption behind the Coleridge dictum that juries could decide the offensiveness of the material discussed. As repealers could point out, the increasing proximity of blasphemy trials in the last 30 years and the appearance of moral panics in localities, such as the Leeds prosecutions, indicated that another of Coleridge's assumptions was misplaced. In suggesting that the Coleridge dictum would adapt itself to progressive liberalisation of the law at no point did it, at least publicly, entertain the prospect that in response to a changing climate of belief or religious perception the law could in future instances be applied in a more draconian manner.

Another important line of critique was that the application of the Coleridge dictum gave power to Christian opinion which was formed and nurtured at the grass roots. This power and its exercise effectively did more to polarise the competing opinions into self-fulfilling caricatures of Christian opinion and 'intellectual' doubt and atheism. Repealers and many blasphemers since Foote believed that society should be gravitating towards one culture regulated by taste, expertise, reason and the development of critical faculties. Indeed the attempts in the court room to equate the blasphemy being indicted with the works of intellectual reason should potentially be seen in this light. That the blasphemy laws effectively widened the cleave in culture was recognised by many. John Mackinnon Robertson put this succinctly when he noted the class dialogue used to accuse Gott of more than blasphemy. In writing to Mckenna about one of Gott's pamphlet's he noted

> .... It is as bad as possible in its kind. But the fact remains that the offence is vulgarity. You wouldn't send Haeckel to jail for calling the orthodox deity 'a gaseous vertebrate' though the blasphemy is quite as bad!

A different hand appended to this letter a note which indicated that some in the Home Office considered the offence to be purely a legal matter with no class or cultural dimension, effectively shutting the door to any wider discussion of this important area: 'He might just as well say that the indecent exposure of the person or even the public practice of sodomy is mere "vulgarity".'[39]

The failure of this attempt to draw culturally distant tendencies together simultaneously turned repealers and secularists into defenders of a morality they had nurtured since the mid-nineteenth century. Purveyors of this same morality and their seriously held views appeared alternative and dangerous to Christianity which still motivated many 'from below' initiatives from street evangelism to street politics. Statements like Stewart's famous quip that the Almighty was unfit company for him and his grotesque depiction of Crippen being absolved in heaven are instances of this in action. These examples indicate the long-term assertion that Christianity was a bankrupt morality but also reflected popular street idioms. Whilst there was obviously a cat-and-mouse game of incitement involved the fact remains that Stewart and Gott must have felt they had effectively exposed the fact that 'Christianity from below' could summon considerable support to break its opponents.

In the next chapter the power of this swathe of opinion 'from below' was demonstrated graphically by an episode which followed the last attempt to repeal the blasphemy laws described above. This particular incident combined the repealers' twin fears of opinion wielded 'from below' and the ability of the 'spirit of the age' to be enveloped by irrationalism. It also demonstrated that significant social and ideological forces could be mobilised with the intention of taking society in a very different direction from the one consensually and cosily accepted as progress.

Notes

1. HO 45 24619 217459/1.
2. Ibid., 217459/2, Greenwood to Mckenna, 26 December1911; Mckenna to Greenwood, 27 December 1911.
3. Ibid., 217459/8.
4. Ibid., copy of memo signed 'H. B.' *circa* early May 1913.
5. Ibid., 217459/9 (heavily underlined in original).
6. Ibid.
7. *Daily Herald* cuttings 31/5/23 and 5/6/23 in HO 45 24619 217459/16.
8. HO 45 24619 217459/17.
9. Ibid.
10. Ibid., memo from Sir Charles Schuster House of Lords, 5 May 1923.
11. Society for the Abolition of the Blasphemy Laws (1924), *The Blasphemy Laws: Verbatim Report of the Deputation to the Home Secretary on April 16 1924. Issued by the Society for the Abolition of the Blasphemy Laws*, London: RPA, p. 7.
12. Ibid.
13. Ibid., p. 10.
14. Ibid.
15. Hansard, 11 March 1927 and 1 July 1927.
16. Society for the Abolition of the Blasphemy Laws (1929), *The Blasphemy Laws: Verbatim Report of the Deputation to the Home Secretary the Right Honourable J. R. Clynes M.P. Thursday November 7th 1929. Issued by the Society for the Abolition of the Blasphemy Laws*, London: RPA, p. 7.
17. Ibid., p. 10.
18. Ibid., p. 12.
19. HO 45 24619 217459, notes prepared for Home Secretary as briefing for above meeting, document date 6 November 1929, words underlined in original.
20. Hansard, 24 January 1930.
21. Ibid.
22. HO 45 24619 217459/33, Hansard 24 January 1930.
23. HO 45 24619 217459/34, memo from 'A. L.', 11 February 1930.
24. Ibid.
25. Ibid., letter from 'CR' to Home Office, 11 February 1930.
26. Nash, D. S. (1995), 'Look in her face and Lose thy dread of dying': The ideological importance of death to the secularist movement in Victorian England', *Journal of Religious History*, vol. 19, no. 2, pp. 158–80.
27. HO 45 24619 217459/42, memo from DPP to USS Home Office.
28. Ibid.
29. HO 45 24619 217459/42, letter, 13 February 1930, J. A. Stainton to Sir John Anderson GCB, Home Office.
30. Ibid.
31. Bradlaugh-Bonner, op cit., p. 132.
32. HO 45 24619 217459/43, notes on the Blasphemy Law Amendment Bill.
33. Ibid., report on Committee Stage of the Bill to amend the Blasphemy Laws, 1930.
34. Ibid., notes on the Blasphemy Law Amendment Bill.
35. Ibid., letter from J. A. Stainton to Right Hon. Sir John Anderson, GCB, Home Office.

36. HO 45 24619 217459/48.
37. Ibid.
38. HO 45 24619 217459/57 and HO 45 24619 217459/60.
39. HO 45 10665/216120, letter from J. M. Robertson, 5 January 1912.

CHAPTER SEVEN

'Perish Judah' and Save the Empire: Christianity 'From Below', the 'Godless Congress' and the Attempted Extension of the Blasphemy Laws in 1938

In the first week of December 1937 a number of government departments were sent scurrying in search of information about a proposed Russo-Communist inspired 'Congress of the Godless' which was rumoured to be taking place in London during the summer of 1938. This heightened level of urgent activity was in response to questions asked in the Commons and to an extremely large number of petition coupons clipped from the *Catholic Herald* that had been received at the Home Office from the last week of November onwards.[1] These petitions are of considerable historical value because individuals went to some trouble to go beyond the action of merely signing them. A majority enclosed letters, often of some length, that represented a substantial outpouring of religious and anti-rationalist sentiment. Taken together these letters are a remarkable testimony to the level of grassroots 'from below' sentiment attached to Christian belief in 1930s Britain. More importantly they testify to the centrality of this belief to an image of Christian Britishness and Britain's central, God-given, imperial role. This particular image was seen as under concerted attack from challenges such as the deteriorating international state in Europe, the pathological fear of war that still haunted many, the increased visibility of communists – some currently engaged in systematic anti-clericalism in Spain, right through to the lingering effects of the abdication crisis. These letters contain a range of voices which vary from the indignant to the intensely alarmed. The more fearful paint a picture of the sacred and secure protestant state unravelling with potentially incalculable consequences in forthright, and sometimes breathlessly urgent style.

Mrs White of Grantham urged the Home Secretary

> ... to use every effort against holding of a godless Congress which is anti-christ everyone should believe in almighty God & I am sure we cannot expect GOD'S blessing unless we stand for Him in such an

effort as this He has graciously blessed our country by giving us peace. But as we see signs of the end of the Gospel Age approaching upon us and the dawning of that millenial day when Christ Jesus shall reign with his saints for a thousand years the kingdoms of this world shall one day become the Kingdoms of our Lord & of this Christ it will benefit you in your own soul to stand for Christ and not let antichrist come in from Russia.[2]

The rhetoric of imperial Christian achievement was echoed in a letter from Mr E. S. Wingate from Woking in Surrey:

> Convinced Christians are not as a rule very vocal, so the authorities do not realise (though our King's Coronation revealed it) what a large number in the nation still believe in the external verity & blessing of the Christian faith & these people will be solidly behind any steps taken by the government to prevent the holding of the Godless Congress in London on April 6th 1938. Our nation owes its unique peace and prosperity hithertho, to its acknowledgement of God & God will judge us nationally if we abandon that position. The Russians with a madman at their head are everyday losing weight in the councils of the nations. They would not dare to hold such a congress in Rome or Berlin. Why should they use England as an innoculation centre for the principle that has brought them to their present discredited position?[3]

by B. Owens of East Ham:

> Why do the Heathen rage and the people imagine a vain thing? The kings of earth set themselves and the rulers take counsil [sic] together, against the Lord and against his anointed (Psalm 2 v. 1–2).
> Recently I read in a publication of one of our daily papers the proposed meeting of the 'anti-God Congress' to be held in London on April 6th 1938.
> I am only a British workman. But I <u>love</u> my country and hold dear the liberty which was bought me, and unto us all, at the cost of the BLOOD of MY LORD & SAVIOUR JESUS CHRIST also of the martyrs who laid down their lives for the word of God which has brought to us all Liberty, Peace, Love, Purity & worship. Righteousness exalteth a nation, it has exalted our nation must we tolerate such heathen invasion against God, in this nation, whom God has Blessed. I speak as a Proud Briton. I enclose my protest from your humble and obedient servant.[4]

The equation of Christianity with a constructed British identity is highlighted in the letter of Janet Kydd from Glasgow:

> As a worker in a Soldier's Home, may I join the many others in recording my whole-hearted protest against the 'Godless Institute' in Moscow, holding a Congress in London during the month of April 1938. We pray ours may be a Christian land of which no one need be ashamed. We would be ashamed if the godless element were allowed to interfere in even a very small way, with their faith in the Lord Jesus Christ in whom no fault could be found.[5]

There was also an interesting number of letters from representatives of the imperial periphery that contained the clear implication that the heart of the empire was preparing to renege upon its Christian duty and leave these pioneers alone in an age of gathering atheist darkness. Petitions from all over the empire totalled 40 000 names, some from far-flung branches of the British Israelite Association. One of these, from Cape Town, declared:

> The British race being a Christian race, and the very foundations of the British order of civilisation being God and the Bible, and the proposed blasphemous gathering at the heart of the Empire, being thus an insult not only to God but to his Majesty King George VI and the British race, and a manifestation of the dark forces which are striving to destroy the British order of civilisation, we most vigorously protest against the holding of the said gathering and respectfully call upon His Majesty's Government in Great Britain to forbid the same.[6]

To set alongside an imperial rhetoric was one which argued for women being seen as the special custodians of morality, Dorothy Holms from Camberley, Surrey wrote:

> I write to thank you for your recent remark in the House, that you would deplore the holding of a congress by the Moscow League of MILITANT Godless, in this country: which congress has for its *openly avowed purpose the arousing and fomenting of class hatred, disorder, revolution and civil war, in THIS country* – hitherto the most civilised and sanest in the world – by the holding of openly seditious public (and no doubt private) meetings. All loyal and patriotic – or even merely *sane* – British subjects, and especially all British *women*, will most fervently hope that no such congress will be permitted to be held in this country, and will most ernestly [*sic*] support you in any action you may be able to take to prevent such congress being held here.[7]

Letters were received from all corners of Britain and beyond.[8] Most remarkable of all was a letter from Thomas Milner of Tickhill near Doncaster who used this opportunity to launch a tirade against many manifestations of modern life, seeing in them the inherent secularising evil that was stalking the land. The letter is an astonishing document that indicates how ingrained attitudes to the preservation of religious culture could in some areas remain scarcely untouched from the previous century.

> May I humbly beg of you to use your full powers to urge parliament make the nation keep the sabbath day holy. Ask them to make an act, that will forbid the opening of all inns, publick-houses, clubs, welfares, and stop all sunday work, all sunday newspapers, all ice cream selling, all shops from opening, and all trading of any kind. Stop all hiking, byking, motoring, fishing, picture palaces, theatres,

and all pleasuring of any kind. Stop all sunday buses, and women and girls from wearing men's garments, for all such are an abomination to the Lord. Make it a day of rest and gladness, worship, prayer, and praise. Fear not what men may say, but fear the lord, and he will uphold and bless you. Trusting you will do your best.[9]

The somewhat shell-shocked response to these petitions by government was to take them very seriously in the light of the worsening international situation. Indeed it was this which provided one of the catalysts for what was to become a withdrawl of tolerance. Following the Anschluss Britain was asked to accept a significant number of Austrian refugees, many of whom were intellectuals and professionals. As a result of this the Home Secretary was lobbied by the medical and dental professions to ensure that the number of refugees entering their respective professions was strictly regulated.[10] Some in Britain began to identify intellect with communism and semitism and it is certainly true that many of these refugees were both. However as matters proceeded, this was to grow out of proportion to become a stereotype with considerable potency.

The Home Office decided to wait for a full explanation of the conference whilst also sanctioning forms of covert digging. The Home Office paid particular attention to the response of the National Secular Society and the relevant copy of the RPA's *Literary Guide* is among the papers relating to this incident. The *Guide* dismissed the sense of panic as 'unreasoning frenzy' and interestingly turned the Coleridge decency test around and used it unforgivingly against their opponents. After singling out the Catholic Church as a power 'whose seat of government is in a foreign country', the churches more generally were condemned for seeking to proselytise and interfere in the domestic theological affairs of other nations whilst denying the atheists similar freedoms, summing this up with the phrase 'The leopard does not change his spots.'[11]

The covert end of government intelligence gathering was represented by the inquiries of MI5. In a letter to the Home Office marked 'secret' MI5 responded rapidly to scotch the rumour that Jaroslawsky, the 'chief exponent of militant atheism in Russia (and) head of the Union of Militant Atheists ... the chief Comintern organisation for anti-god activity and propaganda', planned to attend. A subsequent memo outlined MI5's investigations of the principal organisations involved in the Congress and their significance. Although it is unclear whether the organisation had actually infiltrated the Rationalist Press Association, the South Place Ethical Society and what it amusingly called the National Sectarian Society (certainly its description of Charles Bradlaw [*sic*] as a rationalist might suggest otherwise), it nonetheless was able to pronounce upon their part in the affair. The Congress had been organised by these three organisations which the report concluded, not surprisingly, to be 'as far as we can say, entirely devoid of political interest'. This was to be held in conjunction with the World Union of Freethinkers which MI5 in the event proved to be considerably more interested in. The 'Godless Congress' was revealed to be the quinquennial conference of this latter organisation scheduled to be held in London in mid-September. From the first it was clear that such a conference intended to be staged behind closed doors, thereby minimising the problems posed by recent public order legislation. The report noted that the World Union of Freethinkers had opened its ranks in 1936 to an older organisation – the International Union of Proletarian Freethinkers – when it had disbanded. The report continued:

> A certain discrepancy of opinion exists as to what happened on the occasion of the amalgamation. The communist periodical 'Inprecor' hailed the event as an important step on the road to anti-fascist unity. According to 'Inprecor's' account of the Congress, 'Dr. Terwagne, the president of the International Freethinker's Union (Brussels International), in his address of welcome, strikingly developed the basic line of the congress – the united struggle against fascism and war – and emphasised the indispensibility of amalgamation.'[12]

The British delegation, according to the report, was adamant that the communist freethinkers came into the organisation only on the condition that the 'strict political neutrality' of the organisation be observed at all times. Although MI5 admitted that in general the Russians had adhered to this request it could not avoid pointing out their one misdemeanour which involved a letter from the Russian branch of the World Union to the corresponding Russian domestic organisation on the occasion of the twentieth anniversary of the Russian Revolution. The letter identified the aims of the two organisations far more closely than many on the executive, including the British section, were prepared to tolerate. The British section apparently was so incensed that it threatened to cancel its invitation to the 1938 conference unless the letter itself was withdrawn. The MI5 report was generally sympathetic to the decorum and attitude of the British end of freethought and felt sure that the relevant organisations would prevent political capital being made out of the conference. Likewise the British societies were considered unlikely to indulge in propaganda that would be 'likely to offend the susceptibilities of Christians'. However it was equally sure that 'the communist Press will hail the Conference as a triumph of the United Front idea, and do their best to make the occasion a sign of anti-Fascist unity among Freethinkers'.[13]

The general tenor of the report suggested that the matter had been exaggerated and laid the blame for the Commons questions and subsequent mountain of petitions squarely at the door of the *Catholic Herald*. The report did concede that the *Herald* had sought to retract the story in its next issue of 19 November 1938 with a correction which noted that the Conference '... is not to be one of militant atheists, but an old-time Conference of the International Union of Freethinkers, or old-fashioned atheists'. The MI5 report thus concluded somewhat wearily that 'this account of the matter appears to be very close to the truth'.[14]

The hysteria created by the churches was swiftly condemned by Chapman Cohen in the *Freethinker*, of which the Home Office again made a point of keeping a copy. Cohen's editorial entitled the 'Great Lie Brigade' went to town on the *Catholic Herald*, the *Catholic Times* and the *Universe* as well as the *English Churchman*, the *Sunday Dispatch* and even the *Daily Sketch* whom he accused of scaremongering and fabrication. In particular Cohen was adamant that no money had been received from Moscow and that had it been offered by 'Moscow, or America, or Timbucktoo, the Archbishop of Canterbury, or the Chief Rabbi then it would be accepted if offered unconditionally'.[15]

Despite this spirited refutation and the comparatively temperate opinion of MI5 some more sinister elements had fastened onto what they saw as the dangerous significance of the 'Godless Congress'. One such organisation was the Christian Defence Union which had as its nominal leader Captain Archibald Maule Ramsay. The appearance of Ramsay at the head of this organisation was significant. He had been elected to the National Government in 1931 as MP for Peebles and had become a violent anti-semite upon reading *The Protocols of the Elders of Zion* at some point in 1938. The historian of Fascism, Richard Thurlow, argues that Ramsay interpreted 'all political phenomena in terms of an anti-semitic conspiracy theory' and was unequivocally 'Britain's most notorious extreme anti-semite'.[16] Ramsay was also the leader of the Nordic League, a swastika-bedecked organisation dedicated to the destruction of the 'so-called Jewish menace' and destined to play a later part in our proceedings.

In fact the activities of Ramsay and the Nordic League offer an interesting comparison with the treatment of those who were either liable to be accused of blasphemy or who sought the repeal of the existing laws. The Home Secretary, Sir Samuel Hoare (himself a Jew) was exercised during these years by the spectre of the Nordic League and other neo-Fascist organisations as public order problems – indeed, these organisations clearly sought to embarrass him. Thurlow also notes that there was confusion in the Home Office as to whether offensive speeches against the Jews – akin to blasphemous utterings – were liable to prosecution for seditious libel. The Director of Public Prosecutions argued that they were unlikely to succeed although a senior civil servant corrected this opinion, suggesting that if they were likely to cause a breach of the peace then they could be prosecuted under the Public Order Act. The context of this legal thinking differs from that of blasphemy, however, since Thurlow suggests the anti-semitic organisations and their meetings were more introspective and 'preaching to the converted'.[17]

Ramsay and the Nordic League were probably behind the leaflet 'The Proposed London Godless Congress' published by the National Constitutional Defence Movement which aimed to publicise the adverse nature of the conference. The leaflet argued that the Russian influx into the International Union of Freethinkers had split the organisation into a politically non-aligned group (in Britain represented by the NSS and the RPA) and a 'Communistic element' which had progressively been the League of Militant Atheists and then the British League of Socialist Freethinkers. The leaflet asserted that the two factions had now reunited.

> It would appear that the International Union of Freethinkers is now a mixed body with a membership overweighted with Communists who have decided to have their International Congress in London this year. *The Communistic element is hidden under the less objectionable name of 'Freethinker', and the fact that the Communistic element will play the larger part in this Congress is camouflaged by the fact that the Congress is being held here at the invitation of the British Freethinker organisations.*[18]

A sinister aspect portrayed by the leaflet was the assertion that this organisation was able to nurture itself and develop under the cover of the tolerance and liberty of meeting that the British organisations had enjoyed up to this point in their history. Effectively this analysis identified the British freethought movement with an international atheist crusade that was an extension of the Soviet design to spread communism to the West.

> It is evident that the Communists are succeeding on the religious front just where they are failing on the political front – in staging a 'United Front' and veiling their activities under the cover of inoffensive organisations *and thus providing themselves with a baisis on which they can recruit the less extremist elements.*[19]

The connection between British freethought, foreign communism and the explicit attack upon the moral basis of British civilisation was made in the final words of the leaflet:

> One has only to make a study of the large numbers of 'Left Wing' books, magazines and papers, which are sold in this country and which give expression to the Marxist interpretation of religion, to realise that militant atheism of the communistic type has been popularised among all classes of people. Outbursts against God and religion are to be found in literature designed to be read by Children,

Young People, University Students, the Workers, and even the Middle and Upper Classes. Anti-religious ideas of a revolutionary nature have thus been widely popularised without arousing the notice or opposition of the religious authorities.

It only needs the careful organisation of these individual units of revolutionary atheism to form, in this Christian country, a mighty force of militant opposition to religion. There is no doubt that the holding of this Congress in London is designed to this end.[20]

As time passed the Home Office gained more intelligence concerning the Conference, its intentions and the prospective delegates. There appears to have been general relief that Jaroslawsky was not coming and that another potentially dangerous anarchist André Roulot (alias Lorulot, alias Hael) was considered to 'no longer to have a taste for dangerous enterprises' since he had inherited a fortune.[21] However Ramsay insisted that the Home Office should take the matter far more seriously and enclosed a report intended for Anti-Comintern International which he said showed that the League of Militant Atheists were behind the Union of Freethinkers and that the whole conference was effectively Communist inspired. The bulletin noted that Jaroslawsky had commended the forthcoming conference and that the 1936 Congress spoke of the struggle for bread, peace and freedom – the slogan of the French Popular Front. The bulletin concluded with the assertion that

... it would therefore be futile to deny that the aims of the Freethinkers, far from being of a purely 'intellectual' order, are distinctly political in character; the coming Congress must therefore be regarded as a vehicle for Communistic propaganda.[22]

By now Ramsay had fully entered the 'Jew Wise' phase of his career and this was evident in his attempt to highlight the Jewish speakers at the conference and the danger posed by their topics of discussion. Stridently underlined were the names of the communist advocate of scientific social change Professor Hyman Levy, Speaking on Science and the Churches; the rational gradualist Professor Harold Laski on 'The Struggle for Peace and Liberty', both of London University and NSS chairman Chapman Cohen on 'The reality of lay morals'.[23] Levy in particular might be seen as the embodiment of what Ramsay feared. Although Levy himself was hardly an emigré he had been involved in the promotion of scientific socialism since the end of the First World War. Moreover Levy had, since 1931, been able to extend the influence of his ideas through radio broadcasting, a medium destined to play a role later on in proceedings. Levy introduced Marxism to the British listening public through a series of talks entitled 'The Web of Thought and Action' which eventually found their way into print under the auspices of the Rationalist Press Association.[24]

By the early summer of 1938 the matter had reached Parliament and a House of Commons committee room was set aside on 4 May to receive a deputation from a recently convened *ad hoc* alliance known as the Christian Defence Movement. Ramsay was present along with, amongst others, Commander P. G. Agnew, Mr G. Balfour, Sir Reginald Blair, Sir Nicholas Grattan-Doyle, Sir Patrick Hannon and Sir Alfred Knox. The meeting pledged itself to cross-denominational co-operation although it fought shy of the concept of a countermeeting or demonstration. Meanwhile Ramsay conveyed the impression that the Home Secretary would have liked to prevent the Conference taking place and that his legal hand should be strengthened. The unanimous conclusion was that a recourse to street politics would be the best way to assist him by making it clear that a breach of the peace was likely to ensue. In some respects this pronouncement was likely to feed Chapman Cohen's growing belief that Hoare's open contempt for the conference was starting to breed active intolerance. Although the meeting purported to recognise the importance of retaining the existing rights of freedom of speech and was overall not in favour of special legislation in the matter it did not baulk at the casual suggestion that all 'foreigners (especially Russians)' should be routinely stopped from entering the country.[25]

The Home Office reasserted that it had no power to stop the Congress and something of the dilemma felt by those involved in issuing this statement is carried in the assessment of the situation by one civil servant:

> The attitude of the right-wing M.P.s who want it stopped because it will cause a breach of the peace is the same as that of the left-wing people who want Mosley's marches stopped. S. of S. gave the answer in his published letter of 28th June 1937 'If a lawful demonstration could be prohibited ... merely because opponents ... threatened to create disorder, there would be an end of free demonstration and free assembly ... and a premium would be put on disorder ... .[26]

Ramsay, however, was not to be thwarted this easily and took his campaign into the pages of *The Times*, declaring: 'I must say it is asking a good deal of a Christian country where the King bears the title of Defender of the Faith to allow people from all over Europe to come and tear the whole faith to pieces ... .'[27] Ramsay's particular crusade was joined by Cardinal Hinsley, the Archbishop of Westminster, who introduced an interesting slant upon the affair by declaring that the decision to host the Congress in Britain constituted 'a breach of the formal agreement between Soviet Russia and the United Kingdom on the subject of propaganda'.[28] Hoare was not rattled by this and continued to argue that he had no power to deal with the Congress in advance, that he expected the organisers to regulate ticket admission and that tolerance and free speech should be upheld and respected.[29]

The briefing notes for this letter reiterated all previous knowledge of the Congress including the MI5 report. Additionally there emerged the unsurprising analysis that the decision to admit the Russian Atheists to the World Union of Freethinkers was motivated by financial gain. The extent of the climate of fear which had been nurtured was demonstrated by the report that Scottish Catholics had taken the lead in condemning the Congress since they saw 'in the project the seeds of another Spanish War' – and presumably the spectre of violent anti-clericalism. The briefing paper, emanating, it has to be remembered, from the comfort and rationality of the Home Office, concluded that the matter was being stirred up for political and religious gain:

> It is difficult to resist the impression that the commission of a breach of the peace is being used as a threat by those who resent the Congress being held in order to prevent its taking place.[30]

The staging of the Congress was, however, more than a matter of domestic policy. The Home Office could counter threats to public order by statements of this nature but could not control the reverberations that the affair had in the realm of foreign policy. The implications for imperial unity are starkly illustrated in a letter received from the Roman Catholic Archbishop of Alberta who once again conjured up the rhetoric of the godfearing periphery betrayed by the secularising rationalist centre.

> The holding of such a Congress would certainly be the worst national insult ever offered by the Empire to God... . Your Majesty's Catholic subjects in this Dominion are loyal; and we their spiritual leaders are most anxious to maintain that loyalty at full strength. We have no difficulty so far as ordinary obstacles are concerned; but we are sometimes dismayed by the highly organised power and influence of the many subversive movements afloat all over the country. Our future efforts will be largely fruitless if this anti-God Congress is permitted in the very heart of the Empire.[31]

Moreover in the strained atmosphere of mid-1938 the Archbishop's equivocal statement concerning the importance of maintaining the loyalty of Canadian subjects had some important resonances. The Home Office's instinct was again to play down the whole matter this time, asserting that the Archbishop had not taken into account the fact that the Congress had been invited by British freethinkers and that he should also not underestimate the desire of those involved in promoting the Congress to exaggerate its importance. Home Office commentaries at this point also showed considerable sympathy with or at least understanding of the motivations of the international freethought movement. One commentator noted, rather waspishly, assessing the potentially extremist temperature of the political atmosphere, that Catholicism might be construed a threat to national liberties by a militant Protestant. Nevertheless the Home Office explanation of the freethinker's actions sensibly noted their self-expressed need for unity occasioned by the rise of Hitler and their oft-repeated declaration that the Russians would only be admitted if the political nature of their atheism be disavowed, at least within the international sphere.[32]

The clamour for action emanating from the Catholic Church was once more joined by Cardinal Hinsley who argued that Hoare had been misled by the freethinking organisations and that Jan Jansen, the secretary of the World Union of Freethinkers had made it clear that the Congress in England would be closely co-ordinated with the Communist League of Militant Atheists. Moreover the Cardinal hinted darkly that while he would do his best to maintain order amongst his compatriots he could not be responsible for 'untoward incidents'.[33]

Ramsay's next move indicated how far the climate of religious tolerance could be eroded by determined pressure 'from below'. The introduction of the Aliens Restriction (Blasphemy) Bill in June 1938 was a complete sea-change from previous parliamentary attempts to grapple with the matter. When it was presented in the early days of June Labour and Communist members greeted it with derision but as the month wore on it was treated with increasing seriousness.[34] Ramsay intended to extend the blasphemy laws to 'prevent the participation by aliens in assemblies for the purpose of propagating blasphemous or atheistic doctrines or in other activities calculated to interfere with the established religious institutions of the country'. To accomplish this end the Bill aimed at also amending the existing Aliens Restriction (Amendment) Act of 1919.[35] Although the Home Office correctly surmised the intention of the Bill was to undermine the Godless Congress and ordered it to be blocked this was conceived of as only a temporary measure since at least one civil servant wanted to 'consider the merits of the Bill when it has been printed'.[36]

As it turned out when the Bill arrived in its final form it was a mass of contradictions and legal anomalies that simultaneously demonstrated Ramsay's single-minded lack of understanding and the constitutional and social minefield that legislation in this area constituted. The Bill's wording sought to

> make it an offence, punishable with imprisonment up to three months and deportátion for an alien to participate in the organisation of any assembly for the purpose of propagating beliefs of an atheistic nature or to deliver speeches calculated to bring Christianity or any other form of religion into contempt; or to sell or distribute, make, publish or have in his possession for sale or distribution any document containing blasphemous matter.[37]

The wording of this Bill contains an interesting insight into the way that religious toleration was becoming tied up with forms of wider religio-imperial street politics. On the one hand the Bill was clearly intended to prevent the arrival of émigres from the European mainland, with the concealed bias against those of Jewish origin. However it also attacked existing religious liberties with a savagery that aimed at undoing the relative tide of tolerance created within the last two generations. Whilst the definition of 'blasphemous matter' would produce the traditional problems and counterarguments associated with the police, juries and judges deciding the offence – the notion of possession constituting an offence took the matter far beyond previous considerations of the subject. Likewise attacks upon assembly and upon 'blasphemous matter' ('words spoken or written, or pictorial representations, whereby it is sought to bring the Christian or any other form of religion into contempt') was taking the law far beyond the pre-Coleridge interpretation. The dangerously wide net it cast could reasonably be said to encompass almost all activites organised by the RPA, the NSS and South Place Ethical Society at which foreign visitors took part.

Despite the fact that the Bill applied to aliens this scarcely comforted British freethinkers who could argue that they had done all they could to purge the movement of untoward political influence and, in the climate of 1938, would not be surprised to see further attempts to extend the law to encompass them. This threat seemed to lie behind the wording of the Bill which tacitly signalled that all involvement in atheistic meetings, publishing and other activities constituted a form of treachery to the British Constitution, Church, Empire and Nation.

The Home Office immediately recognised the legal and civil liberties nightmare that the Bill represented. It threatened to make illegal, actions by foreign nationals which were not themselves illegal for British citizens to commit and it was soon realised that this Bill could not be softened by amendments. The whips were thus instructed to block the progress of the Bill through continual vigilance. As F. A. Newsam noted with considerable understatement '... if this Bill were to slip through at 11 o'clock some night, the position would be very awkward'.[38] Almost immediately the Home Office began the process of dissecting the Bill to show its flaws as well as the process of countering the arguments which it knew Ramsay would be raising. The latter involved the fact that Ramsay's action appealed over the heads of parliament to wider imperial and Christian Britain since he could claim that the failure of Hoare to support the Bill undermined the Home Secretary's contention that he was, in a legislative sense, powerless to stop the Congress.

Objections to the Bill itself turned around the fact that it was wrong as a matter of principle to subject aliens to special penal provisions not covered by the law of the land which, together with the existing Aliens Act, had satisfactorily regulated their conduct up to now. Despite an admission that the Aliens Act contained exceptions related to the fermentation of industrial unrest, sedition and dissaffection amongst HM forces the Home Office dismissed these cases as being clearly matters of national safety. Here there was a clear gulf of understanding between the attitude of government and that of the popular demagogue. For Ramsay the attack upon the British civilisation represented by émigre, communist Jewish freethinkers (and arguably their British counterparts) actually amounted to a form of sedition which placed national security in peril.

A further objection to the Bill surrounded the implications of Ramsay's curious phrase 'or any other form of religion', which was construed as extending the laws of blasphemy beyond Christianity. Not only did this provision reopen the debate concerning the definition of the word 'religion' but the Home Office noted with considerable irony that

> Under the Bill an alien would be liable to conviction and imprisonment for delivering a speech or publishing or having in his possession a pamphlet in which contemptuous reference to the Jewish religion or Buddhism or Mohammedanism were made.

It also added its customary line on the matter that 'there was no reason in a Christian country why these religions should be given such gratuitous protection'.[39]

In addition, the shoddiness of Ramsay's thinking was highlighted by the provision in the Bill of deportation for offenders since this could already be recommended for any imprisonable offence. Although the Bill, introduced under the ten-minute rule, had no realistic chance of becoming law its appearance showed a dramatic level of support for Ramsay's views and the strength of feeling that could be motivated against freethought by groups that had influence in Parliament and were prepared to use it. Ramsay's introduction of the Bill stressed arguments he had already aired – the nature of the International Proletarian Freethinkers, the role of Jaroslawsky and the general soviet infiltration of international freethought movements. He also argued that freethought gangs had been responsible for disrupting United Christian Front meetings and this had been done 'nearly always by aliens'. Whilst Ramsay claimed to have nothing against the domestic 'Victorian agnostic free-thought societies' he nonetheless failed to convince Edmund Harvey who squarely linked an attack upon the foreign emigré as an attack upon all. Indeed, Harvey simultaneously sketched the shamefully pedestrian growth of tolerance alongside an acknowledgement of the martyrological element in atheist culture.

I maintain that truth needs no other shield or weapon than itself. Whether it be political error or religious error, the right way to deal with it is by the weapons of argument and appeals to the highest. The only safeguard that truth needs is the light in which and by which it lives.

Some of the darkest pages in the History of this House have been pages where we have tried as a House of Commons to go contrary to that spirit. Go back 300 years and think of the time when a Puritan House of Commons condemned for blasphemy a Quaker whose tongue was bored with a red hot iron and whose forehead was branded. I think that the House then dishonoured itself more than its victim. Go back some 50 years, and think of how the House shut out from its membership one whom they regarded as an Atheist, some perhaps as a blasphemer, and when he lay dying the House expunged from its Minutes the record of what it had done. We do not want to go back to that sort of thing. We want to remember rather that we are the guardians of the spirit which John Milton expressed in his noblest prose work. We need to remember his words today:

> 'Give me liberty to know, to utter and to argue
> freely according to conscience, above all
> liberties.'

That is a liberty which we ought to be proud and glad to share with men of every other nation.[40]

Despite this spirited libertarian rallying call a resulting Commons division adopted the Bill for consideration at its First Reading by 165 to 134 clearly indicating the level of agreement with Ramsay's plausibly described version of events. It also indicated the ability to ignore the implications for the liberty of minorities within society. Whilst most of those who voted for the measure were Conservatives there was nonetheless a small number of Liberals who approved of the measure. Even Labour members were represented in this group by Sir Ernest Bennett (Cardiff), Robert Gibson (Greenock) and David Logan (Liverpool).[41] These MPs and others constituted a loose confederation known as 'Group 34' which produced a *Manifesto of Witness* which was sent to all church leaders. This was the respectable and more thoughtful version of Ramsay's concerns and strategy since the manifesto pleaded for reconciliation in an age when 'conflict and anxiety prevail on every side'. It urged Christians to work concertedly for Peace and expressed, amongst other wishes, a desire to 'attain harmony with the Divine will'.[42]

Ramsay's exploration of legislative avenues ended, for the time being, with the order for the second reading which resulted in the Aliens Bill's withdrawal two days later.[43] Whilst the Bill itself blundered to ignominious obscurity the Home Office was still framing arguments against it in July, perhaps realising that in many senses they had not heard the last of Ramsay.[44] Meanwhile attention focused once again squarely on the Godless Congress itself. George Mathers MP, placed under pressure by a deputation, wrote to Hoare asking what steps would be taken to ensure blasphemous utterings would not occur during the course of the Congress. Having repulsed Ramsay's attempt to alter the law the government was prepared to take this more reasonable request seriously. Mathers was duly informed that, although it was unlikely blasphemy would occur, such utterances could not be proceeded against in the courts. With this in mind the consensus at the Home Office was that the police should openly buy tickets, keep detailed notes and that their presence would 'keep spokesmen within due bounds'. The need to placate opposition to the Congress was interestingly addressed – by the suggestion that '"independent writers" would be able to refute opposition suggestions that blasphemies were occuring'. Although Lord Harry Snell could be counted upon to use temperate language it was argued, with a charming parochialism, that this police presence would be effective since 'experience shows that foreigners have a wholesome respect for the police'.[45] Nonetheless the Chief Constable expressed concern, however veiled, about the Congress since what he considered to be its avowedly anti-fascist stance would provide a focus for fascist opposition. His concerns about the Congress also echoed, in their own way, the morality versus cultural sedition debate that Ramsay and his quasi-Christian organisation had opened. The Chief Constable declared that:

> One of the principal objects of the movement will be to spread its ideas amongst working men who are believers, in order that they may be free from the influence of clerical reaction and may play their part in the struggle for bread, peace and liberty.[46]

The argument about the dissemination of the propaganda from and about the Congress entered a new phase when Cardinal Hinsley urged that the Home Office should do all it could to curb BBC radio broadcasts from referring to the Congress. The Cardinal hoped to influence Hoare by including a telegram which declared that 100 000 men from the Australian and New Zealand branch of the Holy Name Society had signed a petition against the Congress.[47] Hoare replied with his by now established line that such matters were not for him to regulate. The Cardinal raised the stakes by suggesting that any such broadcasts might be in breach of the League of Nations guidelines on 'Broadcasting in the interests of Peace'. Hoare asked the BBC to ignore the Congress, but was advised to keep this strictly secret from the Congress organisers. He placated Cardinal Hinsley by indicating that the role of broadcasting in the proceedings might be referred to the Postmaster General.[48] However the Cardinal had also previously gone over Hoare's head by writing to the Prime Minister Neville Chamberlain on this matter. He cited the League of Nations recommendations and argued that the broadcast of anything which could be linked to soviet activities abroad could, in the Cardinal's chilling phrase, render 'your wise peace policy largely nullified'.[49] Although the BBC replied that it was not bound by the wording of these recommendations concerning the political and religious sentiments of others it nonetheless noted that such transmissions could be contrary to the spirit of them.

While the international implications of the Congress were being digested by the Prime Minister and the Home Secretary, more violent protests were being formulated as forms of militant Christianity, aided and abetted by Ramsay, and the Nordic League began to flex their muscles in the arena of street politics. The Commissioner of the Metropolitan Police made a point of having observers at Caxton Hall on the night of 9 September 1938 where a meeting was held 'under the auspices of the Militant Christian Patriots' – another fascist organisation with strong links to the Nordic League. This meeting was an amalgam of Christian groups such as the British Bible Union, the Christian Endeavour Society, the Christian Evidence Society, the Salvation Army and members of the Catholic Church. Quasi-imperial organisations were also present including the British Empire Union and the British Israel World Federation as well as Ramsay's Nordic League.[50]

The meeting was attended by approximately 500 people, 'a large percentage of whom appeared to be fascist sympathisers'. The meeting was orderly throughout but many of the fascist element in the audience, whenever the occasion arose, persisted in shouting the Nordic League toast 'PJ' ('Perish Judah') and other anti-semitic remarks.[51] The tenor of the meeting made it clear that the attempt to persuade the government to act had failed and that a recourse to street politics was both necessary and justified. After claiming to appreciate the Home Secretary's dilemma the Earl of Glasgow intimated that: 'there was, however, nothing to stop a gathering of British Citizens from meeting and expressing their disgust at such a congress being allowed to meet in London'.[52]

Newman Watts of the British Bible Union outlined his belief that the World Union of Freethinkers had begun in Soviet Russia and that it was now swamped by the membership from that country. At this point the previously carefully nurtured distinction between the foreign communist semitic targets of the Nordic League and domestic British Freethinkers broke down spectacularly as Watts attacked the works of Bernard Shaw for constituting 'anti-God propaganda', reading several extracts to illustrate his opinon.

The imperialist critique of the Congress was voiced by Commander

Franklin of the British Empire Union, who warned of intense communist permeation of the empire's institutions under the guise of 'free speech'. Blaming every industrial disorder upon creeping communism he railed against Anglican clerics who he declared openly supported the communist party. Again the inaction of Hoare was condemned and the speech concluded with an appeal to individuals to protest against the Congress. Ramsay addressed the meeting by joining the assault upon the domestic branch of freethought. He took up the example of Bernard Shaw, declaring his writings had 'given them all the publicity they required in his anti-religious writings'. The unwelcome publicity consisted of paragraphs from Russian newspapers which contained attempts to ridicule the Commandments as well as declarations that the murder of opponents was politically justifiable. Although this constituted flimsy evidence against the Congress Ramsay pointed out that 'No communist would ever do anything to help the British Empire but they were always working for the overthrow of it.'[53] He then recounted the usual stories of the murder of priests during the Spanish Civil War and reiterated that the World Union of Freethinkers was supported and controlled by Moscow and that 'the communists openly avowed that religion and communism were incompatible'. Ramsay then proposed a resolution to the meeting which,

> ... while recognising the right of British subjects to free speech, expresses its strong disapproval of the International Congress of Free-Thinkers being held in this country. The object of this movement is to actively attack the religious beliefs of the community and it is closely connected with foreign revolutionary organisations. This meeting defines the Congress as a subtle and dangerous manoeuvre on the part of the Communist international.[54]

Immediately after the resolution was put to the meeting Ramsay's arch-partner in anti-Semitism, Arnold Leese, proposed an amendment from the floor which sought to replace the word 'Jewish' for 'foreign' in the phrase 'foreign revolutionary movements'. This was accompanied by the ritual shouting of 'PJ' and considerable excitement in the audience. Although the amendment itself was not put to the meeting Ramsay was clearly pleased by this development. Presumably mindful of a police presence Ramsay replied in transparent vindication of the wishes of Leese and the meeting, hinting at a sinister future direction for policy and action.

> For those who want strong meat, I will say that the time is not yet ripe, but I can take as strong meat as anyone and at some future date I shall be very glad when we shall be able to eat it together.[55]

The policemen in attendance noted the sale of fascist literature in the hall and the presence of BUF and IFL stewards. When the meeting closed at least half of the audience gave the fascist salute.

When the Congress finally took place there was in fact little incident. The Home Office put this down to the role played by a direct appeal by Hoare to Ramsay although the simple logistics involved in disrupting an all-ticket meeting overseen by the police must have also defeated even Ramsay and Leese's ingenuity. It is also likely that the unfolding of events in Prague and Berlin may have occupied the minds of those involved. In some respects the sentiments of the 'Godless Congress' were mirrored by a substantial religious service at Westminster Abbey organised in opposition to it. Organised by the Christian Evidence Society it drew together 2000 worshippers who represented most western and some eastern orthodox denominations in an act of 'positive witness' which sought to extend international understanding.[56]

Nonetheless the policemen attending the Congress still took copious notes and submitted their findings to the Home Office for scrutiny. Some of these with passages marked for possible prosecution included the lecture by the geneticist and communist Professor J. B. S. Haldane, another anxious to link his branch of science and its method directly with socialism, which disproved the story of the creation.[57] The mood of siege and gloom that had surrounded the preparations for the Congress invariably coloured the responses of some who spoke. Resolutions congratulating the Spanish republic in its fight against fascism, protesting against the threat of Germany to use force against Czechoslovakia and a general expression of sympathy for those struggling for liberty in Germany, Italy, Austria, Spain, China, Abyssinia, and also with the Jews were all passed.[58]

Allan Flanders, a representative from Belgium, railed against the Catholic Church 'being ready to use the forces of fascism to further its ends, provided it could bring them under its control, as in Dolfuss Austria, Franco Spain and Quebec'. He attacked its bargaining with Italian fascism and what he saw as its gleeful complicity in the Nazi suppression of liberalism, socialism and freethought in Germany. More poignantly the anarchist Lorulot, whom the Home Office had earlier considered a distinct danger, when asked to speak '... in a light vein felt he could not do so, in view of the present critical situation'.[59]

A particularly distasteful incident occurred on the occasion of the Congress's visit to Bradlaugh's grave in Brookwood cemetery outside Woking. On reaching the graveyard the members of the Congress discovered that Bradlaugh's bust had been replaced by a chamber pot and 'An orange coloured poster bearing the words "P swastika J" – "Judah beware, Christian England is rising against you. CGV". Likewise the legend "Beneath that sod lies another", was found by the grave.'[60]

In the history of public order concerns the prevention of violence on this occasion represented a triumph for the police and government's decision to uphold the liberty of opinion and to be prepared to back this up with a considerable police presence and surveillance of these potentially antagonistic organisations. That there were no physical injuries can have been of little comfort to foreign and British freethinkers alike who found their otherwise unobtrusive Congress a focus for the demands voiced by pressure group and street politics. What the Godless Congress episode demonstrated was that the liberal tolerance and the belief in its constant advance that had been the hallmark of attitudes based upon the Coleridge judgment were fundamentally misplaced. Although the Bill to extend the Blasphemy Laws was ill considered and sank without trace there is at least circumstantial evidence to suggest that a better constructed measure would have gained more sympathy, even support. Irrespective of this the episode proved to freethinkers that the legacy of progressive liberal toleration (that the Coleridge dictum argued was a dominant theme in British society) could be eroded and stripped away in a matter of months. Ramsay and the grass roots 'from below' elements of Christianity had constructed a seductive rhetoric which combined anti-semitism and anti-communism with a grandiose imperial British Christian identity. When this was coupled with a paranoid foreboding concerning the collapse of this system which had made Britain successful and morally triumphant attacks upon the enemies of this system were an effortlessly logical progression. Whilst physical violence did not result, considerable damage to the expectations of British freethinkers and their perception of toleration represented another episode in which 'from below' attempts to recolonise social, religious and political opinion could achieve a victory of sorts.

At the meeting to conclude the Congress at the Scala Theatre in Charlotte Street, John Langdon Davies, aware of hostile crowds outside the theatre, noted the gathering international storm which this local manifestation represented:

> It was really remarkable, he thought, that people were going to walk through the streets of 20th century London to assist God to forget that there were people like freethinkers in existence... . Unless freethought was combined with intelligent action there was the gravest danger of the world returning to the dark ages. In the past, the working class, assisted by a few of the middle class had had to struggle hard for its gains, but today we had to unite to fight religious and fascist forces which threatened to bring us back to the dark ages. Organised religion is only dangerous as a force to maintain social injustice and legalised robbery; it is not enough to say we are defending ourselves against fascism – we have got to defeat fascism by improving our heritage, which we owe to Freethinkers of the past.[61]

On that evening for British and Foreign freethinkers alike the world must have seemed a very dark and illiberal place indeed.

Notes

1. Hansard, 2 December 1937.
2. HO45 24619/ 217459/92.
3. Ibid.
4. Ibid.
5. Ibid.
6. HO45 24619/ 217459/155.
7. Ibid. (Italicised words underlined in original.)
8. Letters arrived at the Home Office addressed from Saskatchewan, Capri, Naples, Cardiff, London, Norwich, Sunderland, Sidcup, Manchester, Ayreshire, Falkland Hall London Mission Men's Fellowship, Battle Sussex, Alverston Hants, West Bromwich, Parkstone Dorset, Co. Down, Bath, Preston, Barnetly Lincs., Worthing, Bedford, Sherborne Dorset, Tunbridge Wells, Ramsgate, Stourbridge, Brierley Hill Staffs., Westbury Somerset, Plymouth, St Leonards, Sevenoaks, Bristol, Wellington Shropshire, Leytonstone, Shrewsbury, Llwyngwril Merioneth, Brockenhurst Hants., Reading, Portrush, Manchester, Derby, various London suburbs, Malvern, Liverpool, Rochdale, High Wycombe, Bedford, Hull, Newquay Strict Baptist Chapel, Bristol, Coventry Bethel Evangelistic society, and Gravesend.
9. HO45 24619/ 217459/92.
10. *The Times*, 6, 15 and 22 July 1938.
11. *Watt's Literary Guide*, December 1937.
12. HO45 24619/ 217459/101.
13. Ibid.
14. Ibid.
15. Ibid., *Freethinker*, 20 February 1938.
16. Crowson, N. J. (1995), 'The British Conservative Party and the Jews during the Late 1930s', *Patterns of Prejudice* 29, 2–3: pp. 15–32. Thurlow, Richard (1987), *Fascism in Britain A History, 1918–85*, Oxford: Blackwell, pp. 78–9.
17. Thurlow, op. cit., p. 77.
18. HO45 24619/ 217459/155 copy of leaflet. (Italicised words underlined in the original.)
19. Ibid. (Italicised words underlined in the original.)
20. Ibid.
21. HO45 24619/ 217459/185.
22. Ibid.
23. For Levy and Laski see Wood, N. (1959), *Communism and British Intellectuals*, London: Gollancz, pp. 46–7, 127, 136–7.
24. Werskey, Gary (1978), *The Visible College: The Collective Biography of British Scientific Socialists of the 1930s*, London: Allen Lane, pp. 170–71.
25. HO45 24619/ 217459/211.
26. HO45 24619/ 217459/229.
27. *The Times*, 4 June 1938.
28. Ibid.
29. Ibid. Letter from Hoare to Ramsay 3 June 1938.
30. Ibid.
31. HO45 24619/ 217459/223. Letter from John Macdonald, Catholic Archbishop of Edmonton to A. S. Hutchinson at Buckingham Palace, 7 May 1938.

32. HO45 24619/ 217459/247.
33. Ibid., Letter from Archbishop A. Cardinal Hinsley Archbishop of Westminster to Sir Samuel Hoare, 12 June 1938.
34. *The Times*, 5 July 1938.
35. HO45 24619/ 217459/250.
36. HO45 24619/ 217459/247.
37. HO45 24619/ 217459/274.
38. Ibid.
39. Ibid., briefing note dated 15 July 1938.
40. Hansard, 28 June 1938.
41. Logan who sat for a seat with a large Catholic presence had given his maiden speech against Thurtle's 1930 bill (Hansard 24/1/30).
42. *The Times*, 6 September 1938.
43. Hansard 30 June 1938.
44. See above and footnote 39.
45. HO45 24619/ 217459/274.
46. Ibid.
47. HO45 24619/ 217459/300 letter from Valentine Elwes, Cardinal's Private Secretary, to Neville Chamberlain, 21 August 1938.
48. HO45 24619/ 217459/300 letter of Samuel Hoare to Cardinal Hinsley, 24 August 1938.
49. Ibid., Cardinal Hinsley to Neville Chamberlain, 8 August 1938.
50. HO45 24619/ 217459/310 Commissioner of Police Report on disturbance 9/9/38 at Caxton Hall, Westminster, submitted by Inspector Whitehead, hereafter 217459/310 Caxton Hall Report.
51. Thurlow, op. cit., p. 81.
52. 217459/310 Caxton Hall Report.
53. Ibid.
54. Ibid.
55. Ibid. On the cover of this file there is a note to say that Ramsay's reply is 'worthy of note' and this section is conspicuously underlined in the report.
56. *The Times*, 3 September 1938 and 11 September 1938.
57. For Haldane see Werskey, op. cit., p. 183, Wood, op. cit., pp. 27, 136–7, 147 and 158.
58. HO45 24619/ 217459/311.
59. Ibid.
60. Ibid.
61. Ibid., speech, 11 September 1938.

CHAPTER EIGHT

Silencing the Love that Dares to Speak its Name: Blasphemy and the *Gay News* Case

As a piece of contemporary history the case of Whitehouse versus Lemon, or as it is popularly known, the *Gay News* case, offers a bewildering challenge to those who would categorise it and its significance. For orthodox progressive histories of the crime of blasphemy the outcome of the case should have been a coda to trends in society which were civilising the law away from prosecution, conviction and punishment towards modern forms of toleration. It should have been the culmination of the optimistic view that Arthur Calder-Marshall expounded in the early 1970s. Certainly the blasphemy laws had remained relatively undisturbed since Gott's time and Levy makes the telling suggestion that the portrayal of Christ as a circus clown in the musical *Godspell* (a production enthusiastically endorsed by numerous clerics) was in fact a depiction for which Gott had been punished half a century earlier.[1] The curtain appeared to have been brought down upon the constitutional issue of governmental protection of religious-inspired morality when the statute laws of blasphemy were very quietly repealed in the context of the Criminal Justice Act of 1967.[2] Whilst this attacked the statute law, in particular the 9 & 10 William III acts, the Common Law offence remained intact. Indeed this particular state of affairs echoed distinctly the Home Office opinion in the context of the earlier century discussions in which the statutory laws were widely admitted to be a dead letter.

Instead of this phasing out of the law constituting the final act the *Gay News* case and its outcome threw the history of blasphemy into turmoil by putting the legal status of the blasphemy laws potentially back to the condition they were in before Coleridge and Stephen brought their considerable legal minds to bear upon the matter. As an indicator of social trends the verdict in the case might be seen to have signalled the end of the permissive 1960s, for it highlighted and fulfilled the wish of Mary Whitehouse and those who might be categorised as moral conservatives that a line be drawn beyond which transgression should become actively punishable. However one further inference which might be made from the verdict, which forms a substantial theme of this chapter, is that this episode represents the apogee of grass-roots 'from below' opinion and its influence upon the construction of socially understood and negotiated morality and religion.

Philip Larkin did much to give the Penguin Books' *Lady Chatterley's Lover* case its modernist pedigree as well as its instantly memorable context. The *Gay News* case deserves no less – not simply for descriptive and narrative purposes but also to highlight an important context which suggests that it deserves greater integration into a history of morality and constructive definitions of culture and society. The case which packed the Central Criminal Court between 7 and 9 July 1977 was played out against a cultural and political backdrop of conflicting messages of social stability and social collapse. Whilst the country basked in the afterglow of the Queen's Silver Jubilee in June of that year the streets of one corner of London were occupied by police and pickets engaged in the two opposing sides of the Grunwick industrial dispute. The pubs and clubs of the land were filled with the raucous sounds of the first wave of punk rock records and performances. The Callaghan government grew more fragile by the month, holding to its prices and incomes policy despite threats from the journalism and postal unions. Even the theatre echoed the country's mood, staging Mike Leigh's 'Abigail's Party' with its images of sterile, amoral and empty bourgeois suburban life. Much of the flavour of this period is conveyed most instantly by Hanif Kureishi's the *Bhudda of Suburbia* as much as by Derek Jarman's *Jubilee*. What is striking about both of these is that they suggest that a form of moral retrenchment in the context of the late 1970s was inevitable. In this respect the *Gay News* case emphatically demonstrates its pedigree as a dynamic of moral conservative retrenchment.

It should, however, be pointed out that there is a wider dimension to both the permissiveness of the late 1970s and to the success of forms of moral retrenchment in British society. As far as the former was concerned there was certainly, in the late 1970s, a wider current of scepticism about the role, credibility and purpose of religious belief that amounted to considerably more than a gratuitous attempt to flout morality. Whilst the attempts to go beyond rational discussion and to associate some of the most cogent moral texts of modern society with pornographic ridicule were thwarted – Jens Jorgen Thorsen's proposed *Sex life of Christ* never troubled the authorities – there were nevertheless challenges to the utility and value of Christianity in 1976–77 which were rather more difficult to ignore, attack or explain away.

Despite the fact that Thorsen's attempt to film in Britain was prevented there is a clear sense in which this was a further assault upon

Christian morality and Mrs Whitehouse's biography leads the reader to believe that such attacks were occurring thick and fast at the end of the 1970s. Her encounter with the James Kirkup poem 'The Love that Dares to Speak its Name' is clearly identified as occurring just as the Thorsen controversy had burnt itself out. Likewise the newspapers around the hearing of the *Gay News* case itself indicate that those who feared for the longevity of Christianity as a religious and ethical system in the modern world would have had much to consider.

The previous month (June 1977) witnessed the release of a book, *The Myth of God Incarnate*, edited by Professor John Higg and containing contributions from a number of noted theologians. The book denied the divinity of Christ but most ominously it appeared to signal the retreat of religion from everyday life in the phrase, contained in *The Times* report, which suggested that 'to describe Jesus Christ as the son of God and the second person of the Blessed Trinity is to use language that has lost its meaning'. As *The Times* also suggested, 'although no one was carried out of the room with apoplexy, it would have suited the atmosphere if some one had been'.[3] This book itself was to resurface in Justice King-Hamilton's summing up in the *Gay News* case. Less than a week before the trial *The Times* also carried an article by Clifford Longley which, in the course of attempting to defend Christianity as more than the apparent sum of its parts, conceded that many theologians now suggested that the Gospels were 'a strange mixture of factual history, legend based on actual events, invention for the sake of argument, and subjective interpretation on the part of the author'. From this point on the article admitted that these same theologians were already asking whether '... the fundamental tenets of Christianity are also myths: is the Trinity a myth, is the doctrine of the incarnation of God and Jesus Christ a myth? and inevitable also, once the question has been asked in this way, the answer has to be yes'.[4] Longley's defence against 'The Myth' was to further assert that an ecumenical recognition of Christ's uniqueness was the answer – a solution that would have dismayed other more orthodox Christians.

Interestingly the next day's issue of *The Times* contained an article reporting the retiring address of the President of the Law Society Sir David Napley who noted that a gathering tide of criticism was currently being levelled against the conduct of judges and lawyers and the commensurately damaging effect this had on respect for the law. This, it was argued, also had the unwelcome effect of discouraging citizens from using the law to uphold their rights.[5] Such a linkage – between the perceived diminishing respect for Christianity and for the law in many respects provides a backdrop to the *Gay News* case. At a popular level it provided a medium through which those in favour of moral retrenchment or even those who worried about the extension of permissiveness could invest their hope upon a reversal of the prevailing trend.

The case itself stemmed from the publication in the June 1976 edition of *Gay News* of the James Kirkup poem 'The Love that Dares to Speak its Name', which described the homosexual love felt by a centurion for the crucified Christ, alongside a similarly graphic illustration. The poem also described Christ engaging in homosexual acts with Judas and the other disciples as well as Scribes and Pharisees – totalling 17 people. Additionally acts of fellatio with the dead body of Christ and sexual congress with his wounds were depicted in the poem. If blasphemy were a purely objectively defined offence then the poem was objectively blasphemous, indeed the Judge Alan King-Hamilton, as a Jew, noted that one didn't have to be Christian to be offended by it – perhaps indicating that the power of the offence had drifted still further away from religious doctrinal belief.[6] The poem's description of Christ's penis as the instrument of salvation, the juxtaposition of Christ's ejaculation with the crucifixion and the portrayal of the resurrection and paradise as bodies entwined in homosexual love were all attacks upon scripture and by definition upon the sacred beliefs of Christians.[7]

However all this was clear and unequivocal only if the poem were intended to be understood at face value as deliberately intended to be blasphemous and a work of unrivalled mischief with wholly dishonourable intentions. A component of the defence was to establish the metaphorical nature of the poem and to try and establish a series of just such honourable motives for Kirkup and honest intentions for his artistic expression. Thus the trial could often appear to the outsider as a struggle between the legitimacy and accessibility of literary forms of an intellectual culture against those unable or unwilling to admit the legitimacy of these forms. Rapidly it became clear that Kirkup, who had written religious works before,[8] intended the poem to be allegorical and hoped it would show the redeeming love of Christ in a homosexual context as well as to illustrate the proximity of sexual to religious ecstacy – a theme later to be developed by Nigel Wingrove. What is also illuminating is that Kirkup also belonged to that group of blasphemers who ostensibly were using the medium of their blasphemy as a means of investigating and confronting their own religious feelings and nature. Kirkup portrayed himself as an agnostic anxious to believe whilst living with a legacy of repugnant fascination for the doctrines and images conjured in the mind by orthodox Christianity. Terrified as a child by stories of the torments of the damned, likewise revolted by the apparent cannibalism of the communion and the brutality of the crucifixion, Kirkup was a figure culturally excluded from the Christianity he felt should have been his birthright. 'The Love that Dares to Speak its Name' was thus an attempt to confront Kirkup's search for an alternative spirituality but also significantly to produce an image of Christ more in keeping with the modern world. Thus Kirkup's Christ was open to all, permissive in theology and behaviour and significantly human with 'the same lusts, failings, ecstasies and sexual equipment as the rest of us'.[9] In this respect the poem offended orthodox Christians who themselves had been fighting a rear-guard action against liberal theology's denial of the divinity of Christ. The Kirkup poem appeared to be combining the twin evils of the age – sexual permissiveness and the relegation of Christ to mortality. Mary Whitehouse herself considered the poem to have recrucified Christ only this time 'with twentieth-century weapons'.[10] However, it might equally be argued that the outrage felt against Kirkup and the poem represented also a surprisingly modern chapter in the history of blasphemy's links to fears of anti-trinitarian views of Christ. Its portrayal of an outcast Christ and the court's decision to interest itself in such a matter meant that the *Gay News* case could perhaps be viewed as a trial for heresy.[11]

Mary Whitehouse's attention was drawn to the poem by the arrival of a copy of it on her doorstep and after seeking legal advice she was convinced that it was actionable under the law of blasphemous libel.[12] Acting under a statute of 1866 which required the consent of a judge she instituted a private prosecution against Denis Lemon, the editor of *Gay News*, and also against the publisher, Gay News Ltd.[13] The trial itself took place over the weekend of the 9 July 1977 and was the first airing of the whole issue for over two generations. Although Lemon's counsel, the playwright and novelist John Mortimer, attempted a number of procedural attempts to block the prosecution case – through seeking proof of the identity of the newspaper and of the defendent as well as questioning the nature of the offence – the confrontation between the two conceptions of culture and morality was fused into stark relief. Mortimer did all he could to equate the offence with one of obscenity and thus hoped to use expert evidence to illuminate the nature of neo-Christian allegory and metaphor as well as the honesty of intention exhibited by Kirkup and Lemon. Although Bernard Levin and Margaret Drabble testified to the seriousness of *Gay News* as a publication the wider use of expert testimony was denied. If this had been permitted then the *Gay News* case might well have resembled the Penguin *Lady Chatterley* case. Certainly Mary Whitehouse herself was worried by the prospect of the case taking this course.

> It was at our first legal conference that we discovered that James Kirkup was Professor of Poetry at Massachusetts University with about six column inches to his name in *Who's Who*! Not that that

> really made any difference except that one could see what John
> Mortimer ... would make of it. I could hear the cries of 'Philistine!'
> and 'Censorship' echoing through the land.[14]

Gay News Ltd's counsel, Geoffrey Robertson, attempted to limit the
jury's line of enquiry into establishing whether the prosecution had
proved its case and also tried to undermine the sense of outrage felt by
the prosecution by suggesting that it was far-fetched indeed to regard a
poem as a 'smoking gun ... which would tend to make peoples blood
boil and shake the very fabric of our society'.[15]

Another line of defence attempted by Mortimer and Robertson was to
use expert evidence to assert that Christian theology had changed
sufficiently for the metaphorical and allegorical readings of Kirkup's
poem to be admissable to wider society. The suggestion that the
theological assumptions and beliefs of the 12 members of the jury could
not possibly be aware or knowledgeable about religious matters spoke
volumes. Whilst Mortimer wanted expert evidence to prove this King-
Hamilton thought such evidence would merely confuse and that 'twelve
ordinary people ought to be able to decide amongst themselves, without
getting bogged down in theological controversy'.[16] Once again a clear
attempt to delineate between the liberal naturalistic response to religion
of an educated mind was placed in opposition to a Christianity which
relied upon instinct, faith and steadfast belief. As the case progressed the
two almost became caricatures. Had such a defence been successful it
was possible that the court proceedings would have established a
publicly acceptable face for versions of profoundly heterodox theology.
Mary Whitehouse herself saw this at once and noted in her diary that if
Mortimer and Robertson had been successful then '... before this case is
out, if they have their way, Christ will be a homosexual too'.[17]
Mortimer's assertion that theology had changed was also linked to the
(by now standard) defence that the offence of blasphemy was an
anachronism that should be thrown out and the case dismissed. This
similarly was rejected and the burden of the defence effectively fell upon
the denial on behalf of Lemon and *Gay News* to have displayed the
intent to attack Christianity, to have done so in a deliberately scurrilous
manner and with an intent to cause a breach of the peace. Justice Alan
King-Hamilton rejected this defence and in so doing removed the notion
of intent from this case and was ultimately to do so for the resulting case-
law. This had the double effect of removing from the purview of the
prosecution the requirement to question Lemon directly on his motives
for publication whilst simultaneously eliminating the need to prove that
such intentions were malicious. In his summing up the judge made it
clear that whilst he thought the poem to be blasphemous 'on its face' he
was nonetheless convinced that the jury were responsible for deciding

whether the poem provoked outrage and the desire for revenge irrespective of the intention of the author or publisher.

King-Hamilton's summing up once more contained a reinvention of the casual encounter argument which once more specified the importance of the immediate context of offence in an astonishingly theatrical manner reminiscent of the melodrama which surely clung to its initiation in the previous century:

> When, therefore, ladies and gentlemen, you are considering this poem, you must try to recapture in your minds the impact it made upon you when you first read it. Doubtless, the fact that you were confined in the jury box in a court of law provided its own restraints; but what would your reactions have been had you first read it or had it read aloud to you in your home, or a friend's home, or in a public house? Moreover, now, after over a week you are used to it. It is the first reaction you must try to recall. A medical student present at his first operation quite frequently – not always, of course, but quite frequently – faints at the sight of blood, the shock; but after a time he gets used to it and it does not mean anything to him. So you must not judge it by what you think about it now; it is your first, immediate reaction, because that is the time when, if at all, your anger or anybody else's anger might well be aroused or their resentment provoked.[18]

The jury deliberated for three hours and after receiving further instruction from the judge regarding the tendency to breach of the peace they retired again. The eventual ten to two majority verdict of guilty allowed King-Hamilton to advance his own personal opinion on the nature of the offence. He effectively concurred with the jury that the poem was a gross blasphemy but Levy took him to task for his persistence in using the word 'profanity'as a misuse of a legal term which had previously referred to the 'taking of God's name in vain or an imprecation calling on divine judgement'.[19] The clear implication here was that even legal minds deserted their usual exactitude in the matter of blasphemy – not necessarily for malicious or premeditated motives but quite simply through the lack of exercise of legal skill in the matter. Indeed, this image of lawyers working through dusty legal treatises in search of case-law curios on blasphemy remained one of the lasting popular images painted by the media.[20]

The sentence consisted of a nine-month suspended prison sentence and a fine of £500 for Lemon together with an order to pay a proportion of the prosecution's costs – *Gay News* itself was fined £1000. The suspended sentence was later the subject of considerable remorse on the part of King-Hamilton who was relieved when it was later removed by the court of appeal.[21] The reaction of the newspapers was generally in favour of the verdict, although even here there were qualifications which raised doubts about the wisdom of the law and its prosecution in the courts. *The Times*' editorial of the following day ranged widely in its coverage of the case. Suggesting the conviction was a correct decision, amidst adjectives like 'shocking' and 'offensive', the editorial nonetheless lamented the fact that to dispassionate eyes the prosecution appeared to be an attack upon gay rights and gay forms of expression. The paper similarly criticised King-Hamilton for a blatant disregard of *Gay News*'s previously unsullied reputation as a responsible paper and likewise criticised the severity of the custodial sentence.[22] The *Daily Telegraph* was considerably less inclined to show sympathy for Lemon and *Gay News*. Arguing that forms of restraint rather than permissiveness were the hallmarks of a civilised society the *Telegraph* was unequivocal about the links it drew between various forms of unacceptable behaviour:

> ... there can be no doubt that a poetic fantasy compounded partly of homosexuality, partly of necrophilia and partly of what, in the judgement of ordinary men, must be considered rank blasphemy should not be permitted to appear in Britain even today. If the Old Bailey jury had not found against *Gay News* in the case brought by Mrs Whitehouse and the Crown, the obvious inference would have been that the cause of permissiveness in publishing had wholly prevailed.[23]

Interestingly enough both the *Daily Telegraph* and *The Times* were prepared to offer tolerance to other theistic minorities in Britain. *The Times* saw King-Hamilton's assertion that the current law on blasphemous libel could offer protection to the religious minorities in Britain as over optimistic and its only concern was that such protection, if offered, could be dangerously open:

> There is authority to the affect that it is not blasphemy to vilify the Jewish or any other non Christian religion. It would not have mattered too much until recently that the offence was so narrowly defined. Today, however, substantial minorities of British citizens follow religions other than Christianity, and, indeed, a high proportion of them are devout followers, who would perhaps take even greater exception to derogatorily offensive remarks about their Gods than would most Christians to similar language about Christ. If blasphemy is to remain a crime ... Muslims, Hindus, Sikhs, Buddhists and Jews would clearly need to be placed on the same footing as Christians. But what of the numerable minor sex and quasi religions which have a presence in Britain? The protection should be confined to major religions and not to be extended to the scientologists or Mr Moon. ... Allowing total freedom to insult the religious beliefs of others can also have a profoundly adverse affect on the harmony that exists between different groups, particularly, perhaps, where racial and religious divisions go together.[24]

Likewise the *Telegraph* argued:

> If the habit of gratuitously affronting religious convictions were to
> spread, if it were to be indulged at the expense of the votaries of the
> many world religions other than Christianity which are now so
> powerfully represented in Britain, it could well cause serious
> trouble.[25]

As far as the legitimacy of modern blasphemy prosecutions were
concerned both papers were agreed that the utility of such laws was at
least partly vindicated. *The Times* sought to see the question as one of
maintaining the rights and morality of the community. This, despite
some very slight misgivings, depended upon harnessing the perceptions
and participation of the public at large just as the Home Office had
argued for earlier in the century.

> There is a danger that the success (subject to appeal) of the *Gay
> News* prosecution will encourage other individuals and
> organizations to start similar, perhaps less reasonably founded
> private prosecutions. There is a temptation to urge that the
> prosecution should be able to be brought only with the consent of
> the Director of Public Prosecution or Attorney General. But
> blasphemy is an offence which depends for its existence on the
> public's reaction to such language, and it is right that members of the
> public should continue to be able to play a part in its prosecution.
> The Crown should not normally take over such prosecutions,
> however, as it did in the *Gay News* case. It would then be left to
> juries to determine the validity of the cases before them, and, by
> their verdicts, to throw out those which are unmeritorious.[26]

The clear implication here was that governments and the law should not
be the supreme arbiter of morality and moral transgression, a view
echoed by the *Telegraph* – although the paper also tacitly endorsed
further value judgements concerning homosexuality that should have
had no bearing upon the matter:

> Plainly, the poem condemned at the Old Bailey was obscene no less
> than blasphemous. Because it was prosecuted as blasphemy,
> however, the defence, though it availed itself of the right to object to
> 14 jurors, had no access to the other familiar expedient of trooping
> out 'expert witnesses' to testify to the work's literary merit or
> therapeutic value to the sexually inadequate. Is there not a lesson to
> be drawn from this?[27]

Once again the crime of blasphemy had become a category into which
other concerns about social crisis and moral collapse had been included.
Just as fear of the foreign freethinking Jew had entered the discussion
over the extension of the blasphemy laws in 1938, so concern about gay
rights and gay attempts to colonise morality, religion and even language
were inextricably linked in the case.[28] The verdict that intent on the part
of the author and publisher was irrelevant was a legal decision that had
considerable social and cultural implications. It is certainly clear that the

juxtaposition of Christ with homosexual desire contained in the Kirkup poem was instrumental in persuading Mary Whitehouse to institute proceedings against Lemon and the paper. The conduct of the case not only rejected the allegorical and metaphorical components of the poem as outlined by the defence but any likelihood of homosexual Christian spirituality being recognised was denied. Levy points out that King-Hamilton's argument that the poem was profane because it suggested that the founder of Christianity could behave as a practicing homosexual amounted to an exclusion of them from the Christian religion.[29] Likewise King-Hamilton's rebuke concerning the want of taste and 'disregard for the feelings of Christians' also intimated that homosexual versions of Christianity were not acceptable. This very incident led to the founding of the Lesbian and Gay Christian Society from which followed considerable financial support for the fighting fund established on behalf of *Gay News*.[30] The satirist Peter Cook writing in the *Daily Mail* immediately noted the connection between the concerns of sexual morality, depictions of Christ and the instinctive link made with this blasphemy prosecution. Moreover he also indicated the perennial truism that the case would ensure a much wider readership of the poem than would otherwise have occurred naturally (it was subsequently published by, amongst others, *Socialist Worker*).[31] He also entered into the debate on the disquiet concerning the attempts by homosexual activists to colonise the word 'Gay', a phenomenon which itself provoked a considerable tirade of correspondence in the press during this same month.[32]

> ... I suppose there may still be a few people who might inadvertently buy a copy of *Gay News* under the impression that it was a jolly version of the *Tatler*. Denis Lemon should change the title to Homosexual News. Nobody is forced to buy *Gay News* though I suspect a lot more may read it as a result of the guilty verdict... . Is Mrs Whitehouse really surprised that a newspaper which calls itself *Gay News* should publish a poem about a Gay centurion? I have published what I consider to be a far greater blasphemy a while back in these pages, suggesting that God may be an alcoholic. There was no prosecution presumably because sex didn't rear its ugly head. Apparently a drunken God is acceptable but not a Gay one. I suspect he or she may well be both – and Black to boot.[33]

Writing in the *Daily Telegraph* Christopher Booker, whilst expressing disappointment at the prosecution of the case, saw the trial (or more correctly the content of the poem) as a cause for sadness in that it indicated that homosexuals were excluded from conventional idioms and emotions connected with the notion of salvation:

> I find Professor Kirkup's poem one of the saddest things I have ever read. With its description of the Centurion frenziedly seeking

physical 'union' with the body of the dead Christ, and somehow trying to convince himself that, by his desperate act, he has won sanction and 'salvation' for the act of homosexual physical love for all eternity, the poem seems to express by its very defiance the heartrending admission that homosexuals can in fact never find that sense of 'wholeness' they are seeking – certainly not by physical acts, however desperate. More than a million 'Gay Liberation' banners, the poem seems to be an implicit heartcry of recognition that homosexuals are 'shut out', not from society, but from something infinitely greater and more important – a sense of union with the very spirit of creation.[34]

Attacks upon the moral acceptability of homosexuality and its religious expression could have been expected. But a sympathetic denial of a genuinely spiritual life to the homosexual was a still further bitterly resented exclusion.

Mary Whitehouse always denied that her own motivations in the case were occasioned by malice against homosexuals and homosexuality, despite their violent protestations to the contrary. Contemporary attitudes to Mary Whitehouse, then as now, often amount to extreme reactions upon a wide scale ranging from enthusiastic support to violent vilification. As such she remains a figure about whom it is extraordinarily difficult to advance a neutral attitude. In effect this response is a direct consequence of her involvement in *cause célèbre* episodes such as the *Gay News* trial. Once legal action became an imperative it was almost inevitable that partisans of libertarian attitudes and those in favour of conservative moral retrenchment would enter the fray and exclude other individuals, views and eventually arguments. This polarisation of opinion was an effective bar to John Mortimer's attempt to use expert witness material. Yet Mary Whitehouse's account of the trial is a valuable text for portraying sections of wounded and outraged Christianity and the way this section of opinion sought to justify its actions in the late twentieth century. It is also a highly illuminating text in its exposition of how deeply felt Christian beliefs can motivate public action and intervention in an apparently secular age. What is nowhere in doubt in Mrs Whitehouse's account, in contemporary press reports or even the impressions of her opponents, is her sincerity. She clearly believed that she had undertaken God's work and this heartfelt conviction spared her the personal animosity which such a crusader might have been expected to harbour against opponents. Her book *Quite Contrary* is full of her expressions of sympathy for Denis Lemon and for individual homosexuals and even has her sharing a cup of tea with Geoffrey Robertson, the defence counsel for *Gay News*.[35] A little later in her autobiography, in the section covering the aftermath of the case, there is an interesting encounter between Mrs Whitehouse and a homosexual who had attempted to shout her down at a university meeting. The individual left the hall trembling and in considerable distress. Mrs Whitehouse later offered her hand to the young man to, in her words '... do something to make him feel less isolated'. The young man apologised but maintained that his actions were the result of fear and the animosity of the world at large. In an attempt to comfort the young man Mrs Whitehouse did her best to make him '... understand and accept that because people like me "believe homosexual practices to be wrong that does not mean that we all hate and despise homosexuals as people"'.[36] Whilst this episode depicts Mrs Whitehouse in a more sympathetic and compassionate light than many commentators are used to, it nonetheless also suggests that the *Gay News* case did much to create a climate of fear. The rights of citizenship granted to homosexuals a matter of only ten years previously could be seen to be, at least in the mind, unravelling before the collective gaze. It should be noted that for homosexuals the case was the start of a series of cultural defeats. The *Daily Mail* of 14 July recorded how the altered atmosphere had led them to hurriedly cancel a season of gay films by, amongst others, David Hockney, Fellini and Hitchcock. The director of the National Film Theatre Brian Baxter, considered 'in the present circumstances it was thought rather *risque*'.[37]

The wider correspondence to the national press on the subject of the *Gay News* case proffered a range of opinions which meant clearly that the verdict of the jury could never, as King-Hamilton suggested, be a completely faithful barometer of public opinion. Many letters applauded King-Hamilton's verdict and subsequent pronouncements, one of these suggesting that 'the verdict shows that ten out of twelve people, chosen at random, thought that in this case the line had been over stepped, and suggests that public opinion is not necessarily behind those who shout loudest'.[38] One considered even the existence of the newspaper *Gay News* to be 'a scandal' whilst several Christians, including clergymen, expressed dismay that the prosecution had blackened the name of Christianity. Others went further in this latter direction and suggested that a modern religion should be capable of withstanding the attacks meted out to it by a modern world.[39] A writer to the *Telegraph* wondered:

> How much longer, I wonder, can Mary Whitehouse continue her crusade without doing permanent damage to the popular image of Christianity and Christians in this country?... The image Mrs Whitehouse most readily evokes is not that of Grace Darling battling through the waves, of Elizabeth Fry or Harriet Beecher-Stowe fighting in their own ways for needful reform: it is of Machiavelli ruthlessly manipulating language and laws to his own ends... . The impression is also becoming inescapable that the Festival of Light and the National Front are bloodsisters under the skin.[40]

Several familiar arguments were once more raised as a result of the verdict. The law was condemned as creaking and anachronistic. Nicolas Walter pointed this out in an erudite letter to *The Times*, which also reiterated the argument heard in the Foote case, that there was no logical reason why proscription should stop at the Kirkup poem if the law were allowed to regulate what was acceptable reading matter:

> ... the present law could be used to suppress any religious or anti-religious controversy, and also many writings not only of such minor figures as James Kirkup but as major figures such as Chaucer, Shakespeare, Donne, Milton, Pope, Shelley, Byron, Swinburne, Hardy, Yeats, Joyce, Lawrence and Eliot. Intellectual argument and literary criticism would be overshadowed by the criminal law, as in the bad old days.[41]

However Nicolas Walter also noted that the recent repeal of the blasphemy statute meant the responsibility for bringing the prosecution rested apparently with individuals and that the reasonable thing for a government to do would be to re-establish blasphemy as a statute offence thus allowing government to regulate its use. This was in many respects the ultimate expression of the fear of creeping religiosity 'from below' – a phenomenon that it could be argued had been legitimised by the conduct and success of the *Gay News* case.

In some respects the question of who actually was in charge of the *Gay News* prosecution was itself a cause of considerable debate and comment. Throughout Mary Whitehouse denied that the Crown was ever involved in the prosecution and the Legal Secretary to the Attorney General W. C. Beckett, wrote to correct *The Times* editorial on this point, stating that all indictments contained the Crown title whilst not actually involving the Crown in the prosecution.[42] However there was concern about this particular facet of the case and one correspondent wrote to *The Times* seeking an assurance that '... no tax payers' money was spent on the prosecution'and in any event it was 'surely something of a legal quibble to assert that the case was not taken over by the Crown'.[43] Such assertions, if they had ever amounted to anything, would have proved particularly embarrassing since government would have publicly denied having any role in the making and construction of morality in an age of religious and moral pluralism, whilst maintaining the prerogative of involvement in the prosecution once initiated by a third party. In this respect the appearence of legal procedure arguably mattered more than the legal reality which Beckett had sketched and, had public opinion been led to focus on this point, the Home Secretary might have found himself as uncomfortable as Sir William Harcourt.

The question of religious pluralism in 1970s Britain, a matter opened for debate by the *Gay News* case and reiterated in numerous editorials, did itself emerge in the correspondence. One correspondent applauded the call for a more widespread legal recognition for Muslims as an early stage towards the extension of the blasphemy laws which would have enabled them to institute prosecutions against blasphemous attacks upon the Islamic faith.[44] The question of cultural pluralism and the fear of attacks upon the civil liberties of artists and writers also, however, took the terms of the debate in a manifestly different direction. Whilst the National Council for Civil Liberties condemned the verdict their opponents were ready with accusations that the organisation had no desire and interest in defending the rights and liberties of Christians. One writer mischievously (but not surprisingly) suggested that the organisation was prepared to act far more swiftly if the liberties of Communist Party Members were threatened.[45] Writing in *The Times* Stephen Spender lamented that the acceptance of the conventions of literary form and the willingness to accept metaphor and allegory as components of wider society were brutally dragged into the arena of public scrutiny. These were found wanting in the face of an apparently universal legal sanction which forcibly denied the changing meanings of words and discourses.

> The significance of the poem lies in the realisation of images and ideas as language which are the experience of the poet as an individual writing for readers who are individuals: not in what Mrs Whitehouse and a jury may consider the social effect of the imagery … dragged out of the poem and considered as recommendations of human behaviour.[46]

Spender went on to suggest that the verdict was effectively rewriting the Christian cultural tradition and was denying the mystical concept of Christ as bridegroom of the soul as depicted in numerous paintings. Moreover the poem was considered evidence of a spiritual inner life which led Spender to quote T. S. Eliot's assertion that 'the blasphemous may be closer to the religious than the conventional and pietistic'. Citing Eliot's references to D. H. Lawrence's 'The Man who Died' as an

> attempt is to vitalise Christ within the context of the most vivid modern imagination: this means transforming the Christ figure into terms of our time in which sex is 'recognised as a force point in the individual life which remains resistant to the material values of society'.[47]

This could perhaps have been interpreted as establishing the literary and philosophical merit of works of art as the first stage of an argument for the centrality of expert evidence which others took up. A correspondent to the *Daily Telegraph* suggested that the denial of expert testimony by implication left the field open for attacks upon the work of St John of the Cross or John Donne. Replying to the *Telegraph's* editorial condoning the verdict the correspondent asserted that this was merely a short step away from a dictatorship where 'the emotional reaction of a jury is more important than its informed understanding'.[48] There were also other contributions which took the defence of Kirkup potentially to farcical proportions. John Michell's hastily produced libertarian pamphlet sought to assert that Kirkup's depiction of Christ's sexual organs, 'far from being blasphemous, are an expression of Christian orthodoxy'. This, he claimed, had been suppressed by attempts to sanitise Christianity away from its earliest origins as a fertility cult. Citing iconographical evidence drawn from Roman catacomb graffiti, church architecture, eighteenth-century iconography and other religious painting Michell suggested that:

> To represent the deity as a 'great cock', as in Mr Kirkup's meek poem, is such a timeless, universal and hallowed practice that its orthodoxy needs no labourious proof. ... In fact, human genitals are merely symbols, among many other such, of the dual powers proceeding from one source, that govern the universe. The Phallic nose on the gnostic bust of Our Saviour is an image of the positive, yin or receptive tendency. Nothing could be more chaste and sublime, nothing less obscene.[49]

What Michell failed to point out was that representations of genitalia as fertility symbols were further away from depictions of homosexual acts than he had admitted. In essence such pamphlets did not help and the grandiose assertion that such depictions were chaste echoed some of the earlier, questionable attempts to establish the quasi-religious credentials of *Lady Chatterley's Lover*.

Despite the furore there was a sense of limbo whilst the appeal which Lemon and *Gay News* had lodged was pending. It was the result of this appeal which radically altered the modern face of the offence of blasphemous libel. The appeal was heard early the next year and John Mortimer went into it with two central arguments. First, that the prosecution needed to prove intent to attack Christianity upon the part of Lemon and *Gay News*, supposedly a source of misdirection from King-Hamilton. Secondly that the poem itself did not intend harm to the Christian religion and indeed could be defended as an expression of such belief – although clearly not that intended by Michell. The Bench divided three to two in favour of the verdict and the report, which contains separate opinion from all five judges, makes very interesting reading. The opinions of the minority, Lords Diplock and Edmund-Davies, concentrated upon the case-law and an extensive trawl of the standard authorities – Starkie, Stephen, the Pooley case, the Coleridge judgment and the Gott case produced considerable legal precedent for the notion that intent was an integral and central component of the offence. Both Diplock and Edmund-Davies reiterated that the poem was blasphemous, despite the fact that this was not legally at issue, but nonetheless argued that the appeal should be accepted. Lord Diplock suggested that Parliament in the Criminal Justice Act of 1967 had removed crimes requiring the proof of specific intention from the status of strict liability. This argument suggested that the intention to offend in this case of blasphemy was a central issue which King-Hamilton had ignored.[50] Moreover he expressed concern that the law was being pressurised by an alteration in the moral climate.

> The very fact that there have been no prosecutions for blasphemous libel for more than 50 years is sufficient to dispose of any suggestion that in modern times a judicial decision to include this Common Law offence in this exceptional class of offences of strict liability could be justified upon grounds of public morals or public order.[51]

Lord Edmund-Davies concurred in both these views, stating that 'to treat as irrelevant the state of mind of a person charged with blasphemy would be to take a backward step in the evolution of a humane code'.[52] Lords Scarman, Dilhorne and Russell, who refused the appeal, effectively were in favour of a contemporary response to the law which ostensibly saw it as legitimate because it had been succesfully enacted. They considered that the concept of *mens rea* (i.e. the presumption that an individual intended the consequences of their action) was pertinent only to publication and not any wider motive. As such they saw no reason why the prosecution should need to prove motive in a case of blasphemy. It was perhaps ironic that the judgment actively used and upheld Stephen's interpretation of the law which he had advocated against the milder one proffered by Coleridge. Lord Scarman, in his judgement, was also an enthusiastic advocate of an extension of the laws which would equalise religions before the law – itself also, ironically, a revival of Stephen's Indian Code solution.

As a result of the case and the appeal verdict the law effectively became more draconian, making the matter once more a central component of the offence. Such matters which attacked the central tenets of Christianity at once became punishable and any sense of manner, motive or intention constituted no defence. In a sense the concern of Foote that judge-made law was easily set aside had been at last realised. Indeed the Crown's case, as it was advanced in the appeal, dismantled the previously influential status of the Coleridge judgment. John Smyth and Jeremy Maurice speaking for the Crown argued that the nineteenth-century introduction of intention had never been clearly defined and had, in any case, been an illogical innovation. What Coleridge had actually laid down, according to Smyth and Maurice, was that the tone and spirit of the words published were 'the test of guilt rather than their substance'.[53] This proposition, and the result of the appeal, had the effect of focusing attention once again upon the actual textual matter involved in blasphemy cases – significantly what Stephen had consistently argued. Notions of wider intention or motive were superfluous considerations, the inferences that juries and individuals took from such texts henceforth were to be enough to convict. The medium had effectively become the motive.

Leonard Levy concluded that the law had become more reactionary but also noted that manner remained more important than matter.[54] This particular point is debatable since the capacity for precise words to upset believers and to provide evidence of their intention relied exclusively on their content without external considerations of societal norms or familiarity with artistic or theological conventions. When combined with the erosion of expert evidence the operation of the offence appeared to place an intolerable burden upon a jury in such cases. Henceforth it had to reflect a knowledge of what society, in all its manifestations, was likely to accept as well as exercising their own reactions which the legacy of the immediate casual encounter still enshrined. Levy's citation of examples such as John Updike's *Marry Me*, *The Jesus Hoax*, or the Python's *Life of Brian* of potential blasphemies that escaped prosecution did so only through the ignorance or tolerance of those who had the potential to prosecute. In this respect it could be argued that Mary Whitehouse's familiarity with the range of responses she invoked from admiration to vilification enabled her to be a pioneer of a route which others did not follow, not necessarily because the heart was unwilling but because the flesh was weak or ill-informed. The law and its continued indulgence of the casual encounter seemed to suggest that those who confronted these dangerous nightmares of what modernity might constitute must be trained and prepared for the experience. This casual encounter, it appeared, was to be avoided before the individual was ready or 'braced' for it. As such, British Society seemed to like its investigators and flaneurs to be self-appointed, and that which was investigated should thus be prevented from hurriedly surprising the unprepared and the unsuspecting. In some respects also the very conception of shifting the emphasis to the offence of breach of the peace was a further step in the direction of giving the prerogative on deciding what constituted blasphemy back to the public at large. If this were the case then blasphemy constituted that which was attacked. That no attacks occurred in the years which immediately followed the *Gay News* trial was – for all parties concerned – fortuitous. But as we shall see the establishment of this precedent represented a timebomb ticking under the law.

At its root the *Gay News* case indicated that it was possible, through the use of the offence of blasphemous libel, for a motivated individual like Mary Whitehouse to bring a private prosecution for blasphemy.

Throughout the case she records in her autobiography that she was emphatically engaged upon God's work and even in the courtroom felt his presence. She was aided and comforted by friends and supporters who revived her flagging spirits through encouraging her to rejoice in the apposite nature of specific biblical texts.[55] Interestingly she maintained in her autobiography that the decision of the Bench did not constitute any substantial change in the law. In this respect it is ironic that Mrs Whitehouse wished to avoid the consequences of her own actions. A lone woman motivated by a sincere caring and devout Christianity sought to defend her Saviour through a court of law which upheld her submission. This court insisted that the defence fight upon the same ground without any recognition of the fact that society was in any sense different from the last application of the laws in question. It is particularly at moments like this that the notion that Britain had become a secular country, or had entered a secular age, appears misguided if not ridiculous.

Notes

1. Levy, Leonard W. (1993), *Blasphemy: Verbal Offense Against the Sacred from Moses to Salman Rushdie*, New York: Knopf, p. 535.
2. The law in Scotland had been repealed by the nineteenth-century statute 53 Geo III c. 160 S. The Viscount Dunedin, John L. Wark, and A. C. Black (1928), *Encyclopaedia of the Laws of Scotland*, Edinburgh: W. Green and Son, p. 68.
3. *The Times*, 29 June 1977.
4. *The Times*, 1 July 1977.
5. *The Times*, 2 July 1977.
6. King-Hamilton, A. (1982), *And Nothing But the Truth*, London: Weidenfeld and Nicolson, p. 172.
7. Levy, op. cit., pp. 537–9.
8. Kirkup, J. (1988), *I, of all People*, London: Weidenfeld and Nicolson.
9. Levy, op. cit., p. 537.
10. Whitehouse, Mary (1993), *Quite Contrary*, London: Pan Books, p, 47.
11. Bradney, A. (1993), *Religions, Rights and Laws*, London: Leicester University Press, p. 93.
12. Leonard Levy quotes from the Michael Tracey and David Morrison book, *Whitehouse* (1979) which uses Mrs Whitehouse's own letters to suggest that the potential for prosecution of the poem was a method by which the Thorsen film could be stopped once and for all. This conflicts with Mrs Whitehouse's own account (Whitehouse, 1993, p. 47) which suggests that the poem arrived after the Thorsen threat had been vanquished.
13. Levy's is a succinct account of the proceedings of the trial in accessible form although Nicolas Walter's books should also be consulted.
14. Whitehouse, op. cit., p. 48.
15. *The Times*, 9 July 1977.
16. King-Hamilton, op. cit., p. 176.
17. Whitehouse, op. cit., p. 50.

18. Original typescript of Justice Alan King-Hamilton's summing up in Reg v. Lemon.
19. Levy, op. cit., pp. 54–5.
20. *The Daily Mail*, 5 July 1977.
21. King-Hamilton, op. cit., p. 180.
22. *The Times*, 13 July 1977.
23. *Daily Telegraph*, 13 July 1977.
24. *The Times*, 13 July 1977.
25. *Daily Telegraph*, 13 July 1977.
26. *The Times*, 13 July 1977.
27. *Daily Telegraph*, 13 July 1977.
28. The aftermath of the case witnessed a considerable level of correspondence to the broadsheet newspapers lamenting the homosexual community's colonisation of the word 'gay'.
29. Levy, op. cit., p. 544.
30. Grey, Antony (1992), *Quest for Justice: Towards Homosexual Emancipation*, London: Sinclair-Stevenson, p. 229.
31. *The Times*, 14 July 1977.
32. See *Daily Telegraph*, 6 August 1977.
33. *Daily Mail*, 18 July 1977.
34. *Daily Telegraph*, 16 July 1977.
35. Whitehouse, op. cit., p. 53.
36. Ibid., p. 60.
37. *Daily Mail*, 14 July 1977.
38. *The Times*, 19 July 1977.
39. *The Times*, 16 July 1977
40. *Daily Telegraph*, 18 July 1977
41. *The Times*, 14 July 1977.
42. Ibid.
43. *The Times*, 16 July 1977.
44. *The Times*, 15 July 1977.
45. *Daily Telegraph*, 18 July 1977.
46. *The Times*, 22 July 1977.
47. Ibid.
48. *Daily Telegraph*, 18 July 1977.
49. Michell, John (1977), 'To Represent Our Saviour as "that great cock" [*Kirkup Gay News*] is not Blasphemy but Eternal and Christian Orthodoxy: Furnished with Irrefutable Illustrative Proofs', London: Open Head Press.
50. Reg v. Lemon, H. L. (E.) (1979), p. 637.
51. Ibid., p. 638.
52. Ibid., p. 656.
53. Ibid., p. 627.
54. Levy, op. cit., p. 549.
55. Whitehouse, op. cit., p. 51.

CHAPTER NINE

Conclusion

The years which have followed the *Gay News* trial have not witnessed a dissipation of interest in the subject of blasphemy. Indeed the issue has become of increasing and enhanced relevance to contemporary society. In some respects the subject has remained a touchstone of religious commitment and for many stands as a cultural Rubicon beyond which the moral landscape appears to be distant and hazy indeed. Moreover the growing inexactitude of contemporary definitions of religion – and of what it means to be religious – have added their own gloss to this problem. Whilst it is certainly true that regular attempts have been made to repeal the law in the years since the *Gay News* case by the Law Commission, Lord Willis, Tony Benn and Lord Avebury, it should equally be remembered that there have been numerous instances where blasphemy has been an area where legal and cultural innovation has entered the agenda. Generally the motives behind this have been a genuine sympathy for a conception of human rights which desires to protect individuals from having their sacred beliefs ridiculed and tarnished. In Britain this has usually been voiced as a wholly just attack upon the anachronism of the blasphemy laws in Britain as they currently stand.

Unfortunately, unlike the work of previous generations, this has not been to suggest that laws against the expression of opinion are illiberal and not in keeping with the 'spirit of the age' but that the laws as they exist are partisan in their protection and ultimately discriminatory in their action. Blasphemy thus stands as a pivotal point where conflicts about late modern culture meet in explosive fashion. Within its understood boundaries the law is tested to breaking point by making society cope with the modern multiplication of tastes and cultures and the pluralisation of new religious influences alongside the resurgence of pre-modern forms of belief. These pre-modern beliefs also, however, have to live with the liberal urge to rationalise and accommodate disparate and often opposing interests. Put in these stark terms it is no surprise to see one commentator describe the future of blasphemy as 'one of the most decisive indicators of the future of the modern state'.[1]

To this day the protection afforded by the laws of blasphemy extends solely to the doctrines of Christianity. The partisan nature of this protection is itself increasingly viewed by a range of commentators as an anachronistic facet of the law in this area. In an age which has seen the growth of multiculturalism in Britain and attendant laws against forms of what some lawyers term 'hate speech' and other public order offences the partisan and selective nature of the blasphemy law appears dangerous and outmoded. Even the forms of belief protected in this fashion have themselves not remained static. In many respects the history of Christianity itself also has undermined the law as it now stands. The absolute decline of Anglican adherence has been to a large extent counteracted by the growth and development of more compact and heterogeneous forms of evangelical Christianity. The 1980s were also the decade which saw the Archbishop of Canterbury Robert Runcie seriously suggest that the Anglican Church should strongly consider the option of disestablishment. This would have removed what some seeking to rejuvenate the Anglican Church saw as a more than uncomfortable encumbrance – yet it might further have muddied the waters with regard to the law of blasphemy. With no protection for a church established by law it might be argued that the jurisdiction which the law sought to protect would have lapsed in spectacular fashion. At the very least the moral/theological justification for such protection, were it indeed a primary consideration, could be said to be growing increasingly tenuous. Much recent thinking has sought to remedy this perceived anomaly through the suggestion that the laws of blasphemy should be extended to cover all religious faiths. Certainly Lord Scarman suggested that an extension would amount to an overdue realignment of the law – although it is interesting to note that he retracted this opinion in favour of abolition in 1990.[2] Such reactions should be seen in the context of the increased concern about equality between faiths and religious experience so that, for the first time, modernisation of the law appeared to mean extension rather than abolition.

The most fundamental and important event which occasioned forceful argument for the extension of the blasphemy laws was the national and international campaign against the writings of Salman Rushdie. As I have already suggested there is not room to investigate this affair here without abridging it or doing it considerable scholarly injustice. However it is worth noting a number of aspects which highlight the conclusions reached here concerning the operation of the laws since the eighteenth century. As has already been pointed out the recognition of the inequality of protection offered by the law of blasphemy is of some antiquity. However this anomaly appeared to exert particularly strong forms of pressure on opinion as a result of the publication of Rushdie's *Satanic Verses* which extended the British experience of dealing with blasphemous rhetorics beyond Christianity. Whilst the motives of Rushdie in publishing the *Satanic Verses* are the source of considerable controversy, the content of his attacks upon Islam clearly contain elements of apostasy and portray an author working out his grievances against an individual religious faith. Indeed it is particularly interesting to note that Rushdie's status as a novelist has led him to claim 'special freedoms since his purpose is the remaking of worlds'.[3] Some arguments have sensibly suggested that this in itself is not the issue and that our traditional questions of manner and intention are very important. However, attempting to analyse the affair in terms of Rushdie himself adopting a particular theological position have been further complicated by his subsequent attempt to embrace the Islamic faith. What is also notable is the connection of the offence of blasphemy to immorality which Rushdie's critics claim should have outraged English monarchists and western women as much as Muslims.[4] In this respect the depth of these grievances and their frank expression have provoked sharp and powerful reaction. Some sections of the Islamic community in Britain demanded protection for their religious faith from the attacks of what they saw as an individual motivated variously by malice or greed. Throughout the argument was couched in terms which displayed this community of British citizens' fear that it was being betrayed by the British legal system and that its faith was being actively discriminated against in this area and others. Despite initial success in upholding the right to bring a private prosecution against the British Government for being in breach of article 9 of the European Convention on Human Rights which guarantees religious freedom, the matter ended in failure and a firm rebuttal by the then Minister of State at the Home Office, John Patten.[5] In refusing to take the matter further John Patten invoked the notion of freedom of speech as being central to the rights extended both to authors and those who sought to protest against their works. In elaborating upon his reasons Patten outlined objections which have an historically familiar ring to them:

> Firstly, the difficulties in re-defining what should or should not be blasphemous would be immense. People hold with great passion diametrically opposing views on the subject. For example, should protection be extended to all faiths, including the very minor or very obscure? Should it extend only to faiths believing in one God? Or to 'major' or 'mainstream' faiths only? I believe there is no equitable, just or right answer to these questions.[6]

Moreover the issue of blasphemy once more provoked, as it had in the 1930s, a recourse to street politics. This time the refusal of extension of the laws by the government and public liberal defences of the writer provoked demonstrations in Muslim centres of population. The precarious and arguably uncomfortable nature of the orthodox liberal defence of free speech was graphically highlighted when its precepts were transformed into racist chants utilised by the far right to confront Muslims on the streets of Bradford and other English cities. This brought into extremely sharp relief the issue of religious belief linked to ethnicity and produced compelling evidence that the question of society dealing with those who would use such instances to incite race hatred should be considered both seriously and urgently. Government inaction was increasingly seen by the offended as amounting to hostility and ultimately paying only lip service to the conception of religious toleration and a multicultural society. However as we have seen a simple change in the law – by way of extension – was by no means as straightforward a procedure as some in modern society imagined it to be.

Definitions of what constitutes religion and where the boundary falls in this matter would today arguably be a far more complex task than the one that pre-war legislators gave up on in despair. Likewise should the arduous task of defining religion ever be accomplished the law would then have to establish historical ownership of doctrine and belief and how responsibility is to be shared out amongst the religious zealot, the mainstream believer and the nominal sympathiser. The Rushdie affair also highlights the fact that the motifs and beliefs of liberalism adopted by a previous generation in the name of free speech and freedom can seem potentially tyrannical to an audience acclimatised to very different thought processes. Moreover in a world where conflict, particularly in this affair, could have rapid global repercussions the sometimes bland assumption of western liberals that their system was somehow totally value-free needed close and vigilant scrutiny and perhaps renewed defence. However the event also provoked speculation as to whether liberalism as a concept sustaining late modern nation states is itself in crisis in its ultimately unrewarding attempt to resolve conflicts between liberty of expression and liberty to practice religion alongside '... the values of fraternity and equality of respect ... to encompass other faiths'.[7] During the affair Muslims accused western liberalism of behaving as though it were itself a religion with sacred icons, shibboleths and its own conception of blasphemy against notions of free expression. Yet the lesson of attempts to contemplate the extension of the blasphemy laws, to supposedly end the discrimination, is that they are all too easily used as a cloak to exclude the undesirable elements in British Society. In particular lessons from episodes like the campaigns against Carlile and the 'Godless Congress' affair of 1938 is that a sustained offensive against a marginalised group may all too easily result in the attack being extended retrospectively to encompass previously accepted and assimilated groups.

In the wake of the Rushdie affair one commentator, Simon Lee, proposed that it had fundamentally demonstrated the rejuvenated nature of religiosity in society. This he saw as having important long-term effects since he characterised religion as being increasingly a part of our identity – as central and irreversible as skin colour or ethnicity. In rejecting American syle models of the secular state as simplistic and ill-informed about the practicalities of policing attacks on the religious he proposed that the media and the state neglected the religio-legal dimensions to a multi-faith society at their peril. Moreover he rightly asserted that only through serious discussion and enhanced understanding would problems be resolved. Lee was in particular critical of the media's obsession with displaying ideological polarity in any religious discussion it promoted and staged. His contention was that the Salman Rushdie affair had exposed flaws in British Society's very definition of religion and the religious – it was thus necessary for this society to seek a resolution and to thereby modernise itself. Lee's proposed answer was to remove the laws against blasphemy and replace them with ones designed to combat religious hatred.

Whilst at first sight a laudable and impressively elegant solution to the problem – one Lee saw as potentially beloved of the Charter 88 nexus – the proposal was a little glib about resolving the problem of defining religion.[8] It suggested borrowing the Australian High Court definition that religion should exhibit 'First, belief in a supernatural Being, Thing or Principle, and second, acceptance of canons of conduct in order to give effect to that belief' rather uncritically and added without comment that this definition had given Scientology judicial protection.[9] Quite apart from the other definitional problems looming on the horizon (such as what to do about sects of the same sacred belief in apparent conflict over blasphemous ideas) Lee's suggestion perhaps underestimates the public's growing fear of fringe forms of religion. These arguably have a greater culturally disquieting presence in modern Britain than that of blasphemers or those who would incite religious hatred. Ultimately Simon Lee pinned faith in the ability of external legal power to produce standards of tolerance and legal scrutiny which would provide a framework for true multi-culturalism. As we shall see below (in examining the case of Nigel Wingrove) Britain's first engagement with external conceptions of the law did not result in universally agreed standards of morality, procedure and visible justice.

However, another serious alteration in the trends observable in the history of blasphemy deserves mention at this point. That is the changing response of those who receive and respond to the offence which can often turn upon the perceived intention of the cultural product. Foote, Gott and the *Jerusalem Star* all sought to destabilise Christianity through laughter. Taking their lead from the Paineite tradition they undermined orthodox Christian biblical stories and when a dash of anticlericalism was thrown in for good measure a much older tradition was being invoked. The gap of over 50 years culminating in the Kirkup *Gay News* Case brought a fundamental change to the identity of the blasphemer. During this passage of time blasphemers were more likely to be artists and writers seeking a dialogue with religion and seeking to express their responses to this, often transforming both the class and the cultural identity of the blasphemer. This is further proof that the artistic community's relationship to religious narratives is becoming an increasingly engaging area of inspiration, as witnessed by the very recent furore over Irvine Welsh's *Granton Star Cause* which seemed to blend elements of Peter Cook and Nigel Wingrove through the use of images of a drunken deity alongside scenes of masochistic sex.[10] Arguably these examples could be seen as a response to the retreat of religion into the private sphere. Kirkup's poem was clearly a dialogue with a religiosity he found at once compelling and repulsive. In no sense was Kirkup engaged in flippancy nor outright vilification ('contumely' as the law has it) and numerous commentators, including Mrs Whitehouse, admitted this quite readily. What sometimes appeared to be at issue was how far Kirkup could be deemed to have impinged upon other Christian's dialogues with their own religiosity – once again indicating the crucial role of religion's colonisation of a private sphere.

As I moved towards writing the conclusion of this book I became aware that my responses to the material I have read and digested led me, as it has many before me, to move from the role of historian to the necessary role of quasi-philosopher and commentator. It has been easy to castigate the products of such engaged writing and the reader may thus find it ironic that this book has criticised some elements of the history represented by campaign literature and postmodern approaches. Whilst I acknowledge in part the inconsistency of this position, the fact remains that an answer to the problem of blasphemy is no less urgent, nor should society at large cease from trying to solve it or, at the very least, maintain the contemporary debate so that more people become aware of its impact upon their lives. In trying to draw some wider conclusions I am aware that this work perhaps stands in stark contrast to the optimism that characterised Arthur Calder-Marshall's attempt to survey the laws. In this respect it does have rather more in common with David Lawton's assessment of the subject than I initially had any reason to expect. Whilst obviously at odds with many of his central conclusions what strikes me particularly is the air of pessimism which crowds around attempts to think through the cultural and social problems which cluster around the contemporary issue of blasphemy. In this respect the works of both Lawton and Leonard Levy reach an emphatically pessimistic appreciation of the concept's future. Once again it is worth reminding ourselves that the history of this subject compels commentators to pronounce upon its destiny. This is the same not simply of empiricists but also of the postmodernist searching for practices and discourses within their own society which might provide models of behaviour and morals.

As far as producing a resolution to the perpetual problem of blasphemy in western and eastern civilisations is concerned there is an extent to which some of the ethical motives of postmodern approaches to the subject must be applauded. Whilst I hope I have suggested that a postmodern analysis of the history of blasphemy is inadequate and misleading, what it tries to offer to contemporary protagonists in the battle is a genuine message of hope, which unfortunately (I would suggest) is ultimately illusory. The postmodern desire to divest knowledge of *a priori* forms of authority, awe and reverence beyond its mere content could, on its own terms, constitute an attempt to remove the mysticism and moral power behind various religious discourses. If all such discourses were accepted as equal, or rather denied their externalising religious/cultural authority, then battles for supremacy, orthodoxy, apostasy and tyrannical claims for total conformity could become a thing of the past for the future to guard against. This casting off of *a priori* power and authority through forms of cultural attrition would also divest blasphemers and their discourse of similar power, authority, and their ability to offend. Removed of their capacity for offence this would present blasphemy as merely a discourse of creative criticism intended solely to carve out the identity of an individual. Such a state would render blasphemy as just another discourse alongside the various discourses of religious faith.

But there is clearly a problem here since an accusation of blasphemy involves an absolute decision to deny the validity of a discourse. As this book should testify the result is not some form of negotiated plurality but a contest in which victory is paramount for both protagonists. Such battles are about beliefs that cannot so readily be categorised as 'texts' with the inherent logic and premeditation that such a term invites. One commentator, Martin Eden of the Evangelical Alliance, succinctly presses this home by suggesting that religion is clearly about more than texts and relativised discourses:

> There is a chasm in modern society, where on the one side you have a post-modern view in which there are no metanarratives and the Bible is just a book, and on the other side there are people like me... . To me there is such a thing as truth.[11]

However this is also an area in which postmodern attitudes and approaches to religion have actively produced conflict. The implication that the modern blasphemy laws create a notion of 'religious feelings' amounts to a nightmare unenvisaged by postmodernists. Postmodern theologians like Don Cupitt suggest that each age constructs and deconstructs its own sacred individuals and symbols and that religion thus resembles the catalogue of these constructions.[12] Whilst this clearly ends, for those who subscribe to it, the notion of religion as a meta-narrative it also amounts to a relocation of the power of belief to those 'from below' with the ability to rejuvenate Christianity for themselves. Importantly the fracturing of beliefs and meta-narratives into myriad discourses has not produced plurality but rather has caused such discourses to be shunted into a convenient umbrella term which, precisely through its very vagueness, invests them with enhanced and not dwindling importance. The consequences of this slippage of religion into the area of 'feelings' was highlighted as early as 1913 when J. B. Bury suggested that religion should function solely as a self-contained truth for believers and that indulging any wider subsidiary notion of offence was clearly where the problems for the rest of society began.[13]

Many of these concerns have been highlighted by the resolution of the recent Wingrove case – an instance in which Europe (Simon Lee's 'standards of international law')[14] for the first time was asked to pronounce upon the British blasphemy laws. Significantly Lee's optimism about external standards providing guidelines for tolerance were ill-founded. Nigel Wingrove's film *Visions of Ecstasy* was refused a classification by the British Board of Film Classification and was, as a result, banned from sale or public display in Britain under the Video Recordings Act of 1984. The film itself depicts the religious and erotic visions of St Theresa of Avila in which she bestrides and kisses the crucified Christ, mutilates herself and has a sexually intimate encounter with another character intended to represent her own psyche. Many discussions revolved around precisely the role of the Christ figure in the film and whether he had actively responded to St Theresa's actions. Wingrove himself appealed to the European Court of Human Rights, arguing that the British Board of Film Classification had clearly denied him freedom of expression as guaranteed in Article 10 of the European Convention as well as exercising prior restraint. This was backed up with a submission from the organisation Article 19 which highlighted these two objections and drew the Court's attention to the situation in 11 other countries.[15] Wingrove's submission was that the uncertainty surrounding the law of blasphemy meant that he could not reasonably have predicted the reaction of the Board nor a hypothetical jury (whose likely decision the Board was obliged to strongly consider). Wingrove's submission was accepted initially by the European Commission on

Human Rights but was overturned in November 1996 by a decision of the Court considering an appeal by the British Government.

Whilst clearly not to everyone's taste the film was rather more than a simple soft porn offering with added religious *frisson*. Whilst this distinction can be argued too far (in the manner of the Lady Chatterley case) it played a crucial role in influencing the Board's decision. Investigation of a filmmaker's motives in producing a work is not a usual procedure for the Board to undertake and has had no place in determining the suitability of other pornographic or violent films without such religious content. The film was thus explicitly denied a certificate by the Board, citing Wingrove's motives as being akin to those of the soft core pornographer and stating that *Visions* lacked the obvious seriousness of something like Scorsese's *Last Temptation of Christ*. The Board went on to ascertain that it had taken the decision to ban Visions on the grounds that the video 'might be blasphemous'. This last assertion was particularly curious since the entire history of the Common Law offence of blasphemous libel in Britain up to this point, as we have discovered, always maintained that juries are those best equipped to decide what is unacceptable in a particular society at a particular time.

When abolition of the blasphemy laws up until recently has been discussed in government circles a resolution not to take any action to repeal them has generally been forwarded, not simply for reasons of administrative inertia but also because the law was considered to be directly reflective of public opinion. Indeed, the fact that it existed in quasi-organic form as a Common Law offence made successive governments comfortable with the fact that the public could be relied upon as an effective barometer of what was permissible and what was not. Whilst this has been the accepted official opinion for most of this century it is easy to forget that it is founded upon a model of static or retreating Christianity which was enshrined in the notion of how far toleration could be pushed rather than how far religious doctrines should be upheld. This was generally reflected in the legal opinion (at least until the *Gay News* case) that the manner of blasphemy was the most important element. The argument for the retention of blasphemy expressed in this context frequently seemed to run like this: the law of blasphemy could remain on the statute book as a deterrent and will generally function as such, only as long as its sanctions and penalties were not called into play. These could be relied upon to remain dormant because religion itself was secularising – that basically religion was less likely to conflict with freedom of opinion. Successive governments could thus rely upon the discretion and sobriety of public opinion to regulate sensibly the moral outlook and in extreme cases pretensions of religious sections of society.

But this particular argument contained, as time went on, a number of increasingly shaky assumptions. Hopefully one factor that this work on blasphemy has achieved is to assist in the strenuous task of removing the modernisation motif implicit in the concept of secularisation. The trajectory of both blasphemy laws and cultural reactions to the offence do not follow a simple and predictable form from primitive darkness to civilised enlightenment – indeed, as we have noted, the law in England has ostensibly been toughened within the last 25 years. Moreover the evidence presented is that the history of blasphemy does not support the notion that religion is being marginalised by the modern world. The historian investigating the history of the blasphemy laws is apt to expect to find a story of final resolution postponed. Rhetorics concerning the growth of religious toleration in this country are assumed to have evolved in line with the modernisation of the laws – a situation that just awaits the final chapter in this myth of progress. Such optimism, however, is an all-too-regular symptom of accepting secularisation at face value.[16]

Unfortunately, as we have discovered, it is impossible to fit the offence of blasphemy into any acceptable conception of secularisation. Its history is a shambolic procession from misunderstanding to misunderstanding with governments and institutions repeatedly doing their best to avoid accepting responsibility for the policing of the offence. Most worryingly of all, the evidence of the last two invocations of the blasphemy law in relation to Christianity contains trends which erode still further the notion of progressive tolerance. This tolerance should be viewed not simply as a measure of attitudes to religion but also to a whole kaleidoscope of societal concerns around which blasphemy has been historically seen as a convenient place to cluster. The *Gay News* case brought squarely into focus the nature of Christ's divinity at precisely the same time that it was being discussed in learned circles but apparently in no less shocking terms. The Wingrove case also contained an explicit exploration of the erotic potential within female spirituality and it would not be far-fetched to assume that there is some connection between this and wider discussions of female roles in the spiritual and religious world.

Part of the process of modernising Christianity and creating Postmodern Christianity has not resulted in a multiplication of views but their degeneration into 'religious feelings'. Paradoxically it has meant that almost any unorthodox depiction of Christ is ripe for scrutiny and extreme criticism – not simply the ones which are unfavourable or the ones which render the gospel null and void. This is particularly pertinent in relation to the Wingrove case. Whilst the blasphemy laws themselves were not used in this case their frame of reference was partly assumed to apply by the Home Secretary's devolution of powers to the British Board of Film Classification (BBFC). At no point in Wingrove's film did he deny any aspect of the generally agreed canon of Christian beliefs. Indeed Wingrove's defence, concurred in by some Christians, commented that the film could not in itself be blasphemous because it did not attempt to depict an alternative version of events which might be seen to contradict the account outlined in the gospels. Certainly Thorsen's *Sex Life of Christ* did precisely this and a similar objection could be advanced to the Kirkup poem 'The Love that Dares to Speak its Name'. Such distortions could equally be said to apply to a work like Scorsese's *Last Temptation of Christ* which largely escaped censorship and legal action. The Wingrove film portrayed Christ in a dream ecstatic vision sequence and at no point did it attempt to alter the gospel image of Christ. It did, however, depict an individual's responses to that gospel and might reasonably have been considered to allude to the 'intimate religious convictions' which the BBFC consistently claimed their action protected. The Wingrove case also exhibited similarities to instances of other blasphemers seeking to engage culturally and at an artistic level with religion. Whilst Wingrove's own religiosity is opaque he did not exhibit a conscious desire to vilify Christianity. Indeed when interviewed he made a subsequent assertion that he would consider a film investigating the Gnostic gospels. This indicates an, at least passing, artistic interest in diverse Christian traditions. Arguably the attempt to suppress both Kirkup and Wingrove suggests a modern desire to streamline Christianity and to marginalise or even deny other ways of being Christian. Whilst Michell's defence of the Kirkup poem which supported his invocation of phallic imagery as a metaphor for the regenerative capacity of Christ pushed the argument too far, the materials assembled within its covers did suggest that alternative readings of Christian traditions were possible.[17] What is evident is that, however marginal, however apparently anachronistic they may seem, alternative interpretations of Christianity and its central focus had existed unmolested at times in recent and otherwise recorded history. This has led Clive Unsworth to describe the contemporary assertion of religious orthodoxy as forms of threatened religiosity seeking to establish 'intellectual property in these icons deserving of legal protection'.[18]

However the Wingrove case could clearly not be resolved in favour of a liberal interpretation of blasphemy simply by invoking a naive expectation that public opinion can be guaranteed to be forever growing more tolerant. As we have discovered throughout this book, whilst most government discourses around the issue of blasphemy speak the language of protection it is still left largely unappreciated how individuals and groups can use the outrage caused by blasphemy to utter the language of cultural attack. Yet in addition we must not forget that public opinion was being spoken for in the Wingrove case in the shape of the BBFC which, through prior restraint, appeared to be both judge and jury whilst the basic principle which governed the retention of the law until the late twentieth century was quietly usurped by a government agency. Whether this is a good or bad thing is a question that society must persist in asking. Importantly the fact remains that this is a significant departure from the previous history of the offence. Moreover the historically frequent worry of prosecutors that publicity may increase readership of the offending material was neatly, if outrageously, solved by the flat denial of a certificate for Wingrove's *Visions of Ecstasy* video. All of this was not done simply as the creeping hand of the centralised state since there were clearly cultural reasons for this assumption of power. Those who believed that Christianity was going to be a victim of secularisation were proved wrong as it became polarised between active belief and the private world of sentiment and what the judgment called 'religious feelings and convictions'. In particular these words increasingly defy and escape pragmatic definition. Thus the BBFC wording was full of words like 'might', 'could reasonably', 'liable to offend' and others which suggested that the Board was stuck with the thoroughly inadequate process of estimating the effect of any item which should come before it. Once a malleable word like 'feelings' is employed it is even possible to entertain sympathy for legislators who, aware of what a word might encompass, perhaps genuinely did not know who might be offended. However the Board, as a body making subjective judgements in the Wingrove case, offered significant opinions of its own about authorial intention. This moved the matter dangerously towards making religion – in the guise of 'feeling' – a passive entity which need not defend itself since the intervention of a quasi-governmental agency, a jurisdiction and the Home Secretary will do this for it. It is no coincidence that many practising Christians are uneasy about the state protection of religious beliefs offered by the offence because it encourages this form of belief passivity.

*   *   *

All these implications, inherent in the last two blasphemy cases, amount to innovative attitudes towards the offence and offenders which, if accepted, represent a new departure in the history of the offence. This I think may have considerable consequences. The cases in the nineteenth and early twentieth centuries contained lampoons of scripture which were actively intended by their publishers and writers. All defendants from the Commonwealth onwards could be shown to be attacking scripture and/or the Bible and actual recorded beliefs. Judges and prosecuting counsel thus identified specific utterances and sentences as blasphemous because they could, for right or wrong, be measured against texts. Neither the *Gay News* case nor the Wingrove film were like this: neither of them can be shown to be contrary to these two tests of blasphemy since they did not intend to vilify Christianity. But as we have discovered British society is on the verge of reaping the whirlwind of the still harsher definition of the law of blasphemy that has lain in wait in the case-law established by the *Gay News* verdict. Likewise the European Court's reading of the *Gay News* verdict amounted to an optimistic view of English Law which ignored its inherent problems. The post-*Gay News* denial of the need to prove intention in the offence has fundamentally important repercussions. Whilst the Wingrove judgment mentions the *Gay News* case as enshrining the 'manner' of the blasphemy as being more important than the 'matter' – this is clearly inconsistent with the notion of intention. The judgment of the BBFC uses the phrase 'The Question is not one of the *matter* expressed but of its *manner* i.e. the tone, style and spirit, in which it is presented.'[19] Even a mildly disinterested observer might argue profitably that any clear definition of the spirit in which an action is performed contains clear elements of intention.

The Wingrove case, however, also highlighted obliquely the increasingly tenuous and precarious status of forms of expert evidence in blasphemy cases which, it could be argued, have been accorded less tolerance and have been actively undermined over the period covered by this book. This must lead us to ask how cultural change is otherwise to be meaningfully measured or demonstrated to a jury when a search of 'religious feelings' appears to offer only an inadequate and static model on each occasion. As we have noted John Mortimer wanted to produce literary evidence in the *Gay News* trial to suggest that the Kirkup poem was thoroughly in keeping with the changing literary standards of the time. That this was rejected was a substantially material factor in securing Dennis Lemon's conviction. In the Wingrove case the BBFC in its later stages acted almost as his own counsel in considering any expert evidence for him. Its report took considerable pains to rehearse and consider any submission which Wingrove might have made in this direction. Unfortunately these matters were not discussed in anything resembling an open court. Indeed this 'closed' consideration and the suggestion that Wingrove needed to include historical notes and to attempt to place the film in spiritual context means that they acted as judge and jury by imposing their own standards of taste, decency and appropriate criticism upon him and his film.

But as we have discovered blasphemy has also always been a

convenient peg on which people hang their own moral concerns and prejudices. The Wingrove case contained yet a further instance of judicial power seeking to police a perceived landscape of moral collapse. The verdict of the European Court gave one judge the opportunity of offering his opinion on the cause of such collapse. Judge Pettiti found the link between religion and obscene pornographic images particularly shocking and in his statement concurring with the verdict linked this to attempts by video distributors to circumvent the law with misleading packaging which apparently allowed the circulation of videos for consumption by paedophiles. At one point he even suggested that 'The sale in hypermarkets and supermarkets of videos inciting pornographic or obscene behaviour is even more dangerous than the sale of books as it is more difficult to ensure that the public is protected.'[20] In this atmosphere the attempt to scrutinise Wingrove's intentions and status as a quasi-pornographer when coupled with the wider concerns voiced about access to morally dangerous video materials could have made the observer quickly forget that the film was refused a certificate because it was blasphemous, not because it was obscene.

The final decision reached by the European Court in the Wingrove case was to state that Britain had not acted unlawfully in seeking to ban the film and that any decision to the contrary would have indicated the need for an overhaul of the blasphemy laws. Britain could retain and continue to exercise such jurisdiction under the conditions of the 'margin of appreciation' which effectively allows member states to regulate culturally distinct ideas and practices. In some respects the implication of such a decision argues obliquely that religion is once more part and parcel of the law of the land. It also suggests that the control and regulation of religious opinion is an important part of Britain's cultural heritage which needs nurturing and protecting – a view which the Archbishop of York, in a letter to *The Times*, went some way to endorsing.[21] Whilst Article 19 has steadfastly warned that the 'margin of appreciation' is not a legislative licence to persecute, and has been widely understood to need Convention supervision, it is still probably no coincidence that Britain was allowed to regulate religion and morals in this instance. In no other of the 11 countries surveyed could Article 19 find an instance of a healthy and thriving culture of blasphemy prosecution. Denmark had allowed public showing of Thorsen's *Sex Life of Christ* without prosecution whilst Norway was in the process of abolishing the relevant section of its penal code. The German law, meanwhile, was demonstrated to have a clear sense of breach of the peace alongside a strong conception of intention to insult belief and a defence of the rights of adults to decide whether to view or encounter material they were briefed about in advance. Whilst the situation was less clear-cut in Belgium, Spain, France and Italy, the powers to regulate the distribution of publications and films that might be offensive could be argued to be dormant and even awaiting the *coup de grâce* of repeal. Moreover, further investigation by Article 19 revealed that the powers adopted by the BBFC were without parallel in the countries surveyed. Countries that did have compulsory censorship procedures were either concerned with removing violence from films or were prepared to pass the matter over to public prosecutors for decisions as regards further proceedings.[22] The report thus concluded that Britain's current practices were 'incompatible with the guarantee of freedom of expression provided by Article 10 of the European Convention of Human Rights'.

This increasingly points to an enduring belief, now given legislative credence by the Court's acceptance of the 'margin of appreciation', that Britain is somehow culturally distinct from the rest of Europe. It serves to feed the enduring and arguably obsessive belief in a cloistered historical self-definition of one country's own culture as emphatically different and beyond question. Clive Unsworth has also argued persuasively that the effects of globalisation upon the nation state have themselves made the redefinition of its national characteristics draw precisely upon those laws like blasphemy that are liable to reinvigorate traditional state nationhood.[23] This in particular is a matter that requires resolution as the British Government integrates the European Convention of Human Rights into domestic law.

Nonetheless a recognition of the 'margin of appreciation' also fits into our history of blasphemy almost seamlessly. It emerges as yet another concerted attempt to avoid grappling with the fundamental problem of blasphemy. What is so frequently observed from episodes like this is the initial finality of judgments and responses – as though they ended the matter and wrapped it up neatly for lawyers and commentators. Ominously, what is missing is any sense that these decisions might represent a bridgehead and victory for a certain view of society. Such judgements can never be final words on the matter since such decisions do not finalise the religious settlement of any country – they constitute battles in the long-running war for toleration or protected orthodoxy. As we have noted blasphemers such as Foote, Carlile and others have sought protection from what they have seen as dangerous, innovative and vulgar evangelism of various kinds and there remains a fundamentally important factor at work in such pronouncements. It is a lesson of this study that it is naive on the part of the law and of society at large to assume that all religions (or more correctly the religious) will act universally and at all times in a benign and unthreatening way. A simultaneous glance at the preceding pages and across the world will demonstrate that it is capable of militancy and direct action in many forms. Britain, as we all should know, is no longer the culturally insulated society that it was when these laws were framed and it is an illusion to seek comfort in the notion of ideas like the 'margin of appreciation'.

The Wingrove case, however, also further highlights the importance of technology and the generation of new media in the history of blasphemy since so often social attitudes to these developments can easily lag behind. We have seen with Foote's journalism and with Boulter, Gott and Stewart's street anti-evangelism that the creation of new forms of expression frequently activates the machinery of moral crusade. The Wingrove Case is of course the first response to the law after the *Gay News* case and since then the technology of video has entered British culture. In this sense censorship of this medium is at a stage where considerable levels of governmental control are being brought to bear in response to an ever-widening variety of perceived moral panics. The assumption of powers relating to blasphemy in films and video means that the British Board of Film Classification finds itself bound and pressurised to take action. Blasphemy prosecutions and incidents come in waves, not simply because of the activities of serial blasphemers but because private agencies and interests are equally made confident by apparent success. Had some earlier films such as *Life of Brian* and *The Last Temptation of Christ* entered the classification stage in such a climate of close scrutiny it is probable that they would not have reached general release.

To take this issue a little further the profile of the Wingrove case has opened a can of worms concerning the inconsistencies related to the current state of the law. The apparent fluidity of the matter/manner distinction (with an enhanced role for the former) together with the assertion that the 'spirit' in which cultural products are created is important. Both represent serious potential anomalies. That these have not been questioned since 1977 are matters related to the Home Office's trust in public taste. Indeed the progressive blurring of the difference between content and manner may also be said to have encouraged arguments which sought to extend the law to protect wider non-Christian 'feelings'. The potential anomalies of such a course of action can perhaps be demonstrated by applying the tests of 'manner' and 'spirit' to perhaps the three films and publications which did, or would have been likely to, produce such prosecutions. The Kirkup *Gay News* case was a victim of both tests but expert evidence which might have shed light upon alternative spiritualities was declared inadmissable so that the notion of intention was clearly denied full consideration. Any prosecution of the Wingrove *Visions of Ecstasy* film would certainly escape any test related to content since the Bible and tenets of Christian scripture are nowhere attacked or vilified. If intention were ever actively applied through the notion of 'spirit' this particular matter would perhaps be very difficult to prove in court. Whilst Wingrove might be portrayed as a salacious pornographer by some, his artistic interest in matters spiritual can also be advanced with some degree of legitimacy – certainly far enough to entertain an acquittal. *Life of Brian*, should it have reached court, would have had much in common with Foote and Gott's portrayal of religion and would thus have fallen foul of tests of both 'matter' and also of 'manner'/'spirit'.

Martin Scorsese's film *The Last Temptation of Christ* would possibly have circumvented any test related to matter but a prosecution that would have had to untangle the 'manner'/'spirit' confusion could have rent the law asunder and subjected it to considerable scrutiny and perhaps ridicule. Scorsese's 'intention' and 'manner' might have been seen by some as beyond reproach since he was a Catholic seeking to portray on film Nikos Kazantzakis's book which explored an alternative version of Christ's ministry on earth and which had not been previously banned or prosecuted in Britain or the United States. Yet for some others the portrayal of a Christ with human weaknesses (not unlike Dennis Potter's *Son of Man* had done two decades previously) amounted to blasphemy and possibly failed King-Hamilton and Avory's breach of the Peace Test.[24] Moreover the allusion to Christ's fantasy of a normal married life and even the suggestion of adultery with his second wife's older sister – in the context of the biblical temptation it portrayed – would not have outraged as Kirkup had done. Yet its clear alteration of scripture to produce a potentially offensive suggestion to some (but importantly not all) Christians would almost have shattered the distinction between 'manner' and 'matter' had it come to court in Britain.[25]

Still murkier waters lie ahead if we indulge F. LaGard Smith's contention that the real blasphemy of Scorsese's film lay not in the portrayal of temptation but its identification as the source of Christ's real struggle on the cross. The elevation of this to centre stage at the expense of what LaGard Smith calls '… the burden of taking the punishment of our sins and being separated from the Father at the moment of death' constituted the real blasphemous trivialisation of the crucifixion.[26] In some respects such a suggestion invites the reader to search for forms of allegorical blasphemy and indicates still further that the wished-for postmodern multiplication of readers has the potential to multiply the ways and means of offence and not just create value-free and power-free discourses. Perhaps this points clearly to why, on some occasions, the cultural distinctions between 'matter' and 'manner' as components of offence are so frequently merged. No longer are scriptures and doctrines sacred – it is, in the words of the Wingrove judgment, 'convictions' and 'feelings' that matter. One might also consider that such supposed relativism and equal protection for religious feelings which the judgment provides is itself by no means complete. A private consumption and viewing of the Wingrove video which wished to see it as a lampoon of Catholicism (not dissimilar to the Gathercole exposé of the nineteenth century, with its close proximity of nuns and the crucified Christ) is offered no protection under the umbrella of religious feelings. As it stands such feeelings, laudable or otherwise, are denied indulgence. Thus the logic of the law as it now stands is that prosecutions need only trawl the Clapham Omnibus in search of the one person with injured 'feelings' necessary to proceed with a case. As recent history shows, the capacity of religious 'feelings' to be articulated in connection with a wide range of events and institutions, from football to royal funerals, means that such an interpretation of blasphemy in modern culture represents a dangerously open door to those who might wish to profit from the status of the offended.

Whilst the foregoing paragraph has posited hypothetical illustrations it should be remembered that the operation of the law has prevented these instances from occurring largely by accident rather than design. Until recently the status of the Common Law of Blasphemy allowed these incidents to remain products of the imagination since prosecutions were not brought. The devolution of jurisdiction to a Board of Classification effectively means that it could realistically be forced to confront a Wingrove each and every year. Trapped in an institutionally sponsored casual encounter with a whole range of materials the Board is assailed on all sides by government pressures and the need to engage through a glass darkly with, rather than directly reflect, changing moral climates. Faced by the inadequacy of the *Gay News* judgment with only Justice King-Hamilton's fainting medical student and (looking further backwards) Justice Avory's enraged Christian administering thrashings as companions in their arduous task it is no wonder that the Board can only feebly estimate the effect of anything coming before it.

What this situation ostensibly amounts to is a trap in which the current legal standing of the offence of blasphemy in Britain is caught. As such it has three predators seeking to profit from such a trap. The oldest of these is the liberalising lobby in British society which argues the measure's anachronism and which has provided many of the protagonists of this book. As the preceding pages have suggested, their impact upon the law has been rather less than they often hoped. More pertinently the law based upon a religious settlement which the legal philosophers of an earlier age presumed to be static is threatened by innovation in precisely this very area. The second predator, a focus upon literalism by evangelical religion, invites movements 'from below' to recolonise religiosity and to pressurise the state to comply with their wishes and to thus endorse their beliefs through the courts. The third predator is the polar opposite of literalism – diluted postmodernised 'religious feelings'. These offer a dangerous, all-embracing language which undermines 'dogma' and invites all to be religious and to demand almost open-ended protection for beliefs, however diffuse or inchoate. In such a climate the justification for a stable definition of blasphemy grows increasingly untenable. From this point in our reflection there appears to be two routes forward: extension or abolition of the law.

In modern Britain we should avoid the path of extension which beckons so seductively to some. Surrender to this tendency would pull religion still further into the mire of amorphous 'feelings and convictions' – concepts which should frighten both the irreligious and religious. The irreligious should be concerned that such words – as demonstrated by this study – are dangerously open-ended and have the potential to be extended to anything from anti-Semitism to attacks upon other faiths which may upset the feelings of a religious individual. Bhuddists, for example, have rightly pointed out that their belief, which effectively denies a personal God, expressed 500 years before the establishment of Christianity, could effectively be judged blasphemous.[27]

The religious, however, should also fear the implications of taking people's active text- and doctrine-based beliefs away from them. As such the notion of religious 'feelings' and 'convictions' takes us far beyond the scriptural and biblical basis of people's sincere practised religious beliefs and leaves the actively religious as victims to a lazy, neglectful definition of religion. Whilst some argue that religion is essential to modern identity in a way that has not really been appreciated it would also pay us to take note of those who argue that the exercise of free speech is an essential part of the cultural and even quasi-religious identity of others. As they rightly argue, accepting prohibitions upon the exercise of thought and belief is asking individuals to indulge in a charade and 'to be the person they are not'. At the very least those who defend the current situation of the law and take shelter in its disuse perhaps should appreciate how its provisions may have silenced individuals in a range of cultural and religious contexts.[28] That the law still performed this function was reinforced in 1996 when BBC programme makers, in the wake of the Wingrove case, were upbraided for their commonplace use of profanities related to God and reminded that 'blasphemy is a criminal offence'.[29]

The elevation of religion to a state of unsatisfactory limbo can only be solved by a repeal of all blasphemy laws. I am not naive enough to think that this would end religious hurt or religious strife overnight since this is often an intrinsic part of being religious. Indeed, the removal of such a law should also be an occasion for a stringent and far-reaching enquiry into the operation of the laws aimed at re-establishing an equal and enabling community to prevent the incitement of race and religious hatred and other species of public disorder. Only when these laws are clear, practical and generally understood can the fear which urges retention of the law of blasphemy be diffused. Nonetheless some legal commentators are uneasy about this route since they see the dismissal of the link between public order issues and blasphemy as having been widened of late.[30]

But the removal of blasphemy from our religious landscape would also force people to think why they are offended by the criticisms and dialogues of others, which we should not forget are themselves responses to religious stimuli and actively constitute religious feelings. It would also avoid the nightmare result of extension which would force individuals to possess almost encyclopaedic knowledge of other religions (and any potential 'feelings' that might be attached to them) before addressing any audience to avoid causing unwitting offence. As such if the laws were repealed individuals would have to look more critically at their own religion and their faith in it. When they do this most people will realise that their God does not need the inadequate and barely credible protection of a confused Court or a frightened Board of Censors. They might also profitably recall William Blake's concerns about those who consider they know the will of a deity. As such everybody's conception of themselves, their god, their religion, their agnosticism and their atheism deserves better.

Notes

1. Unsworth, Clive (1995), 'Blasphemy, Cultural Divergence and Legal Relativism', *Modern Law Review*, 58 (5): pp. 658–77, p. 677.
2. Ibid., p. 673–4.
3. Bradney, A. (1993), *Religions, Rights and Laws*, London: Leicester University Press, p. 94.
4. Ahsan, M. and A. Kidwai (1991) (eds), *Sacrilege versus Civility – Muslim Perspectives on 'The Satanic Verses' Affair*, 2nd edn, Leicester: The Islamic Foundation, p. 28.
5. *Ex parte* Choudhury case: 1 All ER 306.
6. Ahsan and Kidwai, op. cit., p. 344.
7. Unsworth, op. cit., p. 673.
8. Lee, Simon (1986), 'Religion and the Law: Ways Forward', in David G. Bowen (ed.), *The Satanic Verses: Bradford Responds*, Bradford: Bradford and Ilkley Community College.
9. Ibid., p. 74.

10. *Guardian*, 28 July 1997.
11. *Independent on Sunday*, 24 March, 1996.
12. Cupitt, Don (1987), *The Long-Legged Fly*, London: Xpress Reprints, pp. 1–12.
13. Bury, J. B. (1913), *A History of Freedom of Thought*, Home and University Library of Modern Knowledge, vol. 74, London: Williams and Novgate, p. 245.
14. Lee, op. cit., p. 76.
15. Article 19 and Interights (1995), *Blasphemy and Film Censorship: Submission to the European Court of Human Rights in Respect of Nigel Wingrove V. The United Kingdom*, Article 19 and Interights.
16. Unsworth, op. cit., p. 675.
17. Michell, John (1977), *To Represent Our Saviour as 'that great cock' [Kirkup Gay News] is not blasphemy but eternal and Christian Orthodoxy: Furnished with Irrefutable Illustrative Proofs*, London: Open Head Press.
18. Unsworth, op. cit., p. 675.
19. European Court of Human Rights. Case of Wingrove v. The United Kingdom (19/1995/525/611) Judgment, Strasbourg, 25 November 1996. Earlier BBFC judgment enclosed.
20. European Court of Human Rights. Case of Wingrove v. The United Kingdom (19/1995/525/611) Judgment, Strasbourg, 25 November 1996, p. 28–9.
21. *The Times*, 29 March 1996.
22. Interights, op. cit.
23. Unsworth, op. cit.
24. Smith, F. Lagard (1990), *Blasphemy and the Battle for Faith*, London: Hodder & Stoughton, p. 100–104.
25. The Supreme Court refused to allow a prosecution in the United States citing *Burstyn*, 9343 U.S. 495 (1952) which ruled that the statute pursuant to which it was banned was prior restraint on freedom of speech. Interights, Article 19 and Interights (1995), *Blasphemy and Film Censorship: Submission to the European Court of Human Rights in Respect of Nigel Wingrove v. The United Kingdom*.
26. Smith, op. cit., p. 103.
27. Sangharakshita, Bhikahu (1978), *Buddhism and Blasphemy: Buddhist Reflections on the 1977 Blasphemy Trial*, London: Windhorse Publications, p. 7.
28. Bradney, op. cit., p. 95.
29. *The Times*, 14 November 1996.
30. Unsworth, op. cit., pp. 666–7.

Bibliography

Manuscript Sources

In the Bodleian Library Oxford:

Papers of William Ewart Gladstone
Papers of Sir William Harcourt
Papers of Sir John Simon

In the Public Record Office, Kew:

HO 45

OS299 Prosecution of the Oracle of Reason 1842
OS3017 Refusal of H. O. to prosecute 1850
OS3537 Atheistic lectures by Mr John Stuart Mill: magistrates to prosecute if they thought it advisable 1851
9597/96131 Refusal of magistrates to administer affirmation, 1880
9613/A9275 As to suppression of disturbances and instructions to local authorities re. Salvation Army (1882–88)
9536/49902, Prosecution of the Freethinker, 1882–83
9645/A36331 Religious disturbances in Regents Park, 1884
10406/A46794 Prosecution of the Freethinker, 1887–1908
10665/216120 Prosecutions of T. W. Stewart and J. W. Gott, 1911–14 Memorandum on British Laws by Sir John Simon, Attorney General (1911–14)
24619/ 217459 Blasphemy Laws (amendment) Bills 1913–1938: atheist assemblies

HO 144

114/A25454, letters protesting against the treatment of Foote and the verdict
871 160552 Prosecution for and proposals for repeal of blasphemy laws (1908–1909)

In West Register House (Edinburgh):

AD 43/350 Precognition against Henry Robinson
AD14 43/345 High Court Precognition against Thomas Paterson

Newspapers:

Daily Mail
Daily Telegraph
Freethinker
Guardian
Jerusalem Star
National Reformer
Secular Chronicle
Secular Review
The Times
The Truthseeker
The Movement and Anti Persecution Gazette
Watt's Literary Guide
Independent on Sunday

Publications

Ahsan, M. and A. Kidwai (1991), ed. *Sacrilege versus Civility – Muslim Perspectives on 'The Satanic Verses' Affair*, 2nd edn, Leicester: The Islamic Foundation.

Aldred, G. A. (1941), *Richard Carlile, agitator: his life and times*, Glasgow: Strickland Press.

———— (1942), ed. *Jail Journal and Other Writings by Richard Carlile*, The Word Library, Glasgow: Strickland Press.

———— (1948), *Rex v. Aldred*, Glasgow: Strickland Press.

———— (1955), *No Traitor's Gait! The Autobiography of Guy A. Aldred*, Glasgow: Strickland Press.

Anderson, Patricia (1991), *The Printed Image and the Transformation of Popular Culture 1790–1860*, Oxford: OUP.

Arnstein, W. L. (1957), 'The Bradlaugh Case: a reappraisal', *Journal of the History of Ideas* XVIII (2): 254–69.

———— (1962a), 'Gladstone and the Bradlaugh Case', *Victorian Studies* V (4): 303–30.

———— (1962b), 'Parnell and the Bradlaugh Case', *Irish Historical Studies* XIII (51): 212–35.

———— (1965), *The Bradlaugh Case: A Study in Late Victorian Opinion and Politics*, Oxford: Clarendon Press.

Aspland, L. M. (1884), The Law of Blasphemy: a candid examination of the views of Mr Justice Stephen, London.

Aston, M. E. (1993), *Faith and Fire: Popular and Unpopular Religion, 1350–1600*, Cambridge: Hambledon Press.

Avrich, Paul (1984), *The Haymarket Tragedy*, Princeton: Princeton University Press.

Ayer, A. J. (1988), *Thomas Paine*, London: Faber and Faber.

Bailey, S. H., D. J. Harris and B. L. Jones (1995), *Civil Liberties: Cases and Materials*, London: Butterworths.

Baker, Keith Michael (1994), 'A Foucauldian French Revolution?', in Jan Goldstein (ed.), *Foucault and the Writing of History*, Oxford: Blackwell, pp. 187–205.

Balleine, G. R. (1956), *Past Finding Out: The Tragic Story of Joanna Southcott and her Successors*, London: SPCK.

Barker, A. G. (1938), *Henry Hetherington, 1792–1849*, London: G. W. Foote & Co.

Begbie, Harold (1920), *Life of William Booth: The Founder of the Salvation Army*, London: Macmillan.

Berman, David (1988), *A History of Atheism in Britain: From Hobbes to Russell*, New York: Croom Helm.

Booth, Alan (1983), 'Popular loyalism and public violence in the northwest of England, 1790–1800', *Social History* 8: 295–314.

Bowen, David G. (1992a), 'Can Books be Sacred?', in David G. Bowen (ed.), *The Satanic Verses: Bradford Responds*, 1–4, Bradford: Bradford and Ilkley Community College.

———— (1992b), ed. *The Satanic Verses: Bradford Responds*, Bradford: Bradford and Ilkley Community College.

Bradlaugh, Charles (1870), *Heresy, Its Utility and Morality: A Plea and a Justification*, London: Austin & Co.

Bradlaugh-Bonner, Hypatia (1934), *Penalties Upon Opinion*, London: Watts & Co.

Bradlaugh-Bonner, Hypatia and J. M. Robertson (1894), *Charles Bradlaugh, a record of his life and work*, London: Unwin.

Bradney, A. (1993), *Religions, Rights and Laws*, London: Leicester University Press.

Bristow, Edward J. (1977), *Vice and Vigilance: Purity Movements in Britain since 1700*, Dublin: Gill and Macmillan.

Brooks, Peter (1976), *The Melodramatic Imagination: Balzac, Henry James, Melodrama and the Mode of Excess*, New Haven: Yale University Press.

Brown, Callum G. (1988), 'Did urbanization secularize Britain?', *Urban History Yearbook*: 1–14.

———— (1991), 'Secularisation: A Theory in Danger?', *Scottish Economic and Social History* (II): 52–8.

Brown, Desmond H. (1992), 'Abortive Attempts to Codify English Criminal Law', *Parliamentary History* II (1): 1–40.

Bruce, Stevē (1992), ed. *Religion and Modernisation, Sociologists and Historians Debate the Secularisation Thesis*, Oxford: Clarendon Press.

Budd, Susan (1971), *Varieties of Unbelief*, London: Heinemann.

Bury, J. B. (1913), *A History of Freedom of Thought*, Home University Library of Modern Knowledge, vol. 74, London: Williams and Norgate.

Calder-Marshall, Arthur (1972), *Lewd, Blasphemous and Obscene*, London: Hutchinson.

Carlile, R. (1825), *The Trials with the Defences at Large of Mrs. Jane Carlile, Mary Ann Carlile, William Holmes (etc.)*, London.

Claeys, Gregory (1987), 'Paine's Agrarian Justice (1796) and the secularisation of natural jurisprudence', *Bulletin of the Society for the Study of Labour History* 52 (3): 21–31.

Clifford, Brendan (1993), *Blasphemous Reason: The 1797 Trial of Tom Paine's Age of Reason*, Hampton, Middx.: Bevin Books.

Colaiaco, J. (1983), *James Fitzjames Stephen and the Crisis of Victorian Thought*, London: Macmillan.

Coleridge, Ernest Hartley (1904), *Life and Correspondence of John Duke, Lord Coleridge*, London.

Colley, Linda (1992), *Britons: Forging the Nation*, London: Yale University Press.

Connor, Stephen (1991), *Postmodernist Culture*, Oxford: Blackwell.

Craun, Edwin D. (1983), '"*Inordinata Locutio*": Blasphemy in pastoral literature', *Traditio* 39: 135–62.

Cromartie, Alan (1995), *Sir Matthew Hale 1609–1676: Law, Religion and Natural Philosophy*, Cambridge: CUP.

Crowson, N. J. (1995), 'The British Conservative Party and the Jews during the Late 1930s', *Patterns of Prejudice* 29 (2–3): 15–32.

Cupitt, Don (1987), *The Long-Legged Fly*, London: Xpress Reprints.

Cutner, H. (n.d.), *Robert Taylor (1784–1844). The Devils Chaplain*, London: G. W. Foote & Co.

Dawson, O. (1895), *The Bar Sinister and Licit Love. The first biennial proceedings of the Legitimation League*, London.

———— (1897), *Personal Rights and Sexual Wrongs*, London.

DeLeon, D. (1978), *The American as Anarchist: Reflections on Indigenous Radicalism*, London: Johns Hopkins University Press.

Doolittle, Ian (1983), 'Obsolete Appendage? The City of London's Struggle for Survival', *History Today* 33 (May): 10–14.

Dunae, P. (1979), 'Penny dreadfuls: later nineteenth century boys' literature and crime', *Victorian Studies* XXII: 135–50.

Eagleton, Terry (1996), *The Illusions of Postmodernism*, Oxford: Blackwell.

Eley, Geoff and Keith Nield (1995), 'Starting over: the present, the postmodern and the moment of social history', *Social History* 20 (3): 355–64.

Epstein, James (1994), *Radical Expression: Political Language, Ritual, and Symbol in England, 1790–1850*, Oxford: OUP.

Evans, Richard (1997), *In Defence of History*, London: Granta Books.

Foote, G. W. (1878?), *Mr. Bradlaugh's Trial and The Freethought Party.*

———— (1885), ed. Comic Bible sketches reprinted from *The Freethinker*, Part 1, London.

———— (1886), *Prisoner for Blasphemy*, London.

———— (1889), Defence of Free Speech, being a three hours' address to the jury in the court of Queen's Bench before Lord Coleridge, on 24 April, 1883, London.

———— (1932), Defence of Free Speech, being a three hours' address to the jury in the court of Queen's Bench before Lord Coleridge, on 24 April, 1883. New edition with an introduction by H. Cutner, London.

Foucault, Michel (1976), *The History of Sexuality: Introduction*, London: Penguin.

———— (1980), 'Truth and Power', in Colin Gordon (ed.) *Power/Knowledge: Selected Interviews and Other Writings 1972–1977*, Brighton: Harvester.

———— (1990a), 'On Power', in Lawrence D. Kritzman (ed.) *Michel Foucault: Politics, Philosophy, Culture. Interviews and Other Writings 1977–1984*, London: Routledge, pp. 96–109.

———— (1990b), 'Politics and Reason', in Lawrence D. Kritzman (ed.) *Michel Foucault; Politics, Philosophy, Culture. Interviews and Other Writings 1977–1984*, London: Routledge, pp. 57–85.

———— (1997), *Essential Works, Volume I: Ethics*, London: Penguin.

Foxe, John (1563), *Acts and Monuments*, London.

Ginzburg, Carlo (1976), *The Cheese and the Worms*, London: RKP.

Goldstein, Jan (1994), ed. *Foucault and the Writing of History*, Oxford: Blackwell.

Grey, Antony (1992), *Quest for Justice: Towards Homosexual Emancipation*, London: Sinclair-Stevenson.

Hackwood, F. M. (1912), *William Hone: His Life and Times*, London.

Harvey, David (1989), *The Condition of Postmodernity*, Oxford: Blackwell.

Herrick, J. (1982), *Vision and Realism: a Hundred Years of the Freethinker*, London: G. W. Foote & Co.

Hill, Christopher (1972), *The World Turned Upside Down*, London: Penguin.

———— (1996), *Liberty Against the Law*, London: Penguin.

Hole, Robert (1989), *Pulpits, Politics and Public Order in England 1760–1832*, Cambridge: Cambridge University Press.

Hollis, P. (1970), *The Pauper Press. A Study of Working Class Radicalism of the 1830s*, Oxford: Clarendon Press.

Holyoake, George Jacob (1857), *The Case of Thomas Pooley, the Cornish Well Sinker*, London: Holyoake and Company.

———— (1864), The Suppressed Lecture, at Cheltenham, London.

Hone, William (1876), The three trials of William Hone, for publishing three parodies, with intr. and notes by W. Tegg. [Followed by] Trial by jury and liberty of the press, London.

Hopkins, James K. (1982), *A Woman to Deliver her People: Joanna Southcott and Millenarianism in an era of Revolution*, Austin: University of Texas Press.

Hunter, W. A. (1878), The Past and Present of the Heresy Laws. A lecture delivered before the Sunday Lecture Society on Sunday afternoon, 1 December, 1878. London.

Interights, Article 19 and Blasphemy and Film Censorship: Submission to the European Court of Human Rights in Respect of Nigel Wingrove V. The United Kingdom, Article 19 and Interights, 1995.

Jenkins, Keith (1991), *Re-Thinking History*, London: Routledge.

Joyce, Patrick (1991), *Visions of the People*, Cambridge: CUP.

———— (1993), 'The imaginary discontents of social history: a note of response to Mayfield and Thorne, and Lawrence and Taylor', *Social History* 18 (1): 81–5.

———— (1995), 'The end of social history?', *Social History* 20 (1): 73–91.

Kabbani, Rana (1989), *Letter to Christendom*, London: Virago.

Keane, John (1995), *Tom Paine: A Political Life*, London: Bloomsbury.

Kenny, Courtney (1922), 'The Evolution of the Law of Blasphemy', *Cambridge Law Journal* 1: 127–42.

Keppel, Gilles (1994), *The Revenge of God*, Cambridge: Polity Press.

King-Hamilton, A. (1982), *And Nothing But the Truth*, London: Weidenfeld and Nicolson.

Kirk, Linda (1987), 'Thomas Paine: a Child of the Enlightenment?', *Bulletin of the Society for the Study of Labour History* 52 (3): 3–8.

Kirk, Neville (1995), 'History, language, ideas and postmodernism: a materialist view', *History* 20: 222–40.

Kirkup, J. (1988), *I, of all People*, London: Weidenfeld and Nicolson.

Kritzman, Lawrence D. (1990), 'Introduction', in Lawrence D. Kritzman (ed.) *Michel Foucault; Politics, Philosophy, Culture. Interviews and Other Writings 1977–1984* ix-xxv, London: Routledge.

Lambert, Malcolm (1992), *Medieval Heresy: Popular Movements from the Gregorian Reform to the Reformation*, Oxford: Blackwell.

Lapidus, Ira M. (1996), 'State and Religion in Islamic Societies', *Past and Present* (151): 3–27.

Laws, Society for the Abolition of the Blasphemy (1924), The Blasphemy Laws: Verbatim Report of the Deputation to the Home Secretary on 16 April 1924. Issued by the Society for the Abolition of the Blasphemy Laws, London: RPA.

Lawton, David (1993), *Blasphemy*, London: Harvester Wheatsheaf.

Lee, Simon (1986), 'Religion and the Law: Ways Forward', in David G. Bowen (ed.) *The Satanic Verses: Bradford Responds*, Bradford: Bradford and Ilkley Community College.

Leff, Gordon (1967a), *Heresy in the Later Middle Ages; The Relation of Heterodoxy to Dissent c1250–1450*, New York: Manchester University Press.

——— (1967b), *Heresy in the Later Middle Ages; The Relation of Heterodoxy to Dissent c1250–1450*, New York: Manchester University Press.

Levy, Leonard Williams (1981), *Treason against God: A History of the Offense of Blasphemy*, New York: Schocken Books.

——— (1993), *Blasphemy: Verbal Offense Against the Sacred from Moses to Salman Rushdie*, New York: Knopf.

Linton, W. J. (1880), *James Watson. A Memoir of the Days of the Fight for a Free Press in England and of the Agitation for the People's Charter*, Manchester.

Lyotard, Jean-François (1992), *The Postmodern Condition: A Report on Knowledge*, Manchester: Manchester University Press.

Macdonell, John (1883), 'Blasphemy and the Common Law', *Fortnightly Review*, new series, June, pp. 776–89.

MacKenzie, John M. (1995), *Orientalism: History, Theory and the Arts*, Manchester: MUP.

Maher, G. (1977), 'Blasphemy in Scots Law', *Scots Law Times*, p. 260.

Marsh, Joss Lutz (1991), '"Bibliolatry" and "Bible Smashing": G. W. Foote, George Meredith, and the heretic trope of the book', *Victorian Studies* 34 (3): 315–36.

Mayfield, David and Susan Thorne (1992), 'Social History and its Discontents', *Social History* 17 (2): 165–88.

McCalman, I. D. (1975), 'Popular Radicalism and Free-Thought in Early Nineteenth Century England: A Study of Richard Carlile and His Followers, 1815–32', M.A., Australian National University, 1975.

——— (1984), 'Unrespectable Radicalism: Infidels and Pornography in Early Nineteenth-Century London Movement', *Past and Present* (104): 74–110.

———— (1993), *Radical Underworld: Prophets, Revolutionaries, and Pornographers in London, 1795–1840*, Oxford: Clarendon Press.

Meredith, W. M. (1912), ed. *Collected Letters of George Meredith*, London: Constable & Co.

Mews, Stuart (1988), 'The General and the Bishops: Alternative Responses to De-Christianisation', in T. R. Gourvish and Alan O'Day (eds), *Later Victorian Britain, 1867–1900*, Basingstoke: Macmillan, pp. 209–28.

Michell, John (1977), To Represent Our Saviour as 'that great cock' [*Kirkup Gay News*] is not blasphemy but eternal and Christian Orthodoxy: Furnished with Irrefutable Illustrative Proofs, London: Open Head Press.

Micklewright, F. H. Amphlett (1961), 'The rise and decline of English Neo-Malthusianism', *Population Studies* XV: 32–51.

Moore, R. I. (1987), *The Formation of a Persecuting Society*, Oxford: Blackwell.

Morton, Vivienne and Stuart Macintyre (1979), *T. A. Jackson, a centenary appreciation*, London: History group of the Communist Party.

Nash, David S. (1991), 'F. J. Gould and the Leicester Secular Society: A positivist commonwealth in Edwardian politics', *Midland History*, 16: 126–40.

———— (1992), *Secularism, Art and Freedom*, London: Leicester University Press.

———— (1995a), '"Look in her face and Lose thy dread of dying": The ideological importance of death to the secularist movement in Victorian England', *Journal of Religious History*, 19: 158–80.

———— (1995b), '"Unfettered investigation" – the Secularist Press and the creation of audience in Victorian England', *Victorian Periodicals Review*, Summer 28: 123–35.

Newman, Gerald (1975), 'Anti-French propaganda and British liberal nationalism in the early nineteenth century: Suggestions toward a general interpretation', *Victorian Studies*, 18: 385–418.

Nokes, G. D. (1928), *A History of the Crime of Blasphemy*, London: Sweet & Maxwell.

Oliver, H. (1983), *The International Anarchist Movement in Late Victorian London*, Beckenham: Croom Helm.

Omer, Mutaharunnisa (1989), *The Holy Prophet and the Satanic Slander*, Madras: The Women's Islamic Social and Educational Service Trust.

Pack, E. (1904), *A 'Blasphemer' on 'Blasphemy'. The latest Leeds police fiasco*, Bradford: Freethought Socialist League.

———— (n.d., a), *The Parsons' Doom*, Bradford: Freethought Socialist League.

—————— (n.d., b), *The Trial and Imprisonment of J. W. Gott for Blasphemy*, Bradford: Freethought Socialist League.

Palmer, Bryan D. (1990), *Descent into Discourse: The Reification of Language and the Writing of Social History*, Philadelphia: Temple University Press.

Prochaska, Franklyn K. (1972), 'Thomas Paine's "The Age of Reason" Revisited', *Journal of the History of Ideas* (33): 561–76.

Radzinowicz, L. (1957), *Sir James Fitzjames Stephen 1829–1894*, London: Quaritch.

Roberts, M. J. D. (1984), 'Making Victorian Morals? The Society for the Suppression of Vice and its Critics 1802–1886', *Historical Studies* xxi: 157–73.

—————— (1992), 'Blasphemy, obscenity and the courts: contours of tolerance in nineteenth-century England', in Paul Hyland and Neil Sammells (eds) *Writing and Censorship in Britain*, London: Routledge, pp. 141–53.

Robilliard, St John A. (1984), *Religion and the Law*, Manchester: Manchester University Press.

Robinson, Neal (1992), 'Reflections on the Rushdie Affair – 18 April 1989', in David G. Bowen (ed.) *The Satanic Verses: Bradford Responds*, Bradford: Bradford and Ilkley Community College, pp. 33–44.

Royle, E. (1971), *Radical Politics 1790–1900, Religion and Unbelief*, London: Longman.

—————— (1974), *Victorian Infidels*, Manchester: Manchester University Press.

—————— (1980), *Radicals, Secularists and Republicans: Popular Freethought in Britain, 1866–1915*, Manchester: Manchester University Press.

Said, Edward (1994), *Culture and Imperialism*, London: Vintage.

—————— (1995), *Orientalism*, London: Penguin.

Sangharakshita, Bhikahu (1978), *Buddhism and Blasphemy: Buddhist reflections on the 1977 blasphemy trial*, London: Windhorse Publications.

Sardar, Ziauddin and Merryl Wyn Davies (1990), *Distorted Imagination: Lessons from the Rushdie Affair*, London: Grey Seal.

Sears, Hal D. (1977), *The Sex Radicals: Free Love in High Victorian America*, Kansas: The Regents Press.

Seidman, Steven (1994), 'Introduction', in Steven Seidman (ed.) *The Postmodern Turn*, Cambridge: Cambridge University Press, pp. 1–23.

Sharpe, James (1996), *Instruments of Darkness: Witchcraft in England 1550–1750*, London: Penguin.

Smart, Barry (1985), *Michel Foucault*, London: Routledge.

Smith, F. Lagard (1990), *Blasphemy and the Battle for Faith*, London: Hodder & Stoughton.

Smith, Olivia (1984), *The Politics of Language 1791–1819*, Oxford: OUP.

Stallybrass, Peter and Allon White (1986), *The Politics and Poetics of Transgression*, Ithica and London: Cornell University Press.

Standring, G. (1914), 'Reminiscent Notes on the Neo-Malthusian Movement', *The Malthusian* XXXVIII (3, 15 March): 19–20.

Standring, G. (1919), 'Memories and Musings of an old Malthusian', *The Malthusian* XLIII (6, 15 June): 43–4.

Stephen, James Fitzjames (1884), 'The Law on Blasphemy and Blasphemous Libel', *Fortnightly Review*, March, pp. 289–318.

The Viscount Dunedin, John L. Wark, and A. C. Black (1928), *Encyclopaedia of the Laws of Scotland*, Edinburgh: W. Green and Son.

Thomas, Donald (1969), *A Long Time Burning: The History of Literary Censorship in England*, London: Routledge and Kegan Paul.

Thompson, E. P. (1963), *The Making of the English Working Class*, London: Penguin.

———— (1993), *Witness Against the Beast: William Blake and the Moral Law*, Cambridge: Cambridge University Press.

Thurlow, Richard (1987), *Fascism in Britain A History, 1918–85*, Oxford: Blackwell.

Toohey, Timothy J. (1987a), 'Blasphemy in Nineteenth Century England: The Pooley Case and its Background', *Victorian Studies* XXX (3): 315–33.

———— (1987b), *Piety and the Professions: Sir John Taylor Coleridge and His Sons*, New York: Garland Press.

Tribe, David (1967), *One Hundred Years of Freethought*, London: Elek.

———— (1971), *President Charles Bradlaugh, M.P.*, London: Elek.

Unsworth, Clive (1995), 'Blasphemy, Cultural Divergence and Legal Relativism', *Modern Law Review* 58 (5): 658–77.

Veeser, H. Aram (1989a), 'Introduction', in H. Aram Veeser (ed.) *The New Historicism*, London: Routledge.

———— (1989b), ed. *The New Historicism*, London: Routledge.

Vernon, James (1994), 'Who's afraid of the "linguistic turn"? The Politics of social history and its discontents', *Social History* 19: 81–97.

Visker, Rudi (1995), *Michel Foucault: Genealogy as Critique*, London: Verso.

Walkowitz, Judith (1992), *City of Dreadful Delight: Narratives of Sexual Danger in Nineteenth-Century London*, London: Virago.

Walter, Nicolas (1977), *Blasphemy in Britain: The Practice and Punishment of Blasphemy, and the Trial of 'Gay News'*, London.

———— (1990), *Blasphemy Ancient and Modern*, London: Rationalist Press Association.

Wardroper, John (1973), *Kings, Lords and Wicked Libellers: Satire and Protest, 1760–1837*, London: John Murray.

Warraq, Ibn (1995), *Why I am Not a Muslim*, Amherst New York: Prometheus Books.

Webster, Richard (1990), *A Brief History of Blasphemy: Liberalism, Censorship and 'The Satanic Verses'*, Southwold: Orwell Press.

Werskey, Gary (1978), *The Visible College: The Collective Biography of British Scientific Socialists of the 1930s*, London: Allen Lane.

White, Hayden (1987a), *Metahistory: The Historical Imagination in Nineteenth-Century Europe*, Baltimore.

———— (1987b), *Tropics of Discourse*, Baltimore.

Whitehouse, Mary (1993), *Quite Contrary*, London: Pan Books.

Wickwar, W. H. (1928), *The Struggle for the Freedom of the Press, 1819–32*, London: George Allen & Unwin.

Wiener, Joel (1969), *The War of the Unstamped*, Ithica: Cornell University Press.

———— (1983), *Radicalism and Freethought in Nineteenth-Century Britain: The Life of Richard Carlile*, London: Greenwood Press.

———— (1988), 'Collaborators of a sort: Thomas Paine and Richard Carlile', in Ian Dyck (ed.) *Citizen of the World*, New York: St. Martin's Press, pp. 104–28.

Wood, Marcus (1994), *Radical Satire and Print Culture 1790–1822*, Oxford: Clarendon Press.

Wood, N. (1959), *Communism and British Intellectuals*, London: Gollancz.

Worrall, David (1992), *Radical Culture: Discourse, Resistance and Surveillance, 1790–1820*, London: Harvester Wheatsheaf.

Index